Visual Basic 2019 Handbook

A Concise Guide to VB2019 Programming

By Dr.Liew

Disclaimer

Visual Basic 2019 Made Easy is an independent publication and is not affiliated with, nor has it been authorized, sponsored, or otherwise approved by Microsoft Corporation.

Trademarks

Microsoft, Visual Basic, Excel and Windows are either registered trademarks or trademarks of Microsoft Corporation in the United States and/or other countries. All other trademarks belong to their respective owners.

Liability

The purpose of this book is to provide basic guides for people interested in Visual Basic 2019 programming. Although every effort and care has been taken to make the information as accurate as possible, the author shall not be liable for any error, Harm or damage arising from using the instructions given in this book.

Copyright ® 2019 Liew Voon Kiong

All rights reserved. No Part of this e-book may be reproduced in any form or by any means, without permission in writing from the author.

Acknowledgement

I would like to express my sincere gratitude to the many people who have made their contributions in one way or another to the successful publication of this book.

My special thanks go to my children Xiang, Yi and Xun who have contributed their ideas and help in editing this book. I would also like to appreciate the support provided by my beloved wife Kim Huang and my youngest daughter Yuan. I would also like to thank the millions of readers who have visited my **Visual Basic Tutorial** website at **vbtutor.net** for their support and encouragement.

About the Author

Dr. Liew Voon Kiong holds a bachelor's degree in Mathematics, a master's degree in Management and a doctorate in Business Administration. He has been involved in Visual Basic programming for more than 20 years. He created the popular online Visual Basic Tutorial at www.vbtutor.net, which has attracted millions of visitors since 1996. It has consistently been one of the highest ranked Visual Basic websites.

To provide more support for Visual Basic students, teachers, and hobbyists, Dr. Liew has written this book to complement the free Visual Basic 2019 tutorial with much more content. He is also the author of the Visual Basic Made Easy series, which includes Visual Basic 6 Made Easy, Visual Basic 2008 Made Easy, Visual Basic 2010 Made Easy, Visual Basic 2013 Made Easy, Visual Basic 2015 Made Easy, Visual Basic 2017 Made Easy and Excel VBA Made Easy. Dr.Liew's books have been used in high school and university computer science courses all over the world.

Contents

Disclaimer 1
   Trademarks 1
   Liability 1
Acknowledgement 2
   About the Author 2
Chapter 1 Introduction to Visual Basic 2019 14
   1.1 A Brief History of Visual Basic 14
   1.2 Installation of Visual Studio 2019 15
1.3 Creating a Visual Basic 2019 Project 17
Chapter 2 Designing the User Interface 26
   2.1 Customizing the Form 26
   2.2 Adding Controls to the Form 33
Chapter 3 Writing the Code 38
   3.1 The Concept of Event-Driven Programming 38
   3.2 Writing the Code 40
Chapter 4 Working with Controls 43
   4.1 TextBox 43
      Example 4.1 43
   4.2 Label 45
      Example 4.2 45
   4.3 ListBox 47
      4.3.1 Adding Items to a Listbox 47

a) Adding items using the String Collection Editor 47

b) Adding Items using the Add() Method 49

Example 4.3 49

Example 4.4 50

Example 4.5 Geometric Progression 52

4.3.2 Removing Items from a List Box 54

Example 4.5 55

Example 4.6 56

Example 4.7 57

Example 4.8 59

Example 4.9 60

4.4 ComboBox 61

4.4.1 Adding Items to a ComboBox 62

4.4.2 Removing Items from a Combobox 66

Chapter 5 Handling Images 68

5.1 Loading an Image in a Picture Box 68

5.1.1 Loading an Image at Design Time 68

5.1.2 Loading an Image at Runtime 71

5.2 Loading an Image in a Picture Box using Open File Dialog Control 72

Chapter 6 Working with Data 76

6.1 Visual Basic 2019 Data Types 76

6.1.1 Numeric Data Types 76

Table 6.1: Numeric Data Types 77

6.1.2 Non-numeric Data Types 78

Table 6.2 Non-numeric Data Types 78

6.1.3 Suffixes for Literals 78

Table 6.3 Suffixes and Data Types 79

6.2 Variables and Constants 79

    6.2.1 Variable Names 80

    6.2.2 Declaring Variables 80

    Example 6.1 81

    Example 6.2 81

    Example 6.3 82

    6.2.3 Assigning Values to Variables 83

    Example 6.4 84

    6.2.4 Scope of Declaration 85

    6.2.5 Declaring Constants 85

    Example 6.5 86

Chapter 7 Arrays 88

7.1 Introduction to Arrays... 88

7.2 Dimension of an Array 88

7.3 Declaring Arrays 89

    Example 7.1 90

    Example 7.2 91

    Example 7.3 91

    Example 7.4 92

Chapter 8 Mathematical Operations 94

8.1 Mathematical Operators.. 94

8.2 Writing Code for Mathematical Operations 95

Example 8.1 Standard Arithmetic Calculations 95

Example 8.2 Pythagorean Theorem 96

Example 8.3: BMI Calculator 96

Chapter 9 String Manipulation 100

  9.1 String Manipulation Using + and & signs 100

    Example 9.1 100

    Example 9.2 101

  9.2 String Manipulation Using Built-in Functions 103

    9.2 (a) The Len Function 103

    Example 9.3 103

    9.2(b) The Right Function 104

    Example 9.4 104

    9.2(c) The Left Function 105

    9.2 (d) The Mid Function 105

    Example 9.5 106

    Example 9.6 106

    9.2(e) Trim Function 107

    Example 9.7 108

    9.2(f) Ltrim Function 108

    9.2(g)The Rtrim Function 108

    9.2(h) The InStr function 109

    9.2(i) The Ucase and the Lcase Functions 109

    9.2(j) The Chr and the Asc functions 110

Chapter 10 Using If...Then...Else 111

  10.1 Conditional Operators 111

10.2 Logical Operators 112

10.3 Using If ...Then...Else 113

    10.3(a) If...Then Statement 113

    Example 10.1 113

    10.3(b) If...Then...Else Statement 114

    Example 10.2 114

    Example 10.3 118

    10.3(c) If...Then...ElseIf Statement 120

    Example 10.4 Grade Generator 121

Chapter 11 Using Select Case 123

11.1 The Select Case...End Select Structure 123

11.2 The usage of Select Case 124

    Example 11.1: Examination Grades 124

    Example 11.2 125

    Example 11.3 126

    Example 11.4 127

Chapter 12 Looping 129

12.1 For...Next Loop 129

    Example 12.1 a 130

    Example 12.1b 130

    Example 12.1c 130

    Example 12.1d 131

12.2 Do Loop 131

    Example 12.2(a) 132

    Example 12.2(b) 133

12.3 While...End While Loop 134

    Example 12.3 135

Chapter 13 Sub Procedures 136

    13.1 What is a Sub Procedure 136

    13.2 Examples of Sub Procedure 136

        Example 13.1 136

        Example 13.2: Password Cracker 138

Chapter 14 Creating Functions 142

    14.1 Creating User-Defined Functions 142

        Example 14.1: BMI Calculator 143

        Example 14.2: Future Value Calculator 144

    14.2 Passing Arguments by Value and by Reference 146

        Example 14.2(a) 147

Chapter 15 Mathematical Functions 150

    15.1 The Abs Function 150

        Example 15.1 150

    15.2 The Exp function 151

        Example 15.2 152

    15.3 The Fix Function 153

        Example 15.3 153

    15.4 The Int Function 154

    15.5 The Log Function 154

        Example 15.4 155

    15.6 The Rnd( ) Function 155

        Example 15.5 156

15.7 The Round Function.. 157

    Example 15.6 157

Chapter 16 The Format Function 159

    16.1 Format Function for Numbers 159

        16.1(a) Built-in Format function for Numbers 159

        Example 16.1 160

        16.1(b) User-Defined Format 161

        Example 16.2 163

    16.2 Formatting Date and Time 164

        16.2(a) Formatting Date and time using predefined formats 164

        Example 16.3 165

        16.2(b) Formatting Date and time using user-defined formats
        166

        Example 16.4 167

Chapter 17 Using Checkbox and Radio Button 170

    17.1 Check Box 170

        Example 17.1: Shopping Mall 170

        Example 17.2 173

        Example 17.3 173

    17.2 Radio Button 176

        Example 17.4 176

        Example 17.5 178

Chapter 18 Errors Handling 182

    18.1 Introduction to Object Oriented Programming 182

    18.2 Using On Error GoTo Syntax 183

Example 18.1: Division Errors 183

18.3 Errors Handling with Try...Catch ...End Try Structure 185

Chapter 19 Object Oriented Programming 187

    19.1 Concepts of Object-Oriented Programming 187

        (a) Encapsulation 187

        (b) Inheritance 187

        (c) Polymorphism 188

    19.2 Creating Class 188

Chapter 20 Creating Graphics 194

    20.1 Introduction to Graphics Creation 194

    20.2 Creating the Graphics Object 194

    20.3 Creating the Pen Object 195

    20.4 Drawing a Line 196

    20.5 Drawing Lines that Connect Multiple Points 198

        Example 20.1 198

    20.6 Drawing a curve that Connect Multiple Points 200

        Example 20.2 200

    20.7 Drawing a Quadratic Curve 202

        Example 20.3 202

    20.8 Drawing a Sine Curve 204

        Example 20.4 205

    20.9 Drawing a Rectangle 206

    20.10 Customizing Line Style of the Pen Object 208

        Example 20.5 208

    20.11 Drawing an Ellipse 210

Example 20.6 212

Example 20.7 213

20.12 Drawing a Circle.. 213

Example 20.8 214

Example 20.9 214

20.13 Drawing Text 215

Example 20.10 216

Example 20.11 218

20.14 Drawing Polygons 219

Example 20.12 Drawing a Triangle............................... 220

Example 20.13 Drawing a Quadrilateral 222

20.15 Drawing a Pie 223

Example 20.14 Drawing a pie that sweeps clockwise through 60 degrees. 224

20.16 Filling Shapes with Color 224

20.16(a) Drawing and Filling a Rectangle with Color 225

Example 20.15 225

20.16(b) Drawing and Filling an Ellipse with Color 227

Example 20.16 227

20.16(c) Drawing and Filling a Polygon with Color 228

Example 20.17 228

20.16(d) Drawing and Filling a Pie............................. 229

Example 20.18 230

Chapter 21 Using Timer 231

21.1 Creating a Digital Clock 231

21.2 Creating a Stopwatch 233

21.3 Creating a Digital Dice..235

Chapter 22 Creating Animation 238

22.1 Creating Motion 238

22.2 Creating a Graphical Dice 240

22.3 Creating a Slot Machine..243

Chapter 23 Working with Databases 247

23.1 Introduction to Database 247

23.2 Creating a Database Application 248

23.3 Creating a Connection to a Database using ADO.NET.......249

23.4 Populating Data in ADO.NET...................................257

    Example 23.1 259

    23.5 Browsing Records 262

23.6 Editing, Saving, Adding and Deleting Records 263

    Example 23.2..264

23.7 Accessing Database using DataGridView 269

    Example 23.3..270

23.8 Performing Arithmetic Calculations in a Database 271

    Example 23.4..272

    Example 23.5..273

    Example 23.6..276

Chapter 24 Reading and Writing Text Files 279

24.1 Introduction 279

24.2 Reading a Text File...279

24.3 Writing to a Text File 284

Chapter 25 Building Console Applications 287

    25.1 Introduction 287

        Example 25.1: Displaying a Message 290

    25.2 Creating a Text File Writer in Console 291

        Example 25.2 292

    25.3 Creating a Text File Reader in Console 293

        Example 25.3 293

    25.4 Creating a Console App using If...Then...Else 294

        Example 25.4 294

Chapter 26 Creating Menu Bar and Toolbar 297

    26.1 Creating Menu Items on the Menu Bar 297

    26.2 Creating the Toolbar 308

Chapter 27 Deploying your VB 2019 Applications 316

    Index 322

Chapter 1 Introduction to Visual Basic 2019

1.1 A Brief History of Visual Basic

Visual Basic is a third-generation event-driven programming language first released by Microsoft in 1991. The final version of the classic Visual Basic was Visual Basic 6. Visual Basic 6 is a user-friendly programming language designed for beginners. Therefore, it enables anyone to develop GUI Windows applications easily. Many developers still favor VB6 over its successor VB.NET.

In 2002, Microsoft released Visual Basic.NET (VB.NET) to replace Visual Basic 6. Thereafter, Microsoft declared VB6 a legacy programming language in 2008. However, Microsoft still provides some form of support for VB6. VB.NET is a fully object-oriented programming language implemented in the .NET Framework. It was created to cater for the development of the web as well as mobile applications. Subsequently, Microsoft has released many versions of VB.NET. They are Visual Basic 2005, Visual Basic 2008, Visual Basic 2010, Visual Basic 2012, Visual Basic 2013, Visual Basic 2015, Visual Basic 2017 and Visual Basic 2019. Although the .NET portion was discarded in 2005, all versions of the Visual Basic programming language released since 2002 are regarded as the VB.NET programming language

Microsoft has released Visual Studio 2019 in early 2019. VS 2019 allows you to code in different programming languages and different platforms, Visual Basic 2019 is one of them. The other Programming languages are C#, C++, F#, JavaScript, Java and Python. Visual Basic

2019 is the latest version VB.NET programming language released by Microsoft.

Learn more about Visual Studio 2019 from the Youtube link below:

https://youtu.be/n5sJ4EewKGk

1.2 Installation of Visual Studio 2019

You can download the free version of Visual Studio 2019 from the following link:

https://visualstudio.microsoft.com/vs/

Clicking the link brings up the Visual Studio 2019 download page, as shown below:

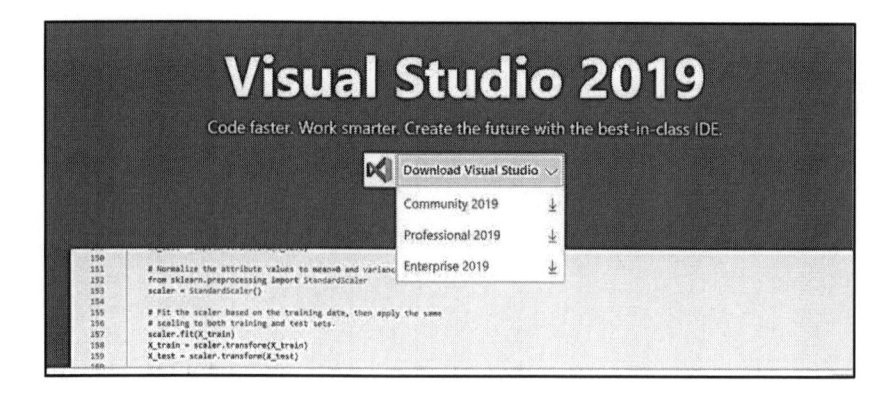

Figure 1.1

You can choose the free Visual Studio Community 2019 or the Full-featured Professional 2019 and End-to-End solution Enterprise 2019 to download. The free version that provides full-featured IDE for students, open source community and individuals. As this book was written based on the free version, proceed to download the free Visual Studio 2019 Community, select community, and download the installer file. The downloaded installer file will appear on your Windows 10 taskbar. Click it to install Visual Studio 2019. Clicking the Visual Studio 2019 Installer will start downloading, unpacking, and installing the files necessary for the installation of Visual Studio 2019, as shown in Figure 1.2

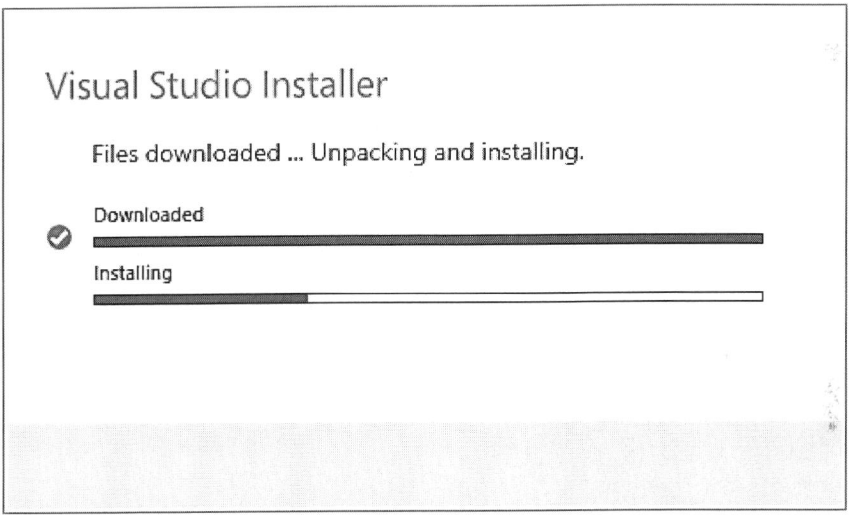

Figure 1.2

You will see several status screens that show the progress of the installation. After the installer has finished installing, it is time to pick the feature set that you wish to install, as shown in Figure 1.3. Since we are focusing on developing Visual Basic 2019 desktop app, we will select the .NET desktop development component. After making your selections, click install.

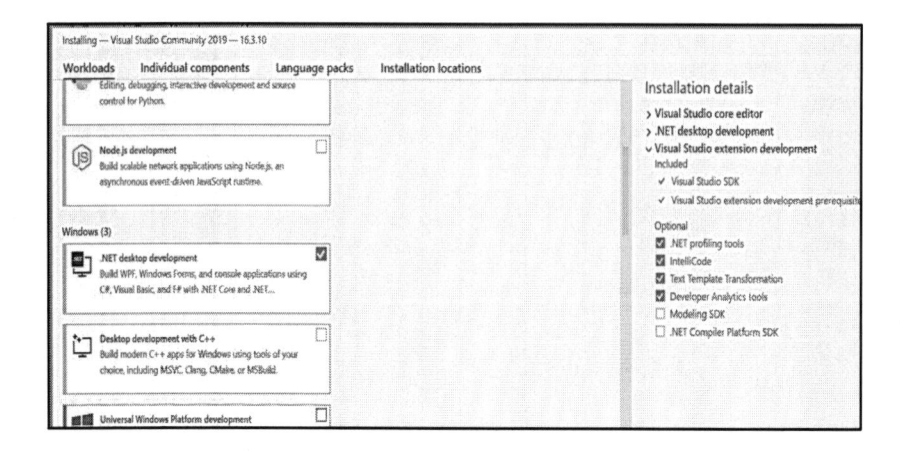

Figure 1.3

Upon completion of the installation, you are now ready to launch Visual Studio 2019 and start programming in Visual Basic 2019

1.3 Creating a Visual Basic 2019 Project

Launching Microsoft Visual Studio 2019 will bring you to the Visual Studio 2019 Start Page, as shown in Figure 1.4

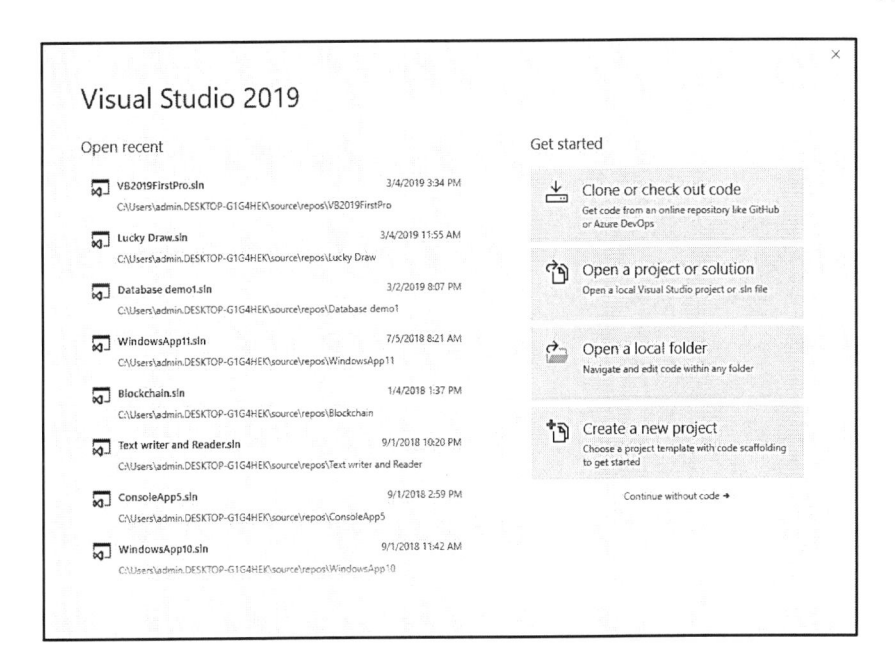

Figure 1.4 Visual Studio 2019 Start Page

The Visual Studio 2019 start page comprises two sections, the Open Recent section, and the Get Started section. In the start page, you can select a recent project file or choose any option in the Get Started section. You can choose to clone a project from GitHub or Azure DevOps, open a project or solution, open a local folder, create a new project, or continue without code.

Let us create a new project by clicking on the Create a new project option. You will now see the Create a new project template page, as shown in Figure 1.5. In the Create a new project page, select the Visual Basic language.

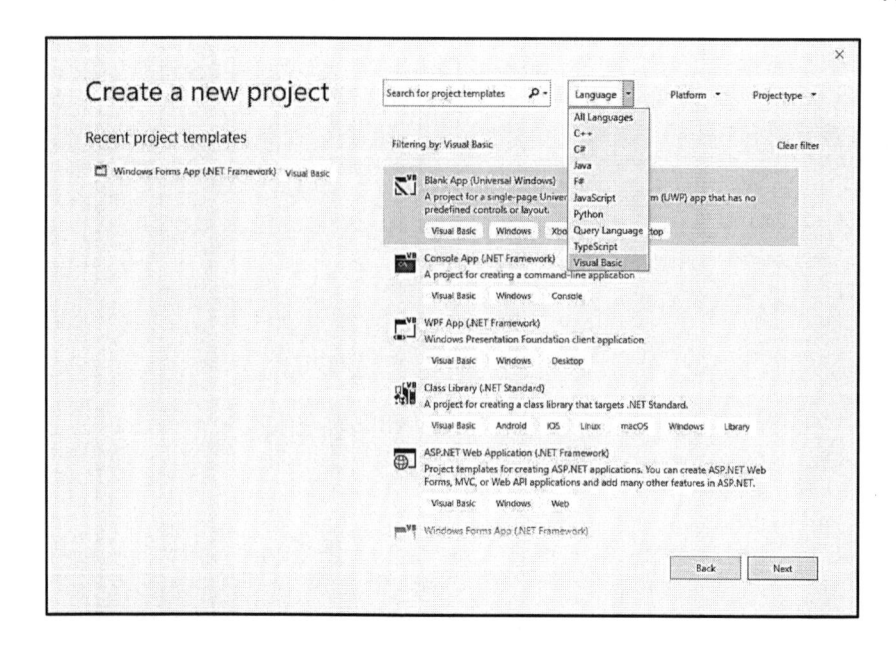

Figure 1.5 Create a new project template

Next, select the Windows Forms App (.Net Framework) template as we want to develop a Windows desktop project, as shown in Figure 1.6

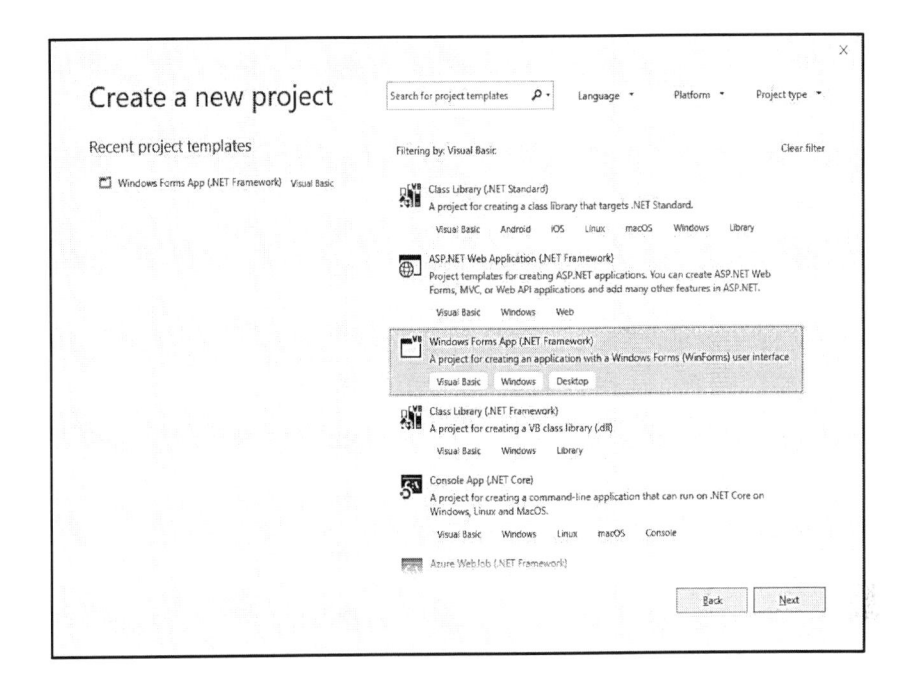

Figure 1.6 Create a new project template

Upon clicking the selected project template, the project configuration page appears, as shown in Figure 1.7. You can configure your project by typing the project name and select a few other options.

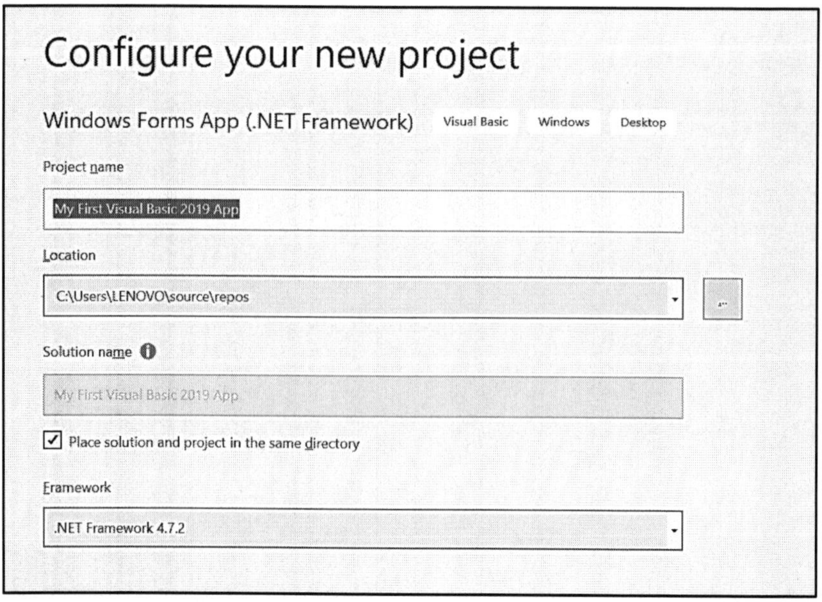

Figure 1.7 Configuring Project

At the bottom of this dialog box, you can change the default project name WindowsApplication1 to some other name you like, for example, My First Visual Basic 2019 App. After renaming the project, click OK to continue. The Visual Basic 2019 IDE Windows will appear, as shown in Figure 1.8. Visual Basic 2019 IDE comprises a few windows, the Form window, the Solution Explorer window, and the Properties window. It also consists of a toolbox which contains many useful controls that allows the programmer to develop his or her Visual Basic 2019 programs.

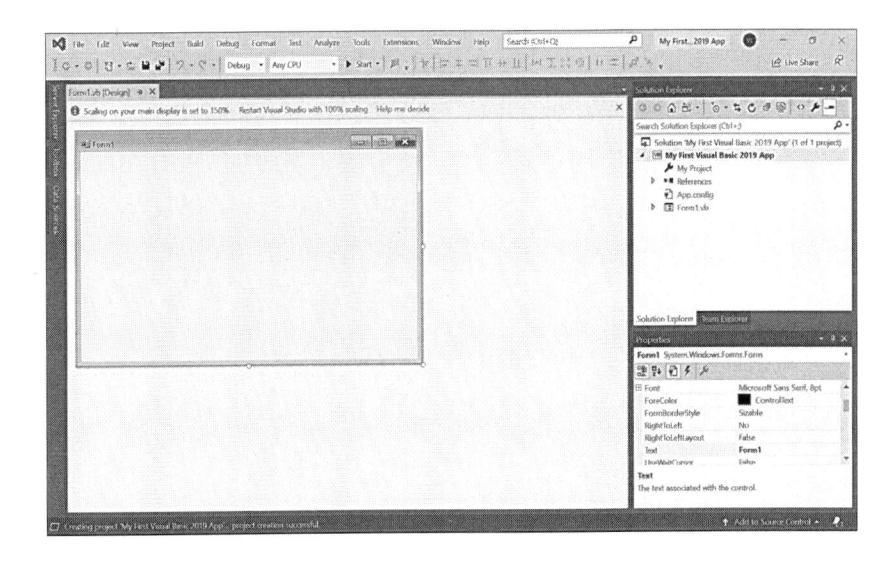

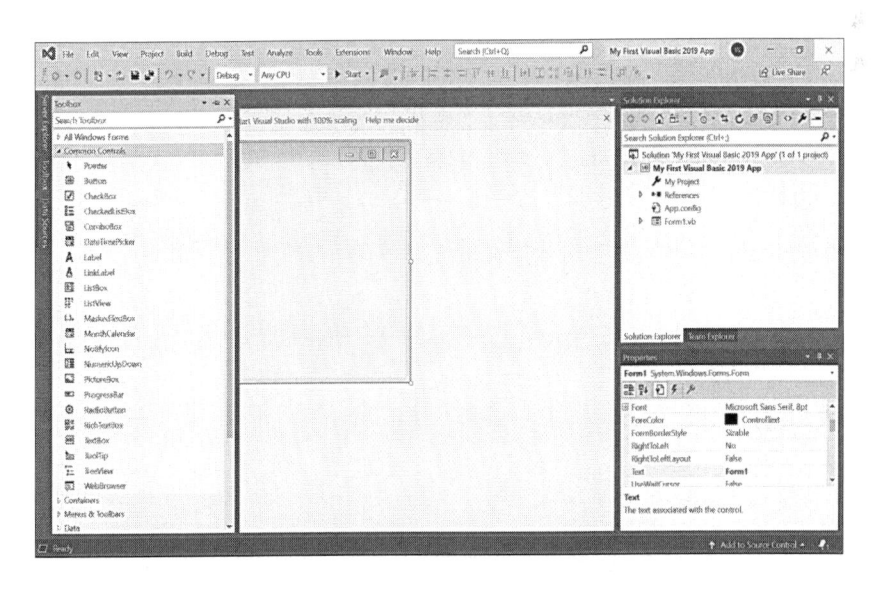

Figure 1.8 The Visual Basic 2019 Express IDE

The Toolbox is not shown until you click on the Toolbox tab. When you click on the Toolbox tab or use the shortcut keys Ctrl+Alt+x, the common controls Toolbox will appear, as shown in Figure 1.9. You can drag and move your toolbox around and dock it to the right, left, top or bottom of the IDE.

Figure 1.9 Visual Basic 2019 Toolbox

Next, we shall proceed to show you how to create your first VB2019 application. First, change the text of the form to 'My First VB 2019 App' in the properties window; it will appear as the title of the application. Next, insert a button and change its text to OK. The design interface is shown in Figure 1.10

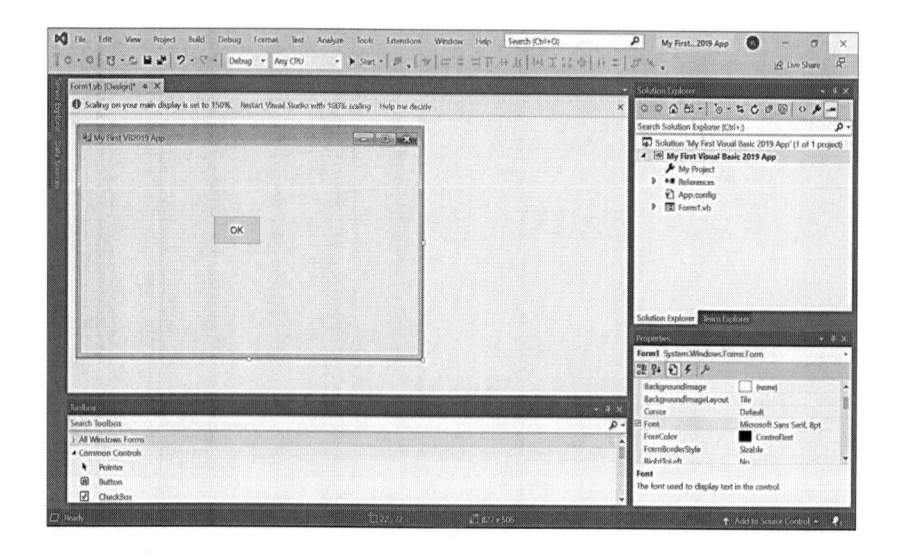

Figure 1.10 The Design Interface

Now click on the OK button to bring up the code window and enter the following statement between **Private Sub** and **End Sub** procedure, as shown in Figure 1.11.

MsgBox("My First Visual Basic 2019 App")

Clicking the Start button on the toolbar or press F5 to run the application will launch the runtime interface, as shown in Figure 1.11. Executing the application by clicking on the OK button will bring up a dialog box that displays the "My First Visual Basic 2019 App" message, as shown in Figure 1.12. The function **MsgBox** is a built-in function of Visual Basic 2019 which can display the text enclosed within the brackets.

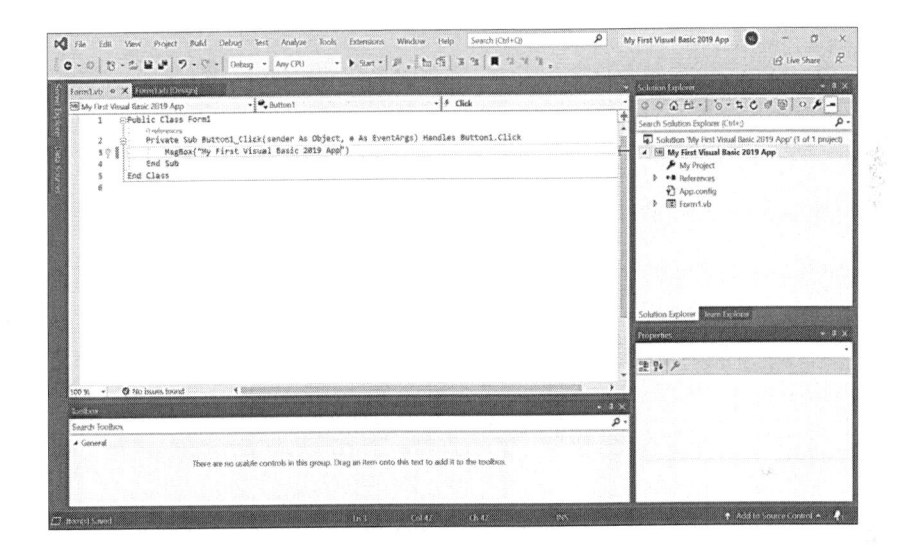

Figure 1.11 Visual Basic 2019 Code Window

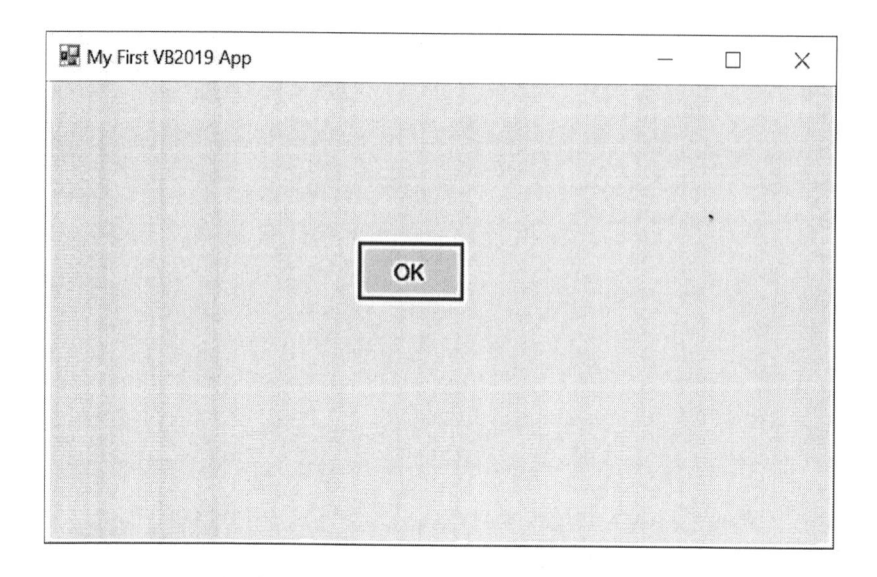

Figure 1.12 The Runtime Interface

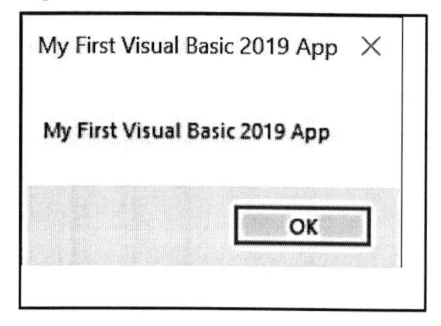

Figure 1.13 The Message Box

Summary

- In section 1.1, you have learned about the history of Visual Basic 2019
- In section 1.2, you have learned how to install and launch Visual Basic Studio 2019
- In section 1.3, you have learned how to launch the new project dialog and the Visual Basic 2019 IDE. You have also learned how to write your first program.

Chapter 2 Designing the User Interface

As Visual Basic 2019 is a GUI-based programming language, the first step in developing an application is to design the user interface (UI). To build a graphical user interface, first of all you need to customize the default form by changing its properties at design phase and at runtime, including its name, title, background color and so forth. After customizing the default form, you may proceed to add controls from the toolbox to the form and then customize their properties.

2.1 Customizing the Form

When you start a new Visual Basic 2019 project, the VB2019 IDE will display the default form along with the Solution Explorer window and the Properties window, as shown in Figure 2.1. The name of the default form is Form1. The properties window displays all the properties related to Form1 and their corresponding attributes or values. You can change the name of the form, the title of the form using the text property, the background color, the foreground color, size and more. Try changing the following properties:

Property	Value
Name	MyForm
Text	My First VB2019 App
BackColor	LavenderBlush
ForeColor	Crimson
MaximizeBox	False

In fact, you do not have to type in the color manually, you can indeed select a color from the color drop-down list that comprises three tabs, Custom, Web, and System, as shown in Figure 2.1. Clicking on the drop-down arrow will bring out a color palette or a list of color rectangles where you can select a color.

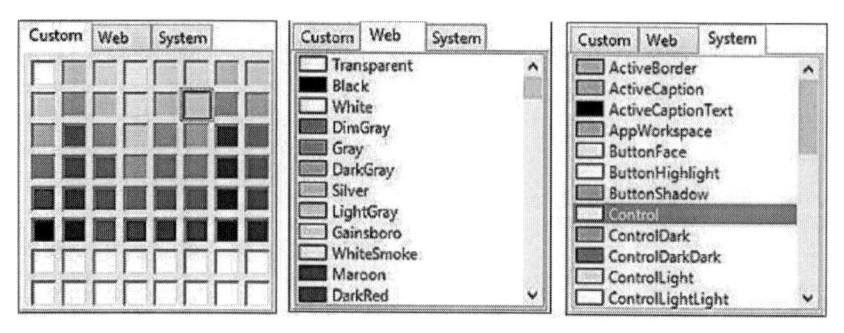

Figure 2.1

Another method of setting the colors is to manually type in the RGB color code or the hex color code. The values of R, G and B ranges from 0 to 255, therefore, by varying the values of the RGB we can obtain different colors. For example, an RGB value of 128, 255, 255 yield the cyan color.

On the other hand, the hex color code system uses a six-digit, three-byte hexadecimal number to represent colors. The bytes represent the red, green and blue components of the color. One byte represents a number ranging from 00 to FF (in hexadecimal notation), or 0 to 255 in decimal notation. For example, `#0000ff` represents the cyan color. However, when you type the Hex color code in the properties window of VS2019, it automatically converts the color to RGB color or the color name. Figure 2.2 shows a list of Hex color codes and the corresponding colors.

color	code	color	code	color	code	color	code	color	code
	eeeeee		ffffcc		ffccff		ff99ff		ff66ff
	dddddd		ffff99		ffcccc		ff99cc		ff66cc
	cccccc		ffff66		ffcc99		ff9999		ff6666
	bbbbbb		ffff33		ffcc66		ff9966		ff6633
	aaaaaa		ffff00		ffcc33		ff9933		ff6633
	999999		ccffff		ffcc00		ff9900		ff6600
	888888		ccffcc		ccccff		cc99ff		cc66ff
	777777		ccff99		cccccc		cc99cc		cc66cc
	666666		ccff66		cccc99		cc9999		cc6699
	555555		ccff33		cccc66		cc9966		cc6666
	444444		ccff00		cccc33		cc9933		cc6633
	333333		99ffff		cccc00		cc9900		cc6600
	222222		99ffcc		99ccff		9999ff		9966ff
	111111		99ff99		99cccc		9999cc		9966cc
	ff0000		99ff66		99cc99		999966		996699
	ee0000		99ff33		99cc33		999933		996633
	cc0000		66ffff		66ccff		6699ff		6666ff
	33ffff		00ffff		00ccff		3399ff		3366ff
	ff00ff		cc00ff		00ee00		0000ff		6600ff

Figure 2.2 Hex Color Codes

The design interface is shown in Figure 2.2 and the runtime interface is shown in Figure 2.4. In the runtime interface, notice that the title has been changed from Form1 to My First Visual Basic 2019 App, background color changed to LavenderBlush , the text OK color is Crimson and the window cannot be maximized.

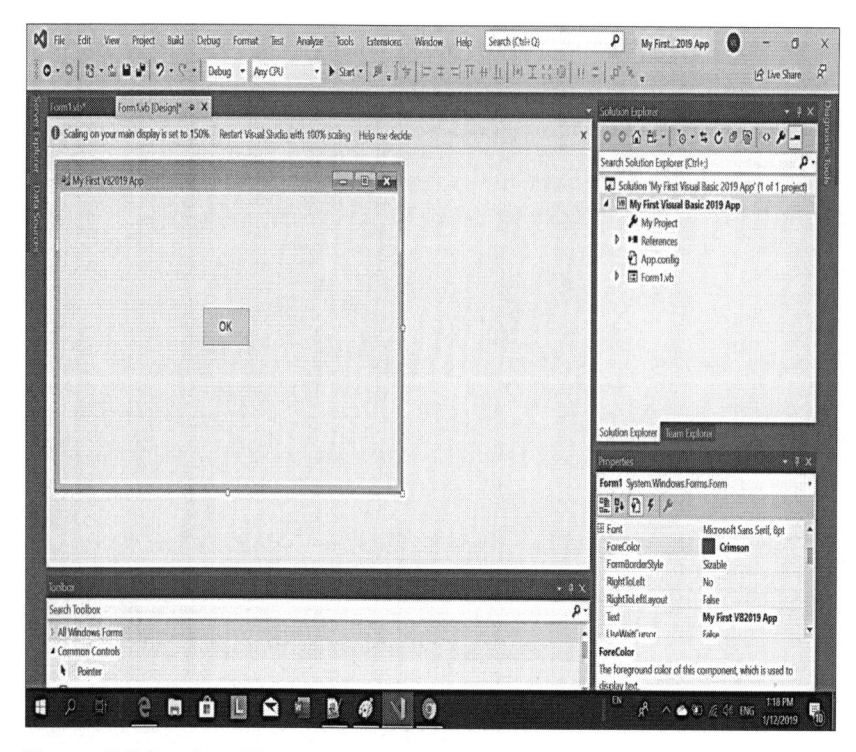

Figure 2.3 Design UI

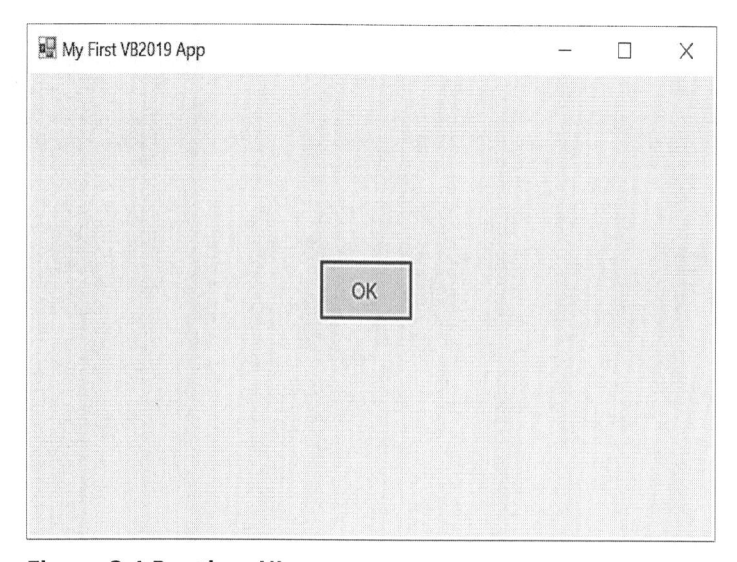

Figure 2.4 Runtime UI

You can also change the properties of the form at runtime by writing the relevant codes. The default form is an object and an instant of the form can be denoted by the name **Me**. The property of the object can be defined by specifying the object's name followed by a dot or period:

ObjectName.property

For example, we can set the background of the form to blue using the following code:

Me.BackColor=Color.Blue

In addition, you can also use the **FromArgb** method to specify the color using the RGB codes, as follows:

Me.BackColor = Color.FromArgb(0, 255, 0)

Now, type in the following code by clicking the form to enter the code window:

```
Private Sub Form1_Load(sender As Object, e As EventArgs)_
Handles_ MyBase.Load
    Me.Text = "My First Visual Basic 2019 Application"
    Me.BackColor = Color.Turquoise
    Me.ForeColor = Color.Ivory
    MyBtn.BackColor = Color.DodgerBlue
    Me.MaximizeBox = False
    Me.MinimizeBox = True
```

End Sub

To runtime UI is shown in Figure 2.5. Notice that is is now different from that shown in Figure 2.4,

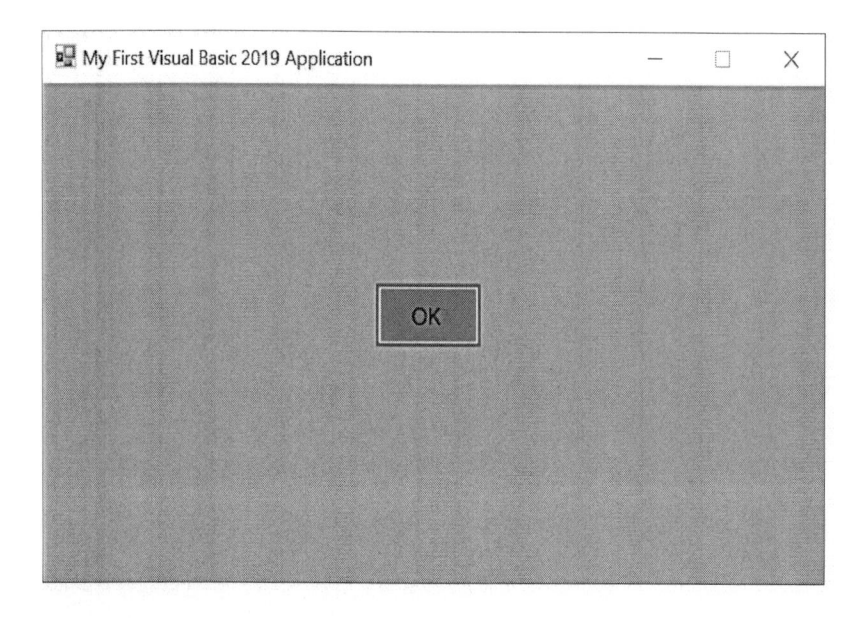

Figure 2.5

In place of Turquoise, you can use RGB code as follows:

Me.BackColor = Color.FromArgb(64,224,208)

In addition, you can also specify the size, the opacity and the position of the default form using the code, as follows:

Private Sub Form1_Load(sender As Object, e As EventArgs_

Handles MyBase.Load

Me.Text = "My First VB2019 App"
Me.BackColor =Color.Beige
Me.MaximizeBox = False
Me.MinimizeBox = True
Me.Size = New Size(400, 400)
Me.Opacity = 0.85
Me.CenterToParent()

End Sub

The property Opacity sets the degree of transparency. The runtime interface is as shown in Figure 2.6

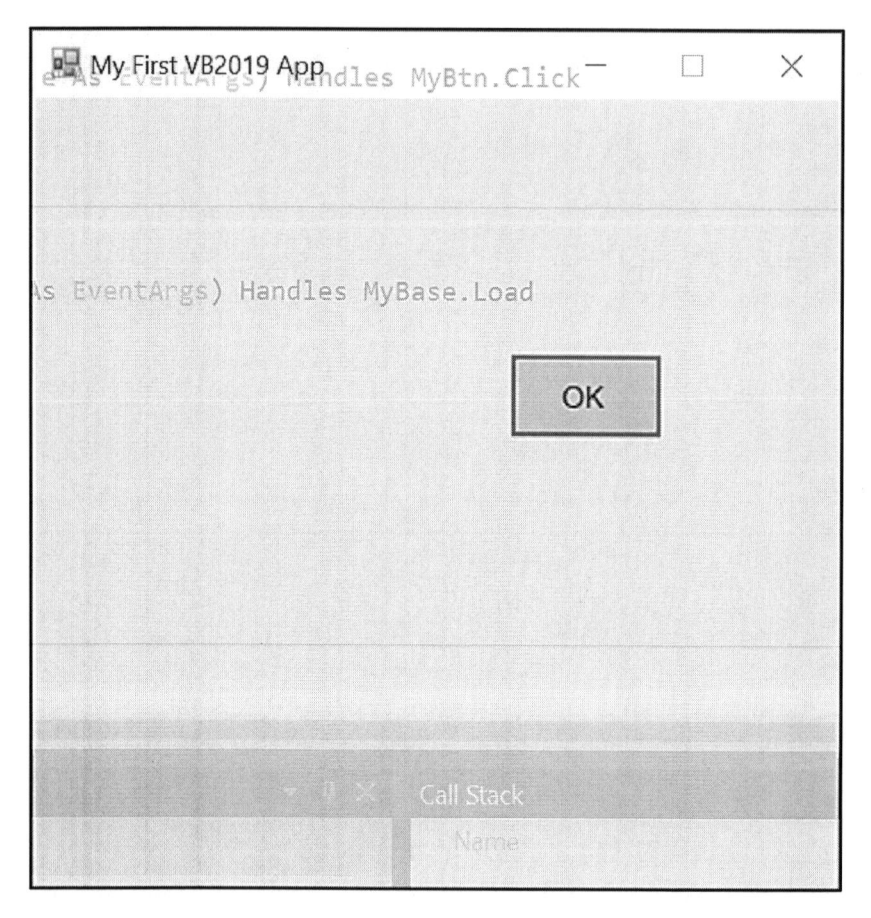

Figure 2.6

2.2 Adding Controls to the Form

In section 2.1, we have learned how to build an initial UI in Visual Basic 2019 by customizing the default form. Next, we shall continue to build the UI by adding some controls to the form. The controls are objects that consist of three elements, namely properties, methods, and events. They can be added to the form from the Toolbox. Among the controls, the most common ones are the button, label, textbox, listbox, combobox, picture box, checkbox, radio button and more. These controls can be made visible or invisible at runtime. However, some controls will only run in the background and never be seen at runtime, one such control is the timer.

The Toolbox is usually hidden when you start Visual Basic 2019 IDE, you need to click View on the menu bar and then select Toolbox to reveal the tool box, as shown in Figure 2.6. You can also use shortcut keys Ctrl+w+x to bring out the toolbox.

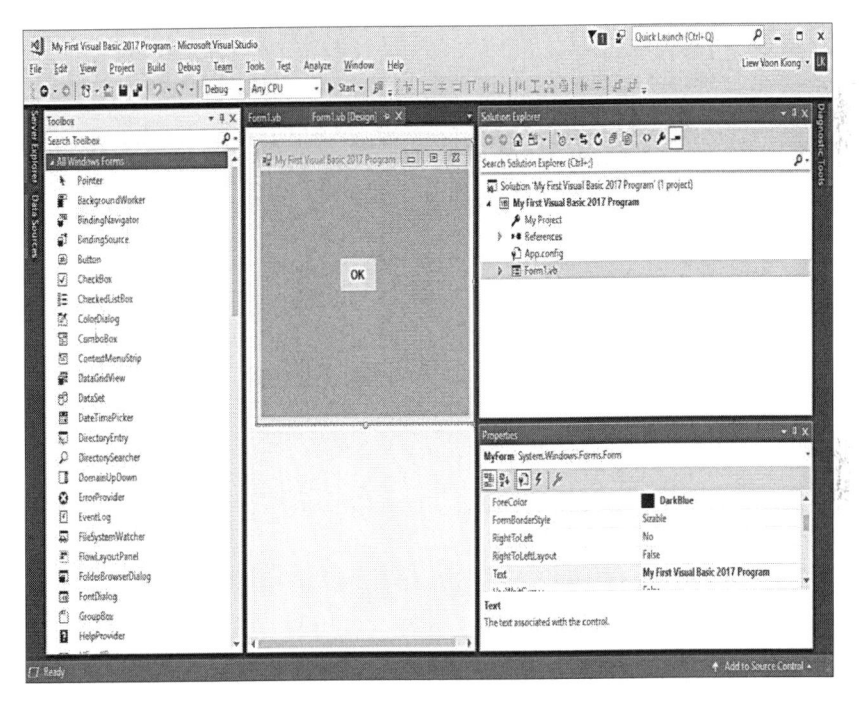

Figure 2.6: Toolbox

You can position the Toolbox by dragging it anywhere you like while its status is set to float. You can also dock the toolbox by right-clicking on the Toolbox and choose dock from the pop-up menu. The docked Toolbox that appears side by side with the Solution Explorer, and as one of the tabbed windows together with the Form Design window and the code window, as shown in Figure 2.7.

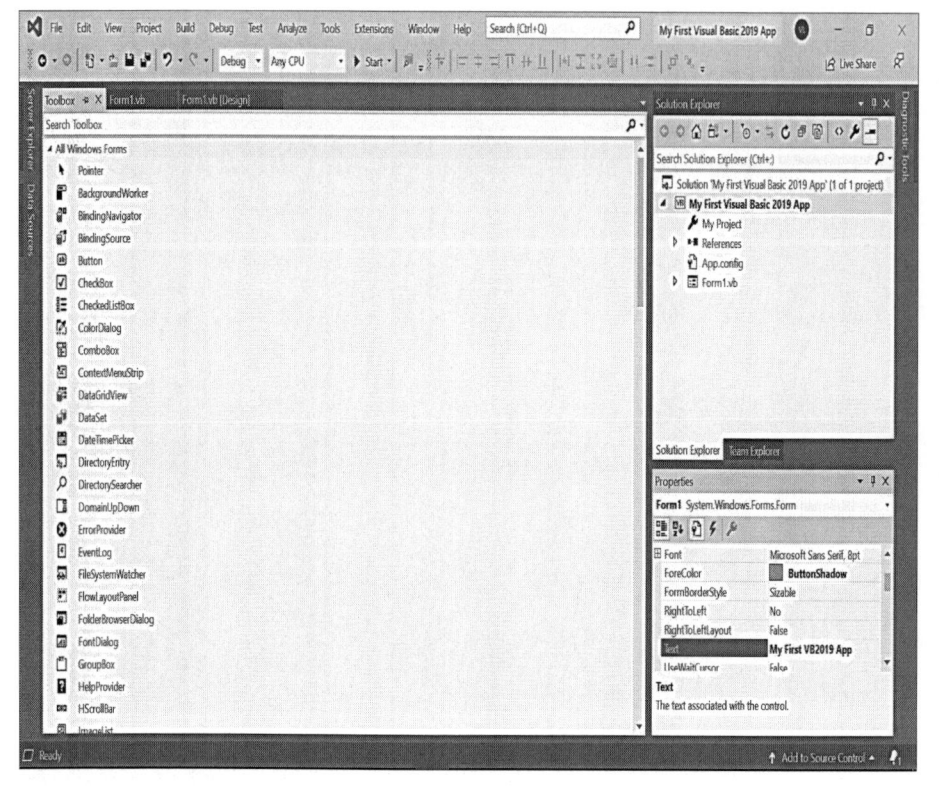

Figure 2.7 Toolbox

You can also dock the Toolbox at the bottom, below the default form, as shown in Figure 2.8. Further, you may also pin the Toolbox to the side bar or the bottom bar by clicking on the pin icon on the menu bar of the toolbox.

How and where you want to position your tool box is entirely up to you but we strongly suggest that you place the tool box alongside or at the bottom of the default form so that it is easy for you to add controls from the tool box into the form. You should never cover the form with the Toolbox because it will be difficult to add controls to the form.

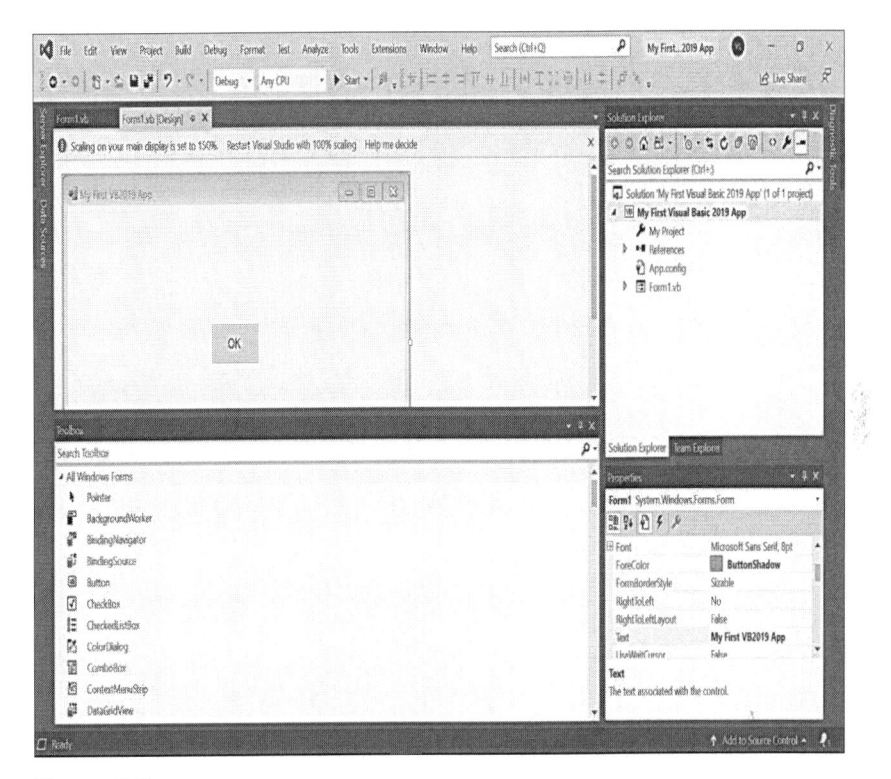

Figure 2.8

Adding a control to the form is an easy task, what you need to do is double click it or drag it onto the form. You can drag the control around the form, and you can also resize it.

To demonstrate how to add the controls and then change their properties, we shall design a picture viewer. First, change the title of the default form to Picture Viewer in its properties window. Next, insert a picture box on the form and change its background color to white. To do this, right click the picture box and select properties in the popup menu, then look for the **BackColor** Property as shown in the properties window in Figure 2.9. Finally, add two buttons to the form and change the text to View and Close in their respective properties windows. The picture viewer is not functional yet until we write code for responding to events triggered by the user. We will deal with the programming part in the coming chapters.

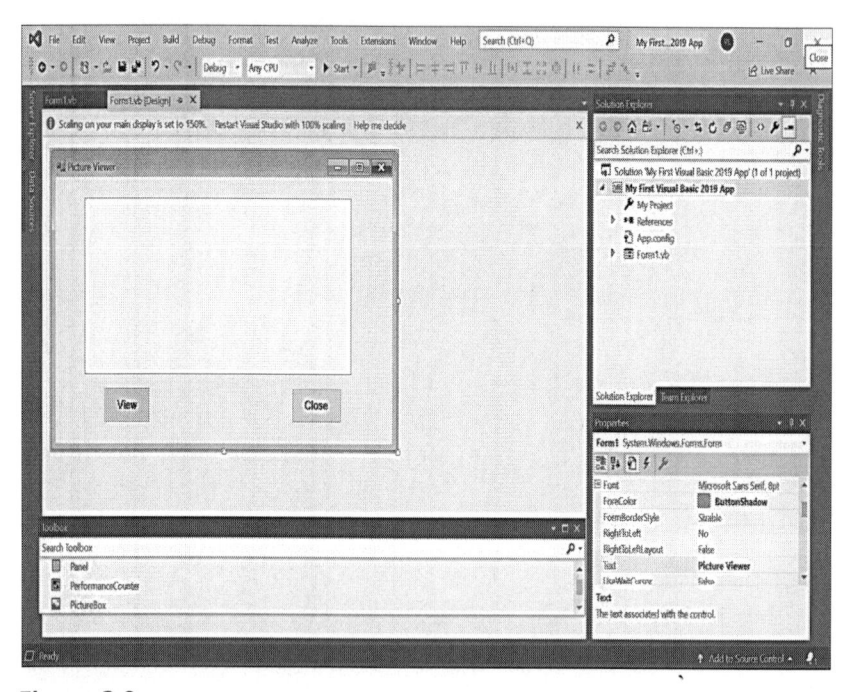

Figure 2.9

Summary

- In section 2.1, you have learned how to customize the form by changing the values of its properties.
- In section 2.2, you have learned how to add controls to the form and change their properties at design phase and at runtime.

Chapter 3 Writing the Code

In the previous chapter, we have learned how to design the user interface by adding controls to the form and by changing their properties. However, the user interface alone will not work without adding code to them. In this chapter, we shall learn how to write code for all the controls so that they can interact with the events triggered by the users. Before learning how to write Visual Basic 2019 code, let us delve into the concept of event-driven programming

3.1 The Concept of Event-Driven Programming

Visual Basic 2019 is an event-driven programming language meaning that the code is executed in response to events triggered by the user like clicking the mouse, pressing a key on the keyboard, selecting an item from a drop-down list, typing some words into text box and more. It may also be an event that runs in response to some other program. Some of the common events in Visual Basic 2019 are load, click, double-click, drag-drop, keypress and more.

Every form and every control you place on the form has a set of events related to them. To view the events, double-click the control on the form to enter the code window. The default event will appear at the top part on the right side of the code window. You need to click on the default event to view other events associated with the control. The code appears on the left side is the event procedure associated with the load event. Figure 3.1 illustrates the event procedure Load associated with the Form (its name has been changed to PicViewer therefore you can see the words PicViewer events) and Figure 3.2 shows the events associated with button.

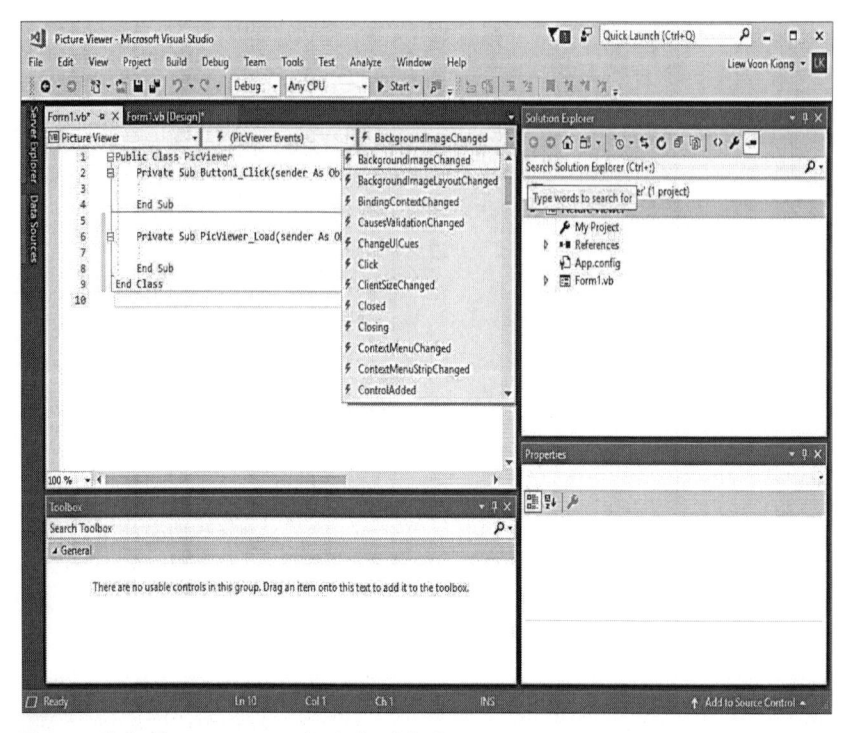

Figure 3.1: Events associated with Form

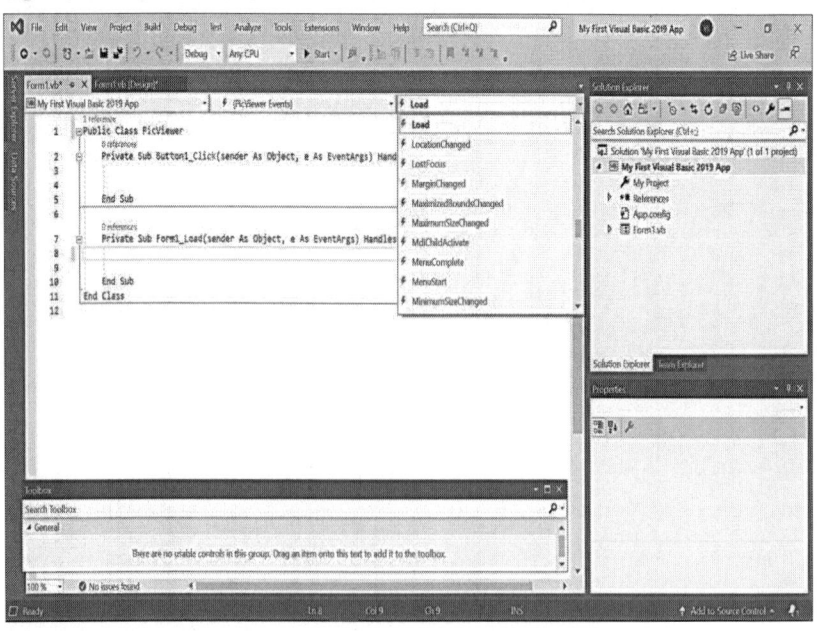

Figure 3.2: Events associated with the button

3.2 Writing the Code

To start writing code in Visual Basic 2019, click on any part of the form to go into the code window as shown in Figure 3.1. The event procedure is to load Form1 and it starts with the keywords **Private Sub** and ends with **End Sub**. This procedure includes the Form1 class and the event Load, and they are bound together with an underscore, i.e. **Form_Load**. It does nothing other than loading an empty form. To make the load event does something, insert the statement.

MsgBox ("Welcome to Visual Basic 2019")

The Code

Public Class Form1
Private Sub Form1_Load(sender As Object, e As EventArgs)_
Handles_ MyBase.Load

MsgBox ("My First Visual Basic 2019 APP", ,"My Message")

End Sub
End Class

MsgBox is a built-in function in Visual Basic 2019 that displays a message in a pop-up message box. The MsgBox function comprises a few arguments, the first being the message that is displayed and the third one is the title of the message box. When you run the program, a message box displaying the text "My First Visual Basic 2019 APP" will appear, as shown in Figure 3.3.

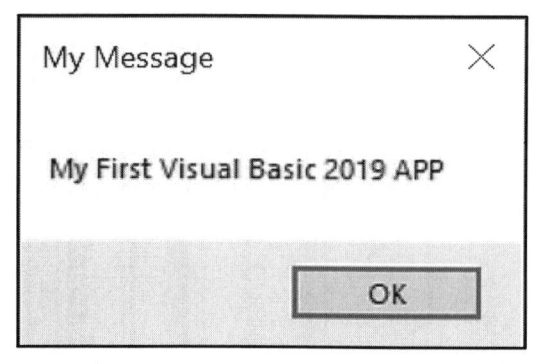

Figure 3.3

You will notice that above the Private Sub structure there is a preceding keyword **Public Class Form1**. This is the concept of the object-oriented programming language. When we start a windows application in Visual Basic 2019, we will see a default form with the name Form1 appears in the IDE, it is actually the Form1 Class that inherits from the Form class **System.Windows.Forms.Form**. A class has events as it creates an instant of a class or an object.

You can also write code to perform arithmetic calculations. For example, you can use the **MsgBox** and the arithmetic operator plus to perform addition of two numbers, as shown below:

Private Sub Form1_Load(sender As Object, e As EventArgs)_
Handles MyBase.Load

MsgBox("2" & "+" & "5" & "=" & 2 + 5)

End Sub

*The symbol & (ampersand) is to perform string concatenation. The output is as shown in Figure 3.4

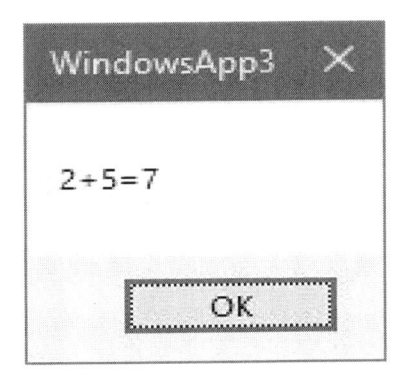

Figure 3.4

Summary

- In section 3.1, you have learned the concepts of event driven programming
- In section 3.2, you have learned how to write code for the controls

Chapter 4 Working with Controls

In the preceding chapter, we have learned how to write simple Visual Basic 2019 code. In this lesson, we shall learn how to work with some common controls and write codes for them. Some of the commonly used controls are Label, TextBox, Button, ListBox and ComboBox. However, in this chapter, we shall only deal with TextBox , Label, ListBox and ComboBox. We shall deal with the other controls later.

4.1 TextBox

TextBox is the standard control for accepting inputs from the user as well as to display the output. It can handle string (text) and numeric data but not images or pictures. String in a TextBox can be converted to a numeric data by using the function **Val(text)**. The following example illustrates a simple program that processes the input from the user.

Example 4.1

In this program, you add two text boxes and a button on the form. The two text boxes are for accepting inputs from the user. Besides that, we can also program a button to calculate the sum of the two numbers using the plus operator. The value entered into a TextBox is stored using the syntax **TextBox1.Text** , where Text is one of the properties of TextBox.

The following code will add the value in TextBox1 and the value in TextBox2 and displays the sum in a message box. The runtime interface is illustrated in Figure 4.1.

```
Private Sub Button1_Click(sender As Object, e As EventArgs)_
Handles Button1.Click

   MsgBox("The sum is" & Val(TextBox1.Text)
+ Val(TextBox2.Text))

End Sub
```

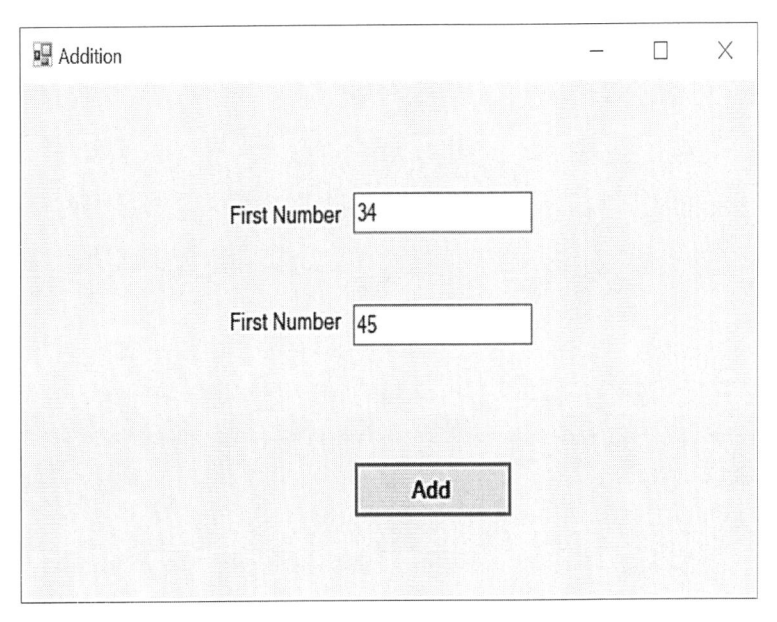

Figure 4.1

After clicking the Add button, you will obtain the answer in a message box, as shown in Figure 4.2.

Figure 4.2

4.2 Label

Label is an especially useful control for Visual Basic 2019 because we can use it for multiple purposes like providing instructions and guides to the users, displaying outputs and more. It is different from the TextBox because it is read only, which means the user cannot change or edit its content at runtime. Using the syntax `Label.Text`, it can display string as well as numeric data . You can change its text property in the properties window or at runtime by writing an appropriate code.

Example 4.2

Based on Example 4.1, we add two Labels, one is for displaying the text **Sum=** and the other Label is to display the answer of the Sum. For the first Label, change the text property of the label by typing Sum= over the default text Label1. Further, change its font to bold and its font size to 10. For the second label, delete the default text Label2 and change its font to bold and the font size to 10. Besides that, change its background color to white.

In this program, instead of showing the sum in a message box, we wish to display the sum on the Label.

The Code

```
Private Sub Button1_Click(sender As Object, e As EventArgs)_
  Handles Button1.Click
    LblSum.Text = Val(TextBox1.Text) + Val(TextBox2.Text)
End Sub
```

*The function Val is to convert text to numeric value. Without using Val, you will see that two numbers are joined without adding them.

The output is as shown in Figure 4.3

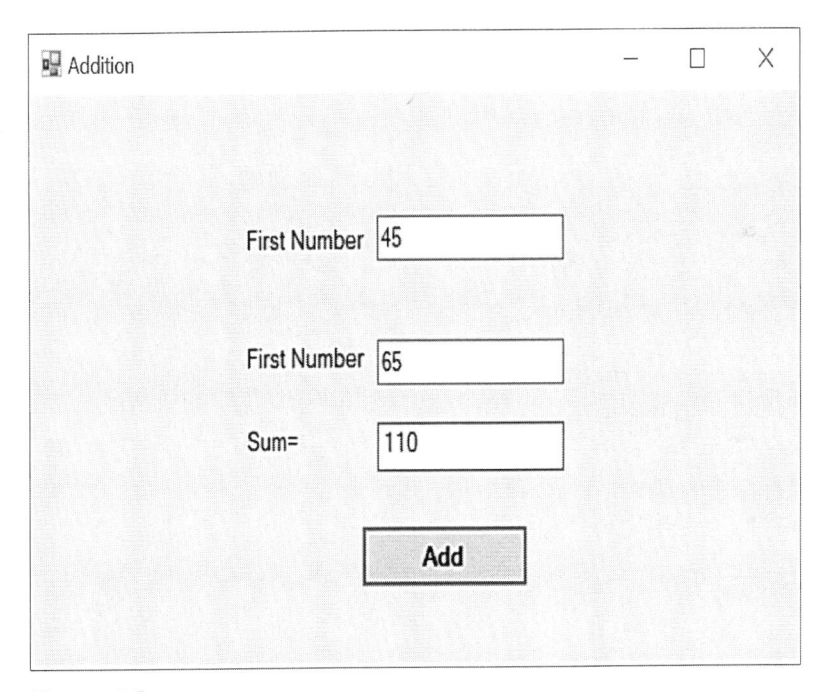

Figure 4.3

4.3 ListBox

The function of the ListBox is to display a list of items where the user can click and select the items from the list. Items can be added by the programmer at design time or at runtime using a code. We can also write code to allow the user to add items to the ListBox or remove the items from it.

4.3.1 Adding Items to a Listbox

a) Adding items using the String Collection Editor

To demonstrate how to add items at design time, start a new project and insert a ListBox on the form then right-click on the ListBox to access the properties window. Next, click on collection of the Item property, you will be presented with the *String Collection Editor* whereby you can enter the items one by one by typing the text and press the Enter key, as shown in Figure 4.4. After clicking on the OK button, the items will be displayed in the text box, as shown in Figure 4.5

Figure 4.4

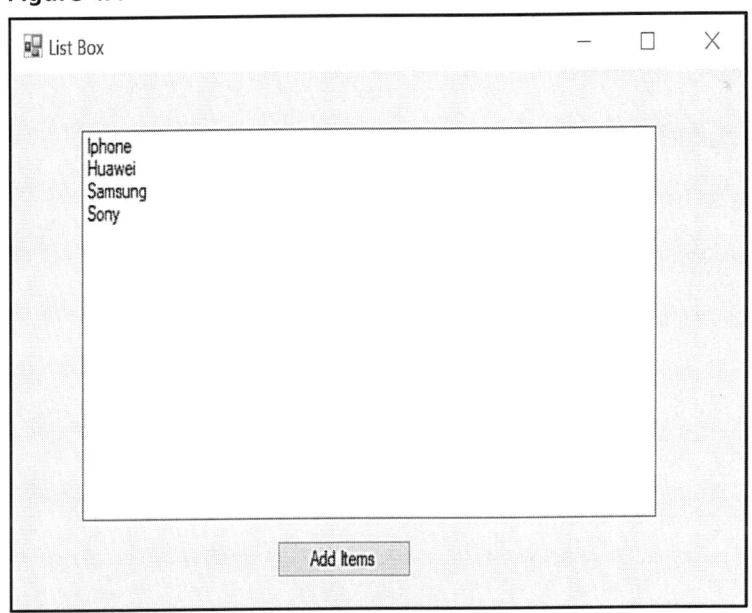

Figure 4.5

b) Adding Items using the Add() Method

Items can also be added at runtime using the **Add()** method. Before we proceed further, we should know that Visual Basic 2019 is an object oriented programming language. Therefore, visual basic 2019 comprises objects. All objects have methods and properties, and they can be differentiated and connected by a hierarchy. For a ListBox, an Item is an object subordinated to the object ListBox. The Item object comprises a method call **Add()** that is used to add items to the ListBox. To add an item to a ListBox, you can use the following syntax:

ListBox.Item.Add("Text")

Example 4.3

In this example, running the program will add the item "Vivo" to the end of the list, as shown in Figure 4.6

```
Private Sub BtnAdd_Click(sender As Object, e As EventArgs)_
Handles BtnAdd.Click
    MyListBox.Items.Add("Vivo")

End Sub
```

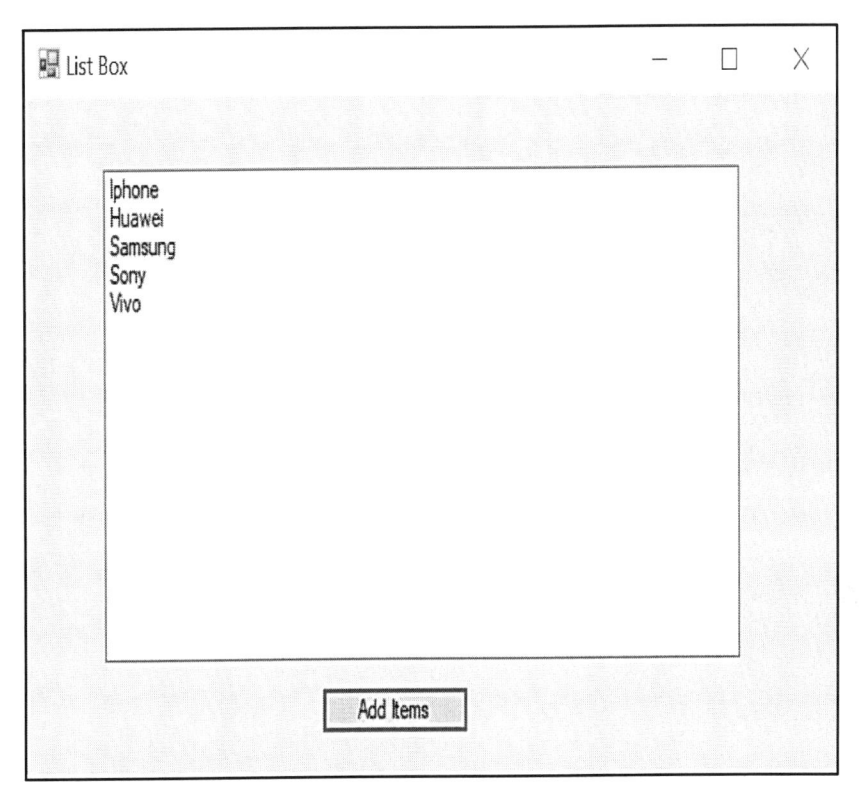

[Figure: List Box window showing items Iphone, Huawei, Samsung, Sony, Vivo with an "Add Items" button]

Figure 4.6

Example 4.4

In this example, you can allow the user to add items via a popup input box. First, we create a variable myitem and then assign a value to myitem via the InputBox function that store the input from the user. We then use the Add() method to add the user's item into the Listbox. The code is as follows:

```
Private Sub Button1_Click(sender As Object, e As EventArgs)_
Handles Button1.Click

Dim myitem                    'declare the variable myitem
myitem = InputBox("Enter your Item")
MyListBox.Items Add(myitem)
```

End Sub

The runtime interface is as shown in Figure 4.7

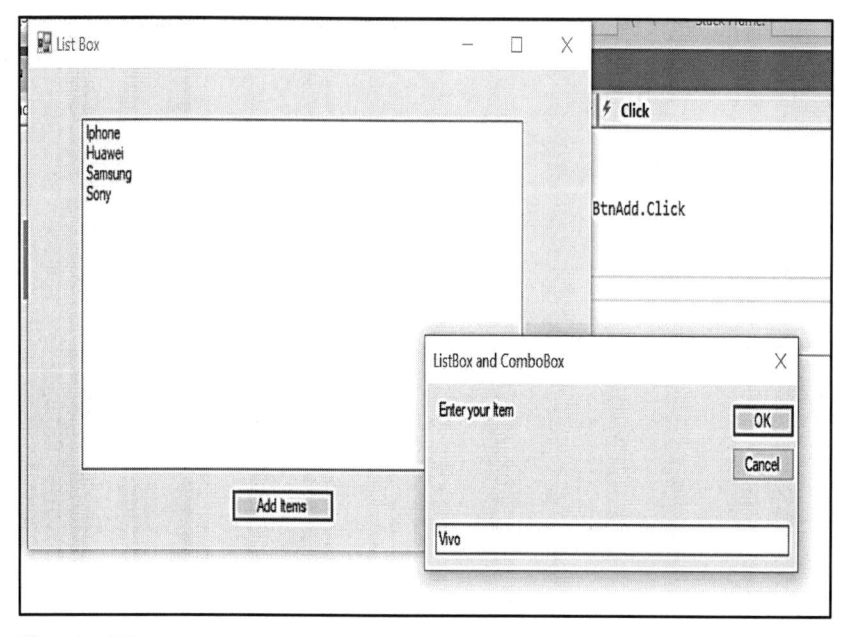

Figure 4.7
After typing the item 'Vivo" in the input box, the item will be added to the Listbox, as shown in Figure 4.8.

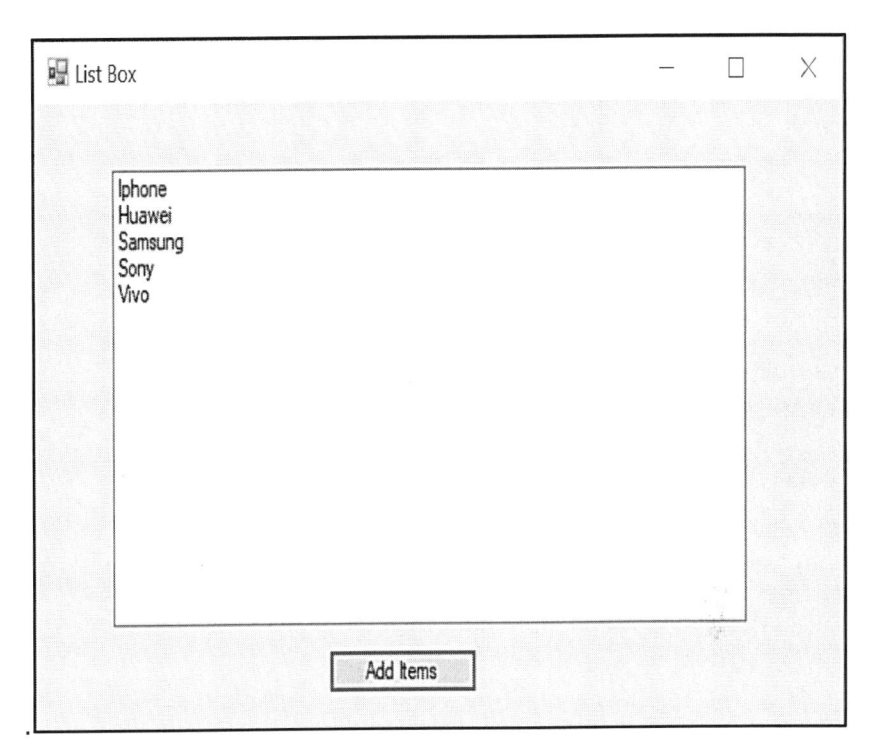

Figure 4.8

Example 4.5 Geometric Progression

This is a Visual Basic program that generates a geometric progression and displays the results in a Listbox. Geometric progression is a sequence of numbers where each subsequent number is found by multiplying the previous number with a fixed number. This fixed number is called the common ratio. The common ratio can be a negative number, an integer, a fraction, and any number but it must not be a zero.

The formula to find the nth term of the geometric progression is ar^{n-1}, where a is the first number and r is the common ratio.

In visual basic 207, we employ the **Do...Loop Until** statement to generate the numbers in a geometric progression. In this program, we need to insert three text boxes for the user to enter the first number, the common ratio and the number of terms. We also need to insert a Listbox to list the generated numbers. Besides that, a command button is needed for the user to generate the numbers in the geometric progression. In addition, we also add another button for clearing the list of generated numbers.

To add the numbers to the list box, we use the **Add()** method. The syntax is `ListBox1.Items.Add(x)`, where x can be any variable.

The code

```
Private Sub BtnComp_Click(sender As Object, e As EventArgs)_
Handles BtnComp.Click
    Dim x, n, num As Double
    Dim r As Double
    x = TxtFirst.Text
    r = TxtCR.Text
    num = TxtN.Text
    MyList.Items.Add("n" & vbTab & "x")
    MyList.Items.Add("_____")

    n = 1
    Do
        x = x * r
        MyList.Items.Add(n & vbTab & x)
        n = n + 1
    Loop Until n = num + 1
End Sub

Private Sub BtnClr_Click(sender As Object, e As EventArgs)_
```

```
Handles BtnClr.Click
    MyList.Items.Clear()
End Sub
```

The output is as shown in Figure 4.9

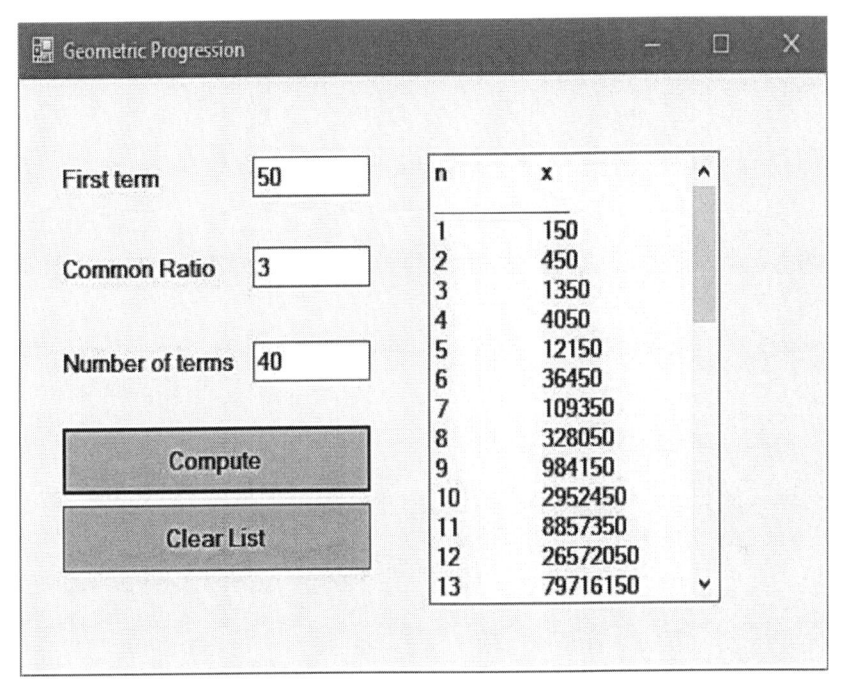

Figure 4.9 The runtime interface

4.3.2 Removing Items from a List Box

To remove items at design time, simply open the String Collection Editor and delete the items line by line or all at once using the Delete key. To remove the items at runtime, you can use the Remove method, as illustrated in the following Example 4.5.

Example 4.5

In this example, add a button and label it "Remove Items". Click on this button and enter the following code

```
Private Sub Button2_Click(sender As Object, e As EventArgs)_
 Handles Button2.Click
MyListBox.Items.Remove("Iphone")

End Sub
```

The item "Iphone" will be removed after running the program, as shown in Figure 4.10

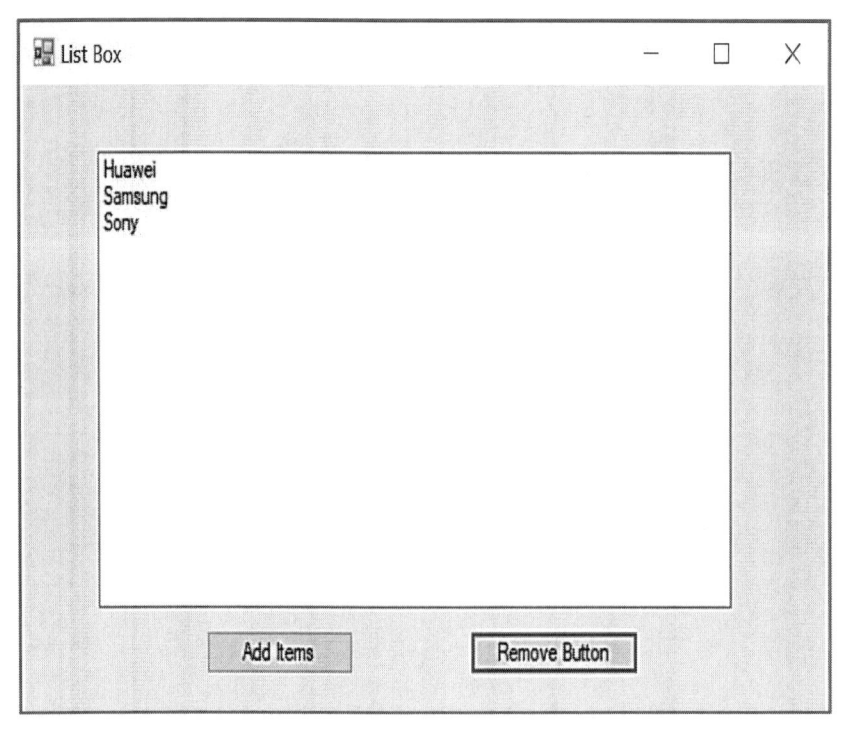

Figure 4.10

Example 4.6

You can also allow the user to choose an item to delete via an InputBox. To add this capability, insert a button at design time and change its text to Delete Item. Click on the button and enter the following statements in the code window:

Private Sub BtnDelete_Click(sender As Object, e As EventArgs)_
Handles BtnDelete.Click
    Dim myitem
    myitem = InputBox("Enter your Item for Deletion")
    MyListBox.Items.Remove(myitem)

End Sub

The runtime interface is as shown in Figure 4.10. After entering the item Ipone in the input box and press OK, the item Iphone will be deleted from the listbox.

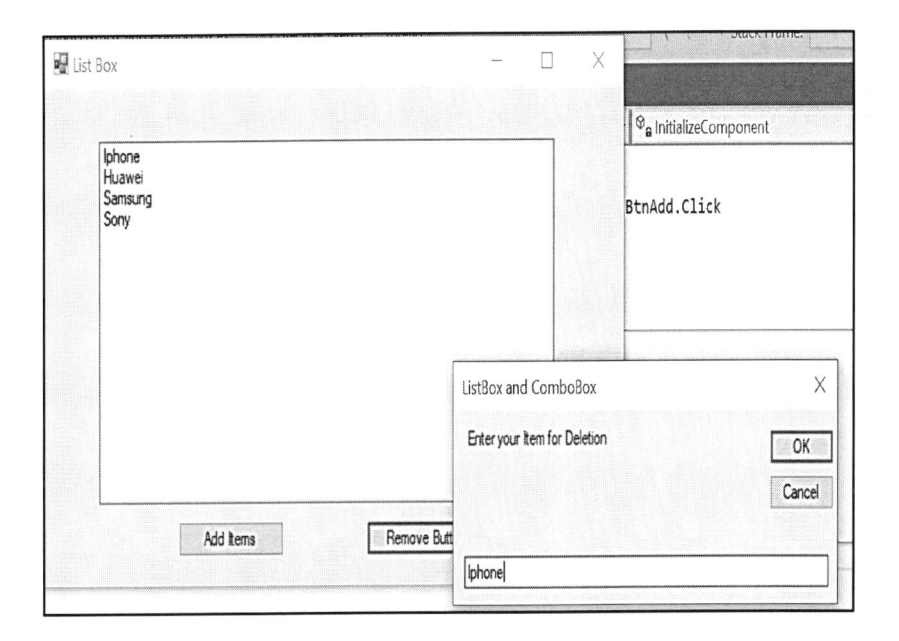

Figure 4.11

To remove a selected item from the Listbox, using the following syntax:

Listbox1.Items.Remove(ListBox1.SelectedItem)

Example 4.7

Private Sub BtnDelSel_Click(sender As Object, e As EventArgs)_
 Handles BtnDelSel.Click

   MyListBox.Items.Remove(MyListBox.SelectedItem)

End Sub

When the user run the program and select an item to delete, the item will be deleted, as shown in Figure 4.12 and Figure 4.13

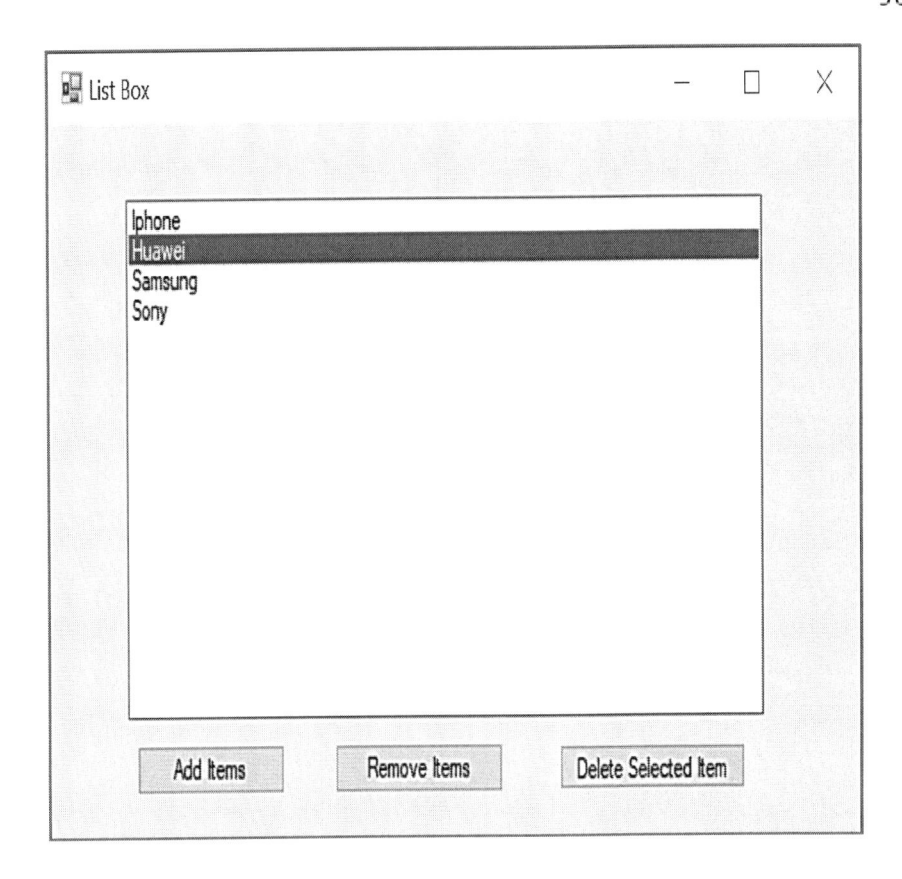

Figure 4.12

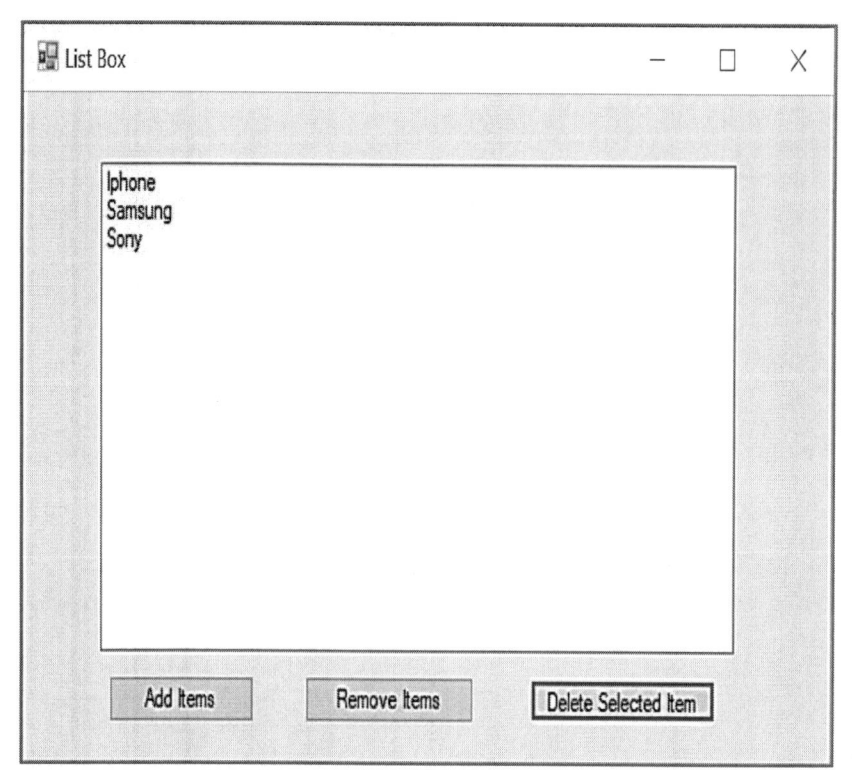

[Figure: List Box window with items "Iphone, Samsung, Sony" and buttons "Add Items", "Remove Items", "Delete Selected Item"]

Figure 4.13

To remove multiple selected items from the Listbox, you need to use the If...End If structure together with the For...Next loop. Besides that, you also need to ensure that the Listbox allows multiple selection. To enable multiple selection, set the selection mode to MultipleSimple in the Listbox properties windows. The code is as shown in Example 4.7.

Example 4.8

In this example, add an extra button to the previous example and label it as Clear Selected Items. Key in the following code:

Private Sub BtnDelSelected_Click(sender As Object, e As EventArgs)_

```
    Handles BtnDelSelected.Click
        If MyListBox.SelectedItems.Count > 0 Then
            For n As Integer = MyListBox.SelectedItems.Count_
- 1 To 0 Step -1
                'remove the current selected item from items
                MyListBox.Items.Remove(MyListBox.SelectedItems(n))
            Next n
        End If
    End Sub
```

To clear all the items at once, use the clear method, as illustrated in Example 4.8.

Example 4.9

In this example, add a button and label it "Clear the List"

```
Private Sub BtnClr_Click(sender As Object, e As EventArgs)_
Handles BtnClr.Click
    MyListBox.Items.Clear()
End Sub
```

When you run the program and click the "Clear the List" button, all the items will be cleared. The complete design interface for remove the items from the Listbox is as shown in Figure 4.14

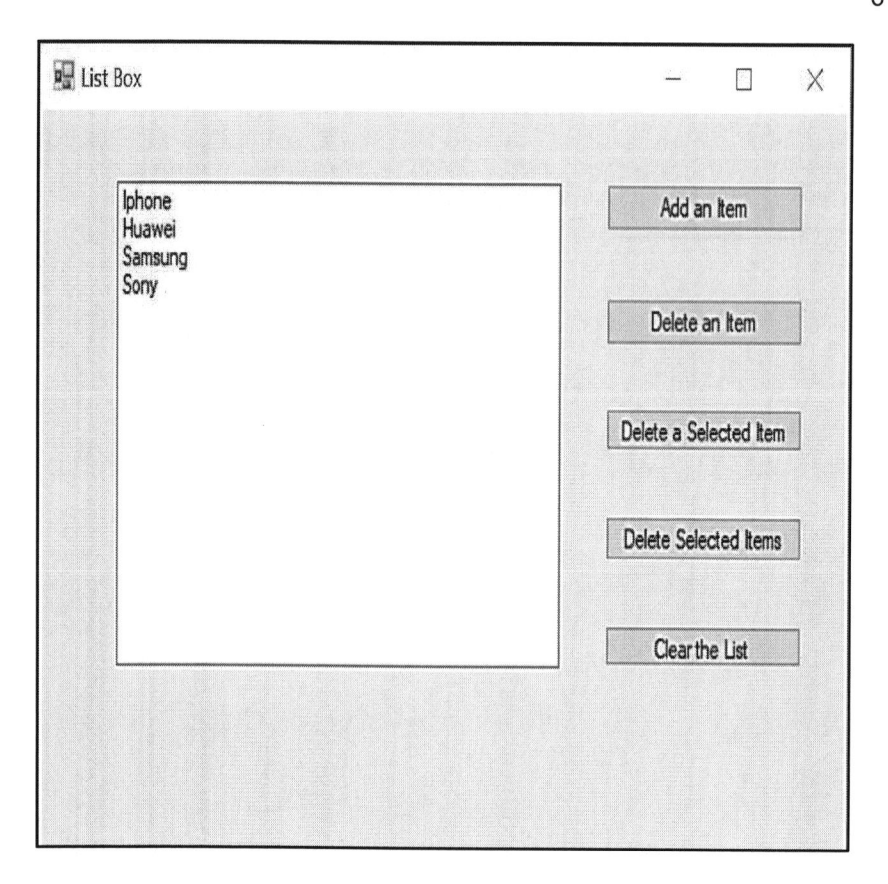

Figure 4.14

4.4 ComboBox

In Visual Basic 2019, the function of the ComboBox is also to present a list of items where the user can click and select the items from the list. However, the ComboBox only display one item at runtime and the user needs to click on the handle (small arrowhead) on the right of the combobox to see all the items that are presented in a drop-down list.

4.4.1 Adding Items to a ComboBox

In order to add items to the combobox at design time, you can also use the String Collection Editor as shown in Figure 4.15. Besides that, if you want to display an item as the default text in the combobox when you run the program, enter the name of the item by replacing the text property of the combobox.

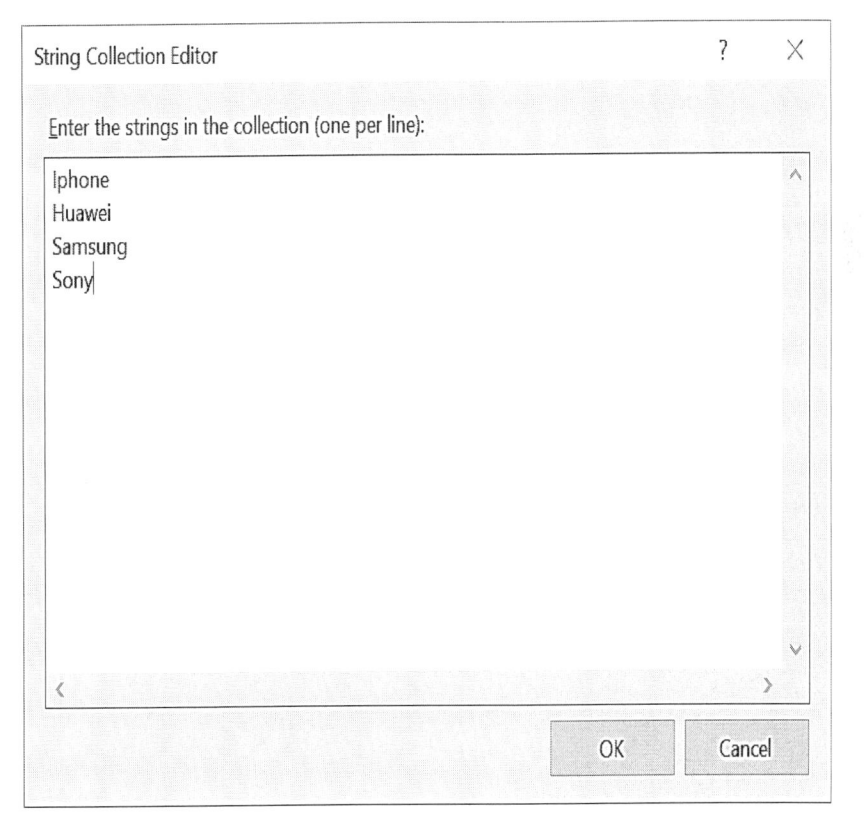

Figure 4.15

After clicking the handle of the right side of the combo box, the user will be able to view all the items, as shown in Figure 4.16.

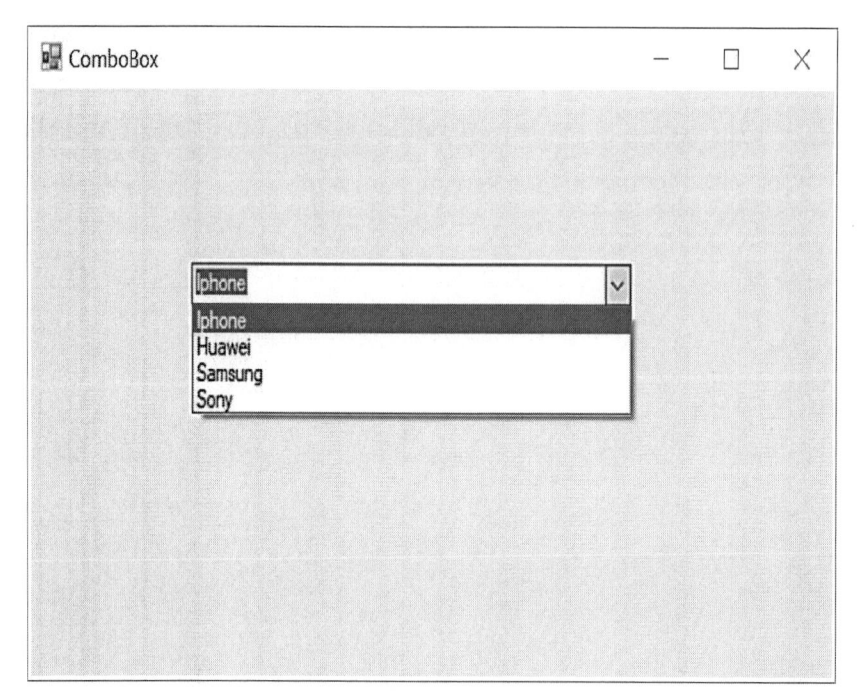

Figure 4.16

Besides that, you may add items using the **Add ()** method. For example, if you wish to add an item to the ComboBox, you can key in the following statement. The output is as shown in Figure 4.17

```
Private Sub Button1_Click(sender As Object, e As EventArgs)_
Handles Button1.Click
MyComboBox.Items.Add("Vivo")

End Sub
```

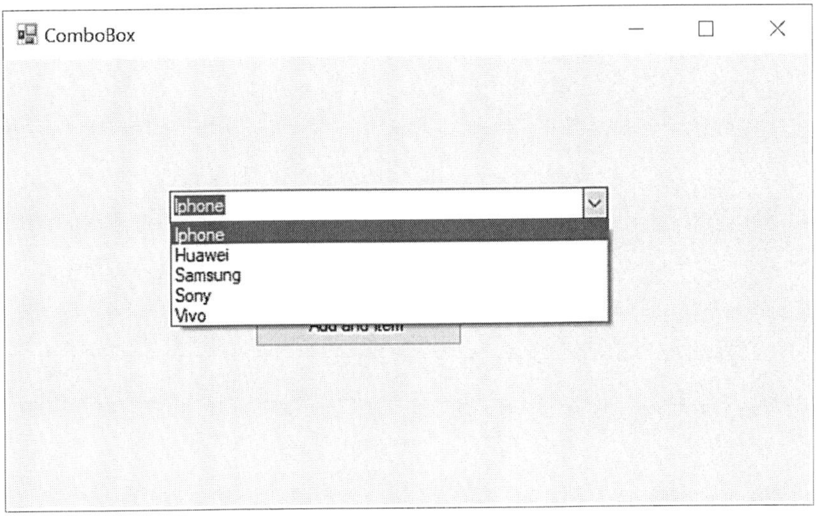
ComboBox
Iphone
Iphone
Huawei
Samsung
Sony
Vivo

Figure 4.17

You can also allow the user to add items using the InputBox function, as follows:

```
Private Sub Button1_Click(sender As Object, e As EventArgs)_
Handles Button1.Click
Dim myitem
myitem = InputBox("Enter your Item")
MyComboBox.Items.Add(myitem)

End Sub
```

The runtime interface is as shown in Figure 4.18

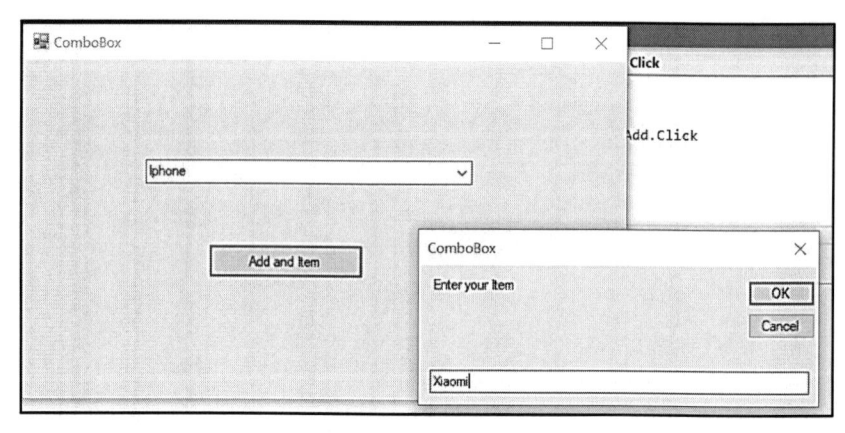

Figure 4.18

After you type the item 'Xiaomi' and click Ok, you can see that the item has been added to the combobox, as shown in Figure 4.19.

Figure 4.19

4.4.2 Removing Items from a Combobox

To remove items from the combobox at design stage, simply open the String Collection Editor and delete the items line by line or all at once using the Delete key.

To remove the items at runtime, you can use the Remove method, as illustrated in the following example. In this example, add a second button and label it "Remove Items". Click on this button and enter the following code:

```
Private Sub Button2_Click(sender As Object, e As EventArgs)_
 Handles Button2.Click
MyComboBox.Items.Remove("Iphone")

End Sub
```

The item "Ipad" will be removed after running the program. You can also let the user select a certain item to delete, the code is as follows:

```
Private Sub Button1_Click(sender As Object, e As EventArgs)_
Handles Button1.Click
MyComboBox.Items.Remove(MyComboBox.SelectedItem)

End Sub
```

To clear all the items at once, use the clear method, as illustrated in the following example. In this example, add a button and label it "Clear Items"

Private Sub Button3_Click(sender As Object, e As EventArgs)_
Handles Button2.Click
MyComboBox.Items.Clear()

End Sub

Summary

- In section 4.1, you have learned how to work with a text box
- In section 4.2, you have learned how to work with a label
- In section 4.3.1, you have learned how to add items to a listbox
- In section 4.3.2, you have learned how to remove items from a list box
- In section 4.4.1, you have learned how to add items to a combobox
- In section 4.4.2, you have learned how to remove items from a combobox

Chapter 5 Handling Images

Image handling is an important component of Visual Basic 2019 programming because it can enhance the aesthetic aspect of your application interface. Besides that, it lets us create multimedia or animation programs that involve the use of graphics. In this chapter, we shall learn how to load an image into the picture box at design time and at runtime. In addition, we shall also learn how to use a common dialog control to browse for image files in your local drives and then select and load an image into the picture box.

5.1 Loading an Image in a Picture Box

5.1.1 Loading an Image at Design Time

To create an image viewer, we insert a picture box in the form. Next, let us change its border property to `FixedSingle` and its background color to white. You might also want to change the `SizeMode` property of the image to `StretchImage` so that the image can fit in the picture box. Now, right click on the picture box to bring out its properties window. In the properties window, scroll to the Image property, as shown in Figure 5.1. In the properties window, click on the grey button on the right of the Image item to bring out the "Select Source" dialog box , as shown in Figure 5.2

Figure 5.1

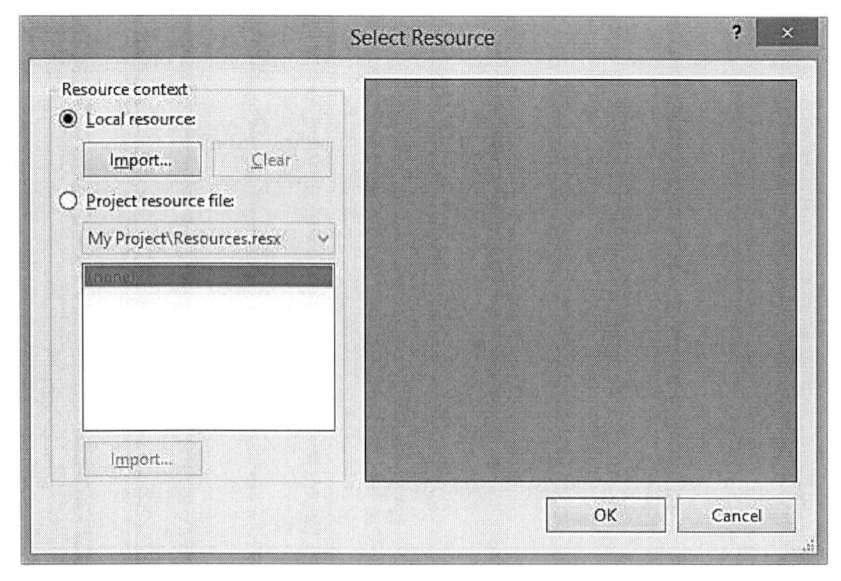

Figure 5.2
The next step is to select local resource and click on the Import button to view the available image files in your local drives, as shown

in Figure 5.3. Finally, select the image you like and then click the open button, the image will be displayed in the picture box, as shown in Figure 5.4

Figure 5.3

Figure 5.4

5.1.2 Loading an Image at Runtime

In Visual Basic 2019, an image can also be loaded at runtime, using the code as follows:

```
Private Sub Form1_Load(sender As Object, e As EventArgs)_
Handles MyBase.Load
MyPicBox.Image = Image.FromFile("C:\Users\LENOVO
\Documents\My Websites\vbtutor\images\vb6_cover.jpg")
End Sub
```

* You need to search for an image in your local drive and determine its path.

Running the program will display the same image in the picture box as in Figure 5.4

5.2 Loading an Image in a Picture Box using Open File Dialog Control

We have learned how to load an image in a picture box at design phase using the properties window. Next, we shall learn how toad an image using the `OpenFileDialog` controls. First, we need to add the `OpenFileDialog` control on the form. This control will be invisible during runtime but it facilitates the process of launching a dialog box and let the user browse his or her local drives and then select and open a file. In order for the `OpenFileDialog` to display all types of image files, we need to specify the types of image files under the Filter property. Before that, rename `OpenFileDialog` as `OFGSelectImage`. Next, right click on the `OpenFileDialog` control to access its properties window. Beside the Filter property, specify the image files using the format:

JPEG Files| *.JPG|GIF Files|*.GIF|WIndows Bitmaps|*.BMP

as shown in Figure 5.5. These are the common image file formats. Besides that, you also need to delete the default Filename.

Properties	
OFGSelectImage System.Windows.Forms.OpenFileDialog	
CheckFileExists	True
CheckPathExists	True
DefaultExt	
DereferenceLinks	True
Filter	JPEG Files|*.JPG|GIF Files|*.GIF|WIndows Bitmaps|*.BMP
FilterIndex	1
Multiselect	False
ReadOnlyChecked	False
RestoreDirectory	False
ShowHelp	False
ShowReadOnly	False
SupportMultiDottedExtensio	False
ValidateNames	True

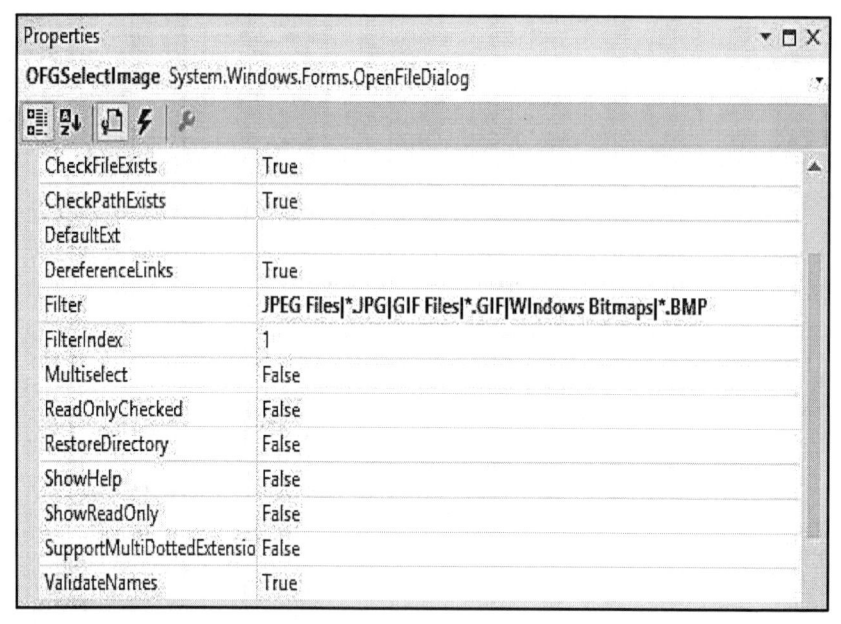

Figure 5.5

Next, double-click on the View button and enter the following code:

Private Sub BtnLoadImg_Click(sender As Object, e As EventArgs)_
Handles Button1.Click
If OFGSelectImage.ShowDialog = Windows.Forms.DialogResult.OK Then
   MyPicBox.Image = Image.FromFile(OFGSelectImage.FileName)
End If
End Sub

Press F5 to run the program and click the View button, a dialog box showing all the image files will appear, as shown in Figure 5.6

Figure 5.6

Notice that that the default image file is JPEG as we have placed it in the first place in the Filter property. Selecting and opening an image file will load it in the picture box, as shown in Figure 5.7

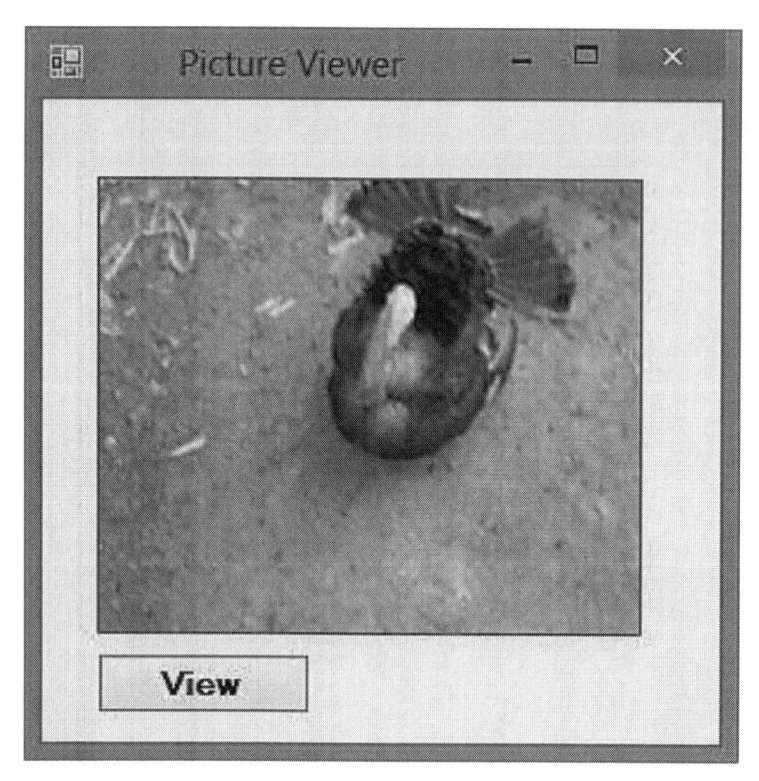

Figure 5.7

Summary

- In section 5.11, you have learned how to load an image at design time using the properties window
- In section 5.1.2, you have learned how to load an image at runtime
- In section 5.2, you have learned how to load an image using the OpenFileDialog control

Chapter 6 Working with Data

We deal with many kinds of data in our daily life. For example, we need to handle data like names, phone numbers, addresses, money, date, stock quotes, statistics, and other data every day. Similarly, in Visual Basic 2019, we must deal with all sorts of data, some of them can be mathematically calculated while some are in the form of text or other non-numeric forms. In Visual Basic 2019, data can be stored as variables, constants, or arrays. The values of data stored as variables always change, just like the contents of a mailbox or the storage bin while the value of a constant remains the same throughout. (We shall deal with variables, constants, and arrays in coming lessons)

6.1 Visual Basic 2019 Data Types

Visual Basic 2019 classifies information into two major data types, numeric data types and the non-numeric data type

6.1.1 Numeric Data Types

Numeric data types are types of data comprises numbers that can be calculated mathematically using various standard operators such as addition, subtraction, multiplication, division and more. Examples of numeric data types are examination marks, height, body weight, number of students in a class, share values, the price of goods, monthly bills, fees, bus fares etc. In Visual Basic 2019, numeric data are divided into seven types based on the range of values they can store. Calculations that only involve round figures or data that do not need high precision can use Integer or Long integer. Programs that require high precision calculation need to use Single and Double precision data types; they are also called floating point numbers. For currency calculation, you can use the currency data types. Lastly, if even more precision is required to perform calculations that involve many decimal points, we can use the decimal data types. These data types are summarized in Table 6.1

Table 6.1: Numeric Data Types

Type	Storage	Range
Byte	1 byte	0 to 255
Integer	2 bytes	-32,768 to 32,767
Long	4 bytes	-2,147,483,648 to 2,147,483,648
Single	4 bytes	-3.402823E+38 to -1.401298E-45 for negative values 1.401298E-45 to 3.402823E+38 for positive values.
Double	8 bytes	-1.79769313486232e+308 to -4.94065645841247E-324 for negative values 4.94065645841247E-324 to 1.79769313486232e+308 for positive values.
Currency	8 bytes	-922,337,203,685,477.5808 to 922,337,203,685,477.5807
Decimal	12 bytes	+/- 79,228,162,514,264,337,593,543,950,335 if no decimal is use

| | | +/- 7.9228162514264337593543950335 (28 decimal places). |

6.1.2 Non-numeric Data Types

Non-numeric data types are data that cannot be manipulated mathematically using standard arithmetic operators. The non-numeric data comprises text or string data types, the Date data types, the Boolean data types that store only two values (true or false), Object data type and Variant data type .They are summarized in Table 6.2

Table 6.2 Non-numeric Data Types

Type	Storage	Range
String(fixed length)	Length of string	1 to 65,400 characters
String(variable length)	Length + 10 bytes	0 to 2 billion characters
Date	8 bytes	January 1, 100 to December 31, 9999
Boolean	2 bytes	True or False
Object	4 bytes	Any embedded object
Variant(numeric)	16 bytes	Any value as large as Double
Variant(text)	Length+22 bytes	Same as variable-length string

6.1.3 Suffixes for Literals

Literals are values that you assign to data. In some cases, we need to add a suffix behind a literal so that VB can handle the calculation more accurately. For example, we can use num =1.3089# for a Double type data. The suffixes are summarized in Table 6.3.

Table 6.3 Suffixes and Data Types

Suffix	Data type
&	Long
!	Single
#	Double
@	Currency

In addition, we need to enclose string literals within two quotations and date and time literals within two # sign. Strings can contain any characters, including numbers. The following are a few examples:

memberName="Turban, John."
TelNumber="1800-900-888-777"
LastDay=#31-Dec-00#
ExpTime=#12:00 am#

6.2 Variables and Constants

In previous section, we have learned about data and various data types in Visual Basic 2019. Data can be stored as a variable or as a constant. Variables are like mailboxes in the post office. The content of the variables changes every now and then, just like the mailboxes. In Visual Basic 2019, variables are areas allocated by the computer memory to store data.

6.2.1 Variable Names

Like the mailboxes, each variable must be given a name. To name a variable in Visual Basic 2019, you must follow a set of rules. The following are the rules when naming the variables in Visual Basic:

- It must be less than 255 characters
- No spacing is allowed
- It must not begin with a number
- Period is not permitted

Examples of valid and invalid variable names are displayed in Table 6.4

Table 6.4

Valid Names	Invalid Names
My_Computer	My.Computer
Smartphone123	123Smartphone
Long_Name_Can_beUSE	LongName&Canbe&Use
	*& is not acceptable

6.2.2 Declaring Variables

In Visual Basic 2019, we must declare the variables before using them by assigning names and data types. If you fail to do so, the program will show an error. Variables are usually declared in the general section of the code windows using the **Dim** statement. The syntax is as follows:

Dim VariableName As DataType

If you want to declare more variables, you can declare them in separate lines or you may also combine more in one line, separating each variable with a comma, as follows:

Dim VariableName1 As DataType1, VariableName2 As DataType2,_
VariableName3 As DataType3

Example 6.1

Private Sub Form1_Load(ByVal sender As System.Object,
ByVal e As_ System.EventArgs) Handles MyBase.Load
Dim password As String
Dim yourName As String
Dim firstnum As Integer
Dim secondnum As Integer
Dim total As Integer
Dim doDate As Date
End Sub

You may also combine the above statements in one line, separating each variable with a comma, as follows:

Dim password As String, yourName As String, firstnum As Integer,...

For the string declaration, there are two possible forms, one for the variable-length string and another for the fixed-length string. For the variable-length string, just use the same syntax as Example 6.1

Example 6.2

Private Sub Button1_Click(sender As Object, e As EventArgs)_

Handles Button1.Click
Dim YourMessage As String
YourMessage = "Happy Birthday!"
MsgBox(YourMessage)
End Sub

When you run the program, a message box that shows the text "Happy Birthday!" will appear, as shown in Figure 6.1

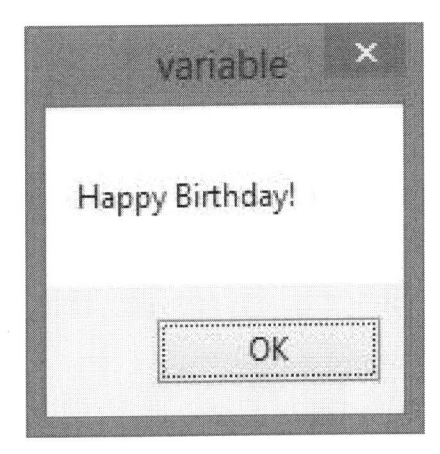

Figure 6.1

For the fixed-length string, you must use the syntax as shown below:

Dim VariableName As String * n

Where n defines the number of characters the string can hold.

Example 6.3

Dim yourName As String * 10

yourName can holds no more than 10 Characters.

6.2.3 Assigning Values to Variables

After declaring various variables using the `Dim` statements, we can assign values to those variables. The syntax of an assignment is

  Variable=Expression

The variable can be a declared variable or a control property value. The expression could be a mathematical expression, a number, a string, a Boolean value (true or false) etc, as illustrated in the following examples:

  firstNumber=100
  secondNumber=firstNumber-99
  userName="John Lyan"
  userpass.Text = password
  Label1.Visible = True
  Command1.Visible = false
  Label4.text = textbox1.Text
  ThirdNumber = Val(usernum1.Text)
  total = firstNumber + secondNumber+ThirdNumber
  MeanScore% = SumScores% / NumSubjects%
  X=sqr (16)
  TrimString= Ltrim ("Visual Basic", 4)
  Num=Int(Rnd*6)+1

An error occurs when you try to assign a value to a variable of incompatible data type. For example, if you have declared a variable as an integer but you assigned a string value to it, an error occurred, as shown in Example 6.4.

Example 6.4

Private Sub Button1_Click(sender As Object, e As EventArgs)_
Handles Button1.Click
Dim YourMessage As Integer
YourMessage = "Happy Birthday!"
MsgBox(YourMessage)
End Sub

When you run the program, the following error messages will appear in a dialog box, as shown in Figure 6.2.

You can either break the program or continue to run the program.

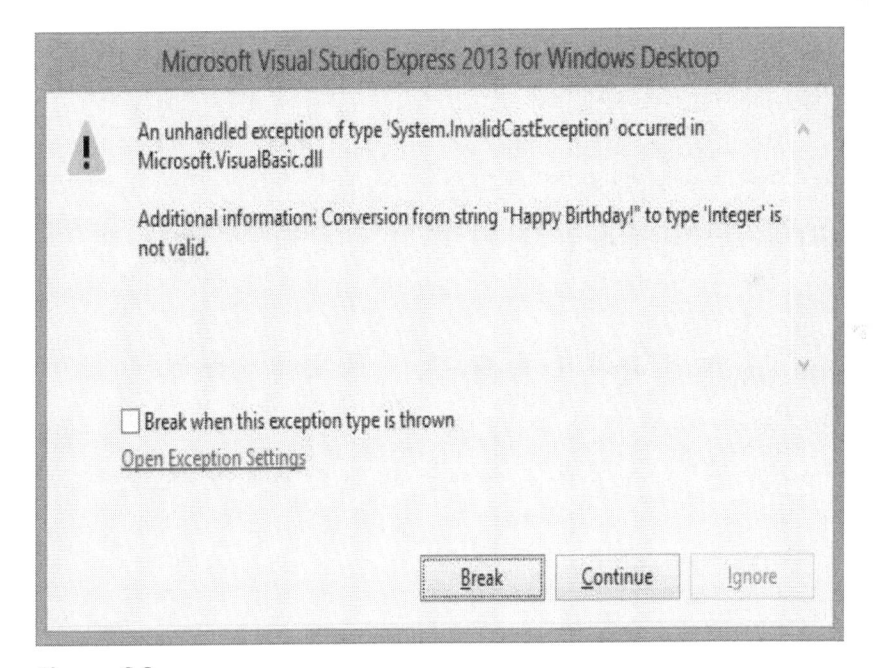

Figure 6.2

6.2.4 Scope of Declaration

Other than using the **Dim** keyword to declare the data, you can also use other keywords to declare the data. Three other keywords are **Private, Static** and **Public**. The forms are as shown below:

Private VariableName As Datatype
Static VariableName As Datatype
Public VariableName As Datatype

The above keywords indicate the scope of declaration. **Private** declares a local variable, or a variable that is local to a procedure or module. However, Private is rarely used; we normally use Dim to declare a local variable. The **Static** keyword declares a variable that is being used multiple times, even after a procedure has been terminated. Most variables created inside a procedure are discarded by Visual Basic when the procedure is completed, **static** keyword preserve the value of a variable even after the procedure is terminated. **Public** is the keyword that declares a global variable, which means it can be used by all the procedures and modules of the whole program.

6.2.5 Declaring Constants

Constants are different from variables in the sense that their values do not change during the running of the program. The syntax to declare a constant is

Const ConstantName As Single=3.142

Private Sub Button1_Click(sender As Object, e As EventArgs)_
Handles Button1.Click
Const Pi As Single = 3.142
Dim R As Single = 10
Dim AreaCircle As Single
AreaCircle = Pi * R ^ 2
MsgBox("Area of circle with " & "radius" & R & "=" & AreaCircle)
End Sub

Example 6.5

Private Sub Button1_Click(sender As Object, e As EventArgs)_
Handles Button1.Click
Const Pi As Single = 3.142
Dim R As Single = 10
Dim AreaCircle As Single
AreaCircle = Pi * R ^ 2
MsgBox("Area of circle with " & "radius" & R & "=" & AreaCircle)
End Sub

Running the program and clicking the OK button will produce the following message, as shown in Figure 6.3

[Dialog box: "variable" — "Area of circle with radius 10=314.2" — OK]

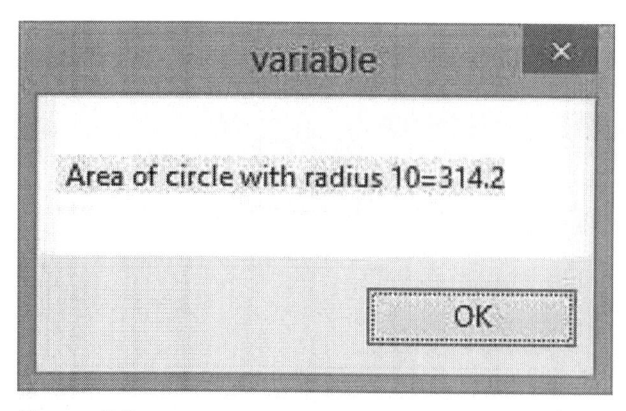

Figure 6.3

Summary

- In section 6.11, you have understood numeric data types
- In section 6.1.2, you have understood non-numeric data types
- In section 6.1.3, you have learned how to use suffixes for literals
- In section 6.2.1, you have understood rules that govern variable names
- In section 6.2.2, you have learned how to declare variables
- In section 6.2.3, you have understood the scope of declaration of variables
- In section 6.2.3, you have learned how to declare a constant

Chapter 7 Arrays

7.1 Introduction to Arrays

An array is a group of variables (elements) with the same data type. When we work with a single item, we only need to use one variable. However, if we are dealing with a list of items of similar type, we must declare an array of variables instead of using a variable for each item

For example, if we have one hundred names, it is very tedious to declare one hundred different names. Instead of declaring one hundred different variables, we need to declare only one array. We differentiate each item in the array by using subscript, the index value of each item, for example name(1), name(2),name(3) ....etc. which will make declaring variables streamline and much more systematic.

7.2 Dimension of an Array

An array can be one dimensional or multidimensional. One dimensional array is like a list of items or a table that consists of one row of items or one column of items. A two-dimensional array is a table of items that are made up of rows and columns. The way to reference an element in a one-dimensional array is ArrayName(x), where x is the index or position number of the element. The way to reference an element in a two dimensional array is ArrayName(x,y) , where (x,y) is the index or position number of the element. Usually it is sufficient to use one dimensional and two-dimensional arrays, you only need to use higher dimensional arrays if you need to deal with more complex problems. Let me illustrate the arrays with tables.

Table 7.1: One –Dimensional Array

Student Name	SName(0)	SName(1)	SName(2)	SName(3)	SName(4)

Table 7.2: Two –Dimensional Array

SName(0,0)	SName(0,1)	SName(0,2)	SName(0,3)
SName(1,0)	SName(1,1)	SName(1,2)	SName(1,3)
SName(2,0)	SName(2,1)	SName(2,2)	SName(2,3)
SName(3,0)	SName(3,1)	SName(3,2)	SName(3,3)

7.3 Declaring Arrays

We can use **Public** or **Dim** statement to declare an array just as the way we declare a single variable. The **Public** statement declares an array that can be used throughout an application while the **Dim** statement declare an array that could be used only in a local procedure or module. The statement to declare a one-dimensional array is as follows:

Dim arrayName(n) As dataType

* n indicates the last index in the array.

Please note that n does not indicate the number of elements in the array, it is one less than the number of elements (n-1) because the first element is always the zeroth element. The first element is arrayName(0), the second element is arrayName(1), the third element is arrayName(2) and so on. The number of elements in an array is also known as length, we can retrieve the length of an array using the syntax **arrayName.length**

For example, the following statement declares an array that consists of 11 elements starting from CusName(0) through to CusName(10)

Dim CusName(10) As String

To find out the length of the array, you can write the following code:

Example 7.1

```
Private Sub Form1_Load(sender As Object, e As EventArgs)
Handles MyBase.Load
Dim CusName As String()
CusName = New String() {1, 2, 3}
MsgBox(CusName.Length)
End Sub
```

Running the program will produce a message box that displays the length of the array i.e. 11, as shown in Figure 7.1

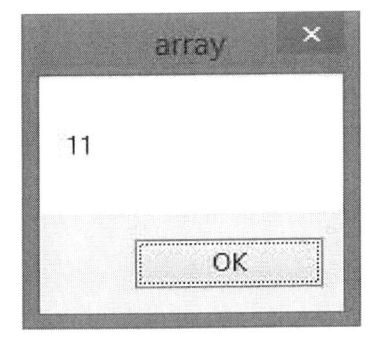

Figure 7.1

You might also declare an array with a non-zero starting index by initializing an index value other than zero, as follows:

```
Dim arrayname As DataType()
arrayName = New String(){1,2,3,....,n)
```

This array will consist of n elements, starting with arrayName(1)

Example 7.2

Private Sub Form1_Load(sender As Object, e As EventArgs)_
Handles MyBase.Load
Dim CusName As String()
CusName = New String() {1, 2, 3}
MsgBox(CusName.Length)
End Sub

The message box will display the length as 3. The statement to declare a two-dimensional array is as follows, where m and n indicate the last indices in the array. The number of elements or the length of the array is (m+1) x (n+1)

Dim ArrayName(m,n) As dataType

Example 7.3

Private Sub Form1_Load(sender As Object, e As EventArgs)_
Handles MyBase.Load
Dim CusName(5,6) As String
MsgBox(CusName.Length)
End Sub

The program produces a message box will display 42, as shown in Figure 7.2

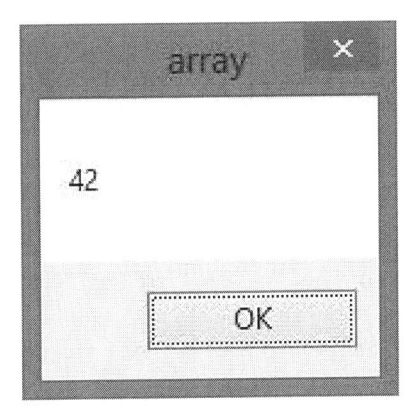

Figure 7.2

Example 7.4

Private Sub Form1_Load(sender As Object, e As EventArgs)_

Handles MyBase.Load
Dim num As Integer
Dim CusName(5) As String
For num = 0 To 5
CusName(num) = InputBox("Enter the customer name", "Enter Name")
ListBox1.Items.Add(CusName(num))
Next
End Sub

This program will prompt the user to enter names in an input box for a total of 6 times and the names will be entered into a list box, as shown in Figure 7.3 and Figure 7.4

Figure 7.3

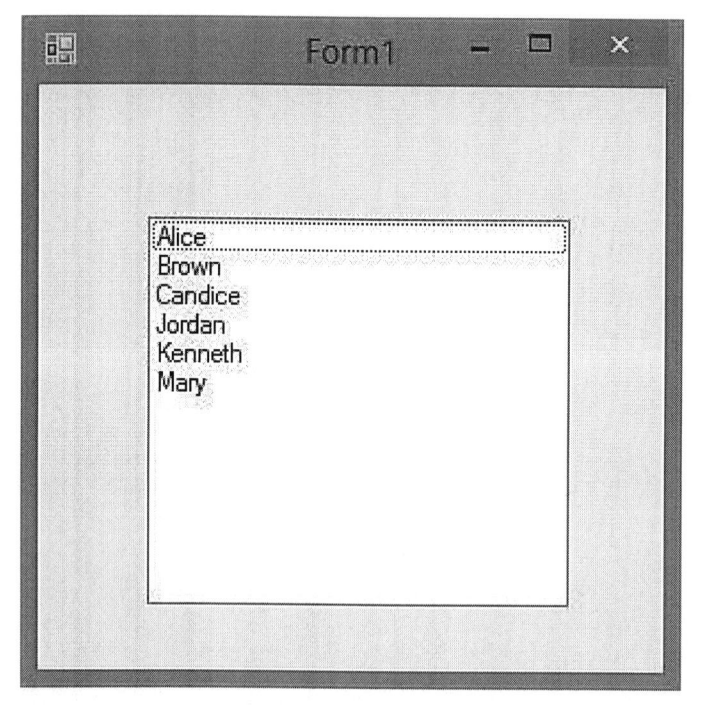

Figure 7.4
Summary

- In section 7.1, you have understood the concept of arrays
- In section 7.2, you have understood dimension in arrays
- In section 7.3, you have learned how to declare an array

Chapter 8 Mathematical Operations

Computers can perform mathematical calculations much faster than human beings do. However, the computer itself cannot perform any mathematical calculations without receiving instructions from the user. In Visual Basic 2019, we can write code to instruct the computer to perform mathematical calculations such as addition, subtraction, multiplication, division, and many other kinds of mathematical operations.

8.1 Mathematical Operators

The Visual Basic 2019 mathematical operators are very similar to the normal arithmetic operators, only with some slight variations. The plus and minus operators are the same while the multiplication operator use the * symbol and the division operator use the / symbol. The list of Visual Basic 2019 mathematical operators is shown in table 8.1.

Table 8.1 Mathematical Operators

Operator	Mathematical function	Example
+	Addition	1+2=3
-	Subtraction	10-4=6
^	Exponential	3^2=9
*	Multiplication	5*6=30
/	Division	21/7=3
Mod	Modulus(returns the remainder of an integer division)	15 Mod 4=3

| \ | Integer Division(discards the decimal places) | 19/4=4 |

8.2 Writing Code for Mathematical Operations

it is relatively easy to write code that can perform mathematical operations in VB2019. First you need to think of a mathematical problem and equations as well as formulas that are required for solving it then write the code using those formulas and equations.

Example 8.1 Standard Arithmetic Calculations

In this program, you need to insert two text boxes, four labels and one button. Click the button and enter the code as shown below. When you run the program, it will perform the four basic arithmetic operations and displays the results on four labels. This program performs standard arithmetic operations involving addition, subtraction, multiplication, and division. The Code is as follows:

```
Private Sub Button1_Click(ByVal sender As Object,
ByVal e As EventArgs) Handles Button1.Click
Dim num1, num2, difference, product, quotient As Single
num1 = TextBox1.Text
num2 = TextBox2.Text
sum=num1+num2
difference=num1-num2
product = num1 * num2
quotient=num1/num2
LblSum.Text=sum
LblDiff.Text=difference
LblPro.Text = product
```

```
LblQt.Text = quotient
End Sub
```

Example 8.2 Pythagorean Theorem

This program uses Pythagorean Theorem to calculate the length of hypotenuse c given the length of the adjacent side and the opposite side b. In case you have forgotten the formula for the Pythagorean Theorem, it is written as
c^2=a^2+b^2

The code is as follows:

```
Private Sub Button1_Click(ByVal sender As Object,
ByVal e As EventArgs) Handles Button1.Click
Dim a, b, c As Single
a = TextBox1.Text
b = TextBox2.Text
c= (a^2+b^2)^(1/2)
Label3.Text=c
End Sub
```

Example 8.3: BMI Calculator

A lot of people are obese now and that could affect their health seriously. Obesity has been proven by medical experts to be one of the main factors that brings many adverse medical problems, including cardiovascular disease. If your BMI is more than 30, you are considered obese. You can refer to the following range of BMI values for your weight status.

Underweight = <18.5
Normal weight = 18.5-24.9

Overweight = 25-29.9

Obesity = BMI of 30 or greater

The BMI calculator is a Visual Basic program that can calculate the body mass index, or BMI of a person based on the body weight in kilograms and the body height in meters. BMI can be calculated using the formula weight/(height)^2, where weight is measured in kg and height in meters. If you only know your weight and height in lb and feet, then you need to convert them to the metric system. The code is as follows:

```
Private Sub Button1_Click(ByVal sender As Object,
ByVal e As EventArgs) Handles Button1.Click
Dim height, weight, bmi As Single
height = TxtBoxHgt.Text
    weight = TxtBoxWgt.Text

    bmi = (weight) / (height ^ 2)

    LblBMI.Text = bmi

    If bmi > 26 Then

        LblComment.Text = "Your are overweight"

    ElseIf bmi <= 26 And bmi > 18 Then

        LblComment.Text = "Your weight is normal"

    Else

        LblComment.Text = "Your are underweight"

    End If
```

End Sub

The output is shown in Figure 8.1 below. In this example, your height is 1.80m (about 5 foot 11), your weight is 75 kg (about 168lb), and your BMI is about 23.14815. The reading suggests that you are healthy.

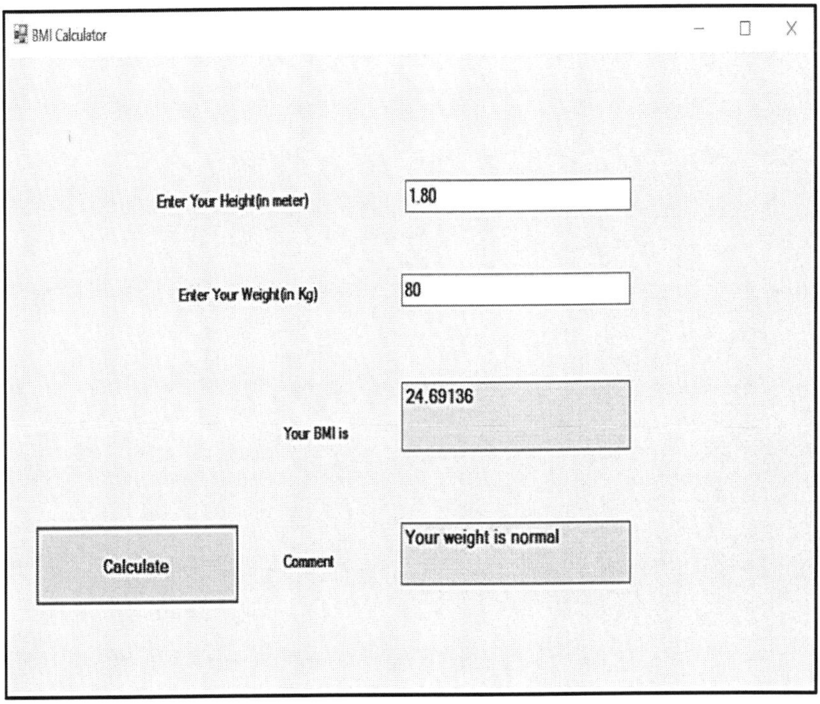

Figure 8.1

Summary

- In section 8.1, you have recognized all mathematical operators in VB2019
- In section 8.2, you have learned to write code that perform arithmetic operations

Chapter 9 String Manipulation

String manipulation means writing code to manipulate characters like names, addresses, gender, cities, book titles, sentences, words, text, alphanumeric characters (@,#,$,%,^,&,*, etc.) and more. String manipulation is best demonstrated in word processing which deals with text editing. In Visual Basic 2019, a string is a single unit of data that is made up of a series of characters that includes letters, digits, alphanumeric symbols etc. It is treated as the String data type and it is non-numeric in nature, which means it cannot be manipulated mathematically though it might consist of numbers.

9.1 String Manipulation Using + and & signs

In Visual Basic 2019, strings can be manipulated using the & sign and the + sign, both perform the string concatenation which means combining two or more smaller strings into a larger string. For example, we can join "Visual"," Basic" and "2019" into "Visual Basic 2019" using "Visual" &" Basic" or "Visual "+"Basic", as shown in the Examples below:

Example 9.1

```
Private Sub BtnShow_Click(ByVal sender As Object,
ByVal e As EventArgs) Handles BtnShow.Click
Dim text1, text2, text3, text4 As String
text1 = "Visual"
text2 = "Basic"
text3 = "2019"
text4 = text1 + " "+text2 + " "+text3
MsgBox(text4)
End Sub
```

The line **text4=text1+ text2 + text3** can be replaced by **text4=text1 & text2 &text3** and produces the same output. However, if one of the variables is declared as a numeric data type, you cannot use the + sign, you can only use the & sign.

The output is shown in Figure 9.1

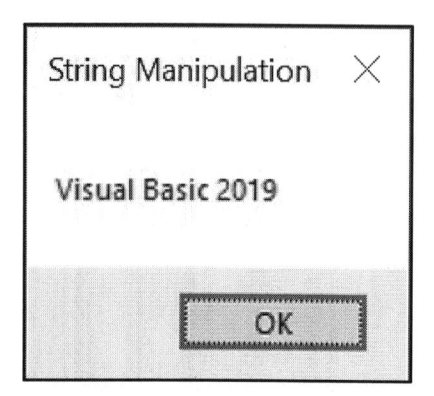

Figure 9.1

Example 9.2

```
Private Sub BtnShow_Click(ByVal sender As Object,
ByVal e As EventArgs) Handles BtnShow.Click
Dim text1, text3 As string
Dim Text2 As Integer
text1 = "Visual"
text2 = 22
text3 = text1 + text2
MsgBox(text3)
End Sub
```

This code will produce an error because of data mismatch. The error message appears as shown in Figure 9.2.

```
Private Sub BtnShow_Click(sender As Object, e As EventArgs) Handles BtnShow.Click
    Dim text1, text3 As String
    Dim Text2 As Integer
    text1 = "Visual"
    Text2 = 22
    text3 = text1 + Text2
    MsgBox(text3)

    End Sub
End Class
```

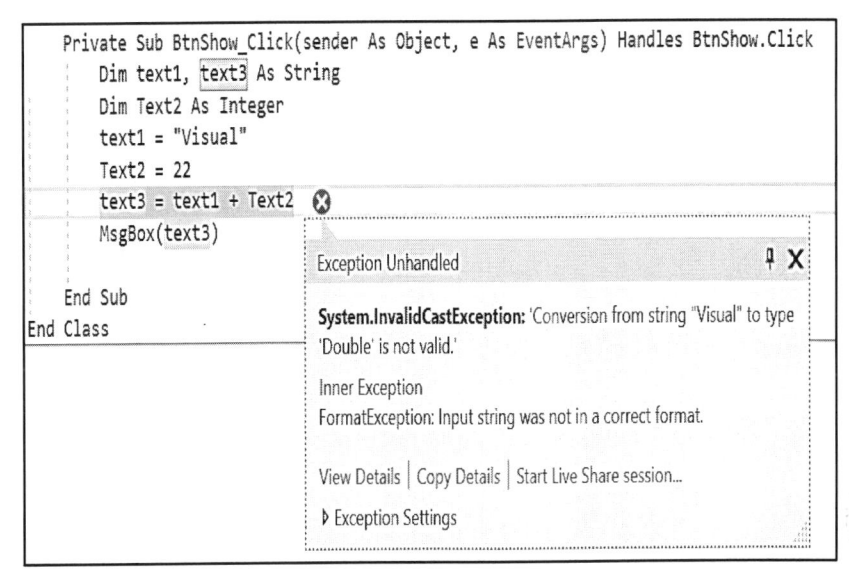

Exception Unhandled

System.InvalidCastException: 'Conversion from string "Visual" to type 'Double' is not valid.'

Inner Exception
FormatException: Input string was not in a correct format.

View Details | Copy Details | Start Live Share session...

▷ Exception Settings

Figure 9.2

However, using & instead of + will be alright.

```
Dim text1, text3 As string
Dim Text2 As Integer
text1 = "Visual"
text2 = 22
text3 = text1 & text2
MsgBox(text3)
```

The output is shown in Figure 9.3

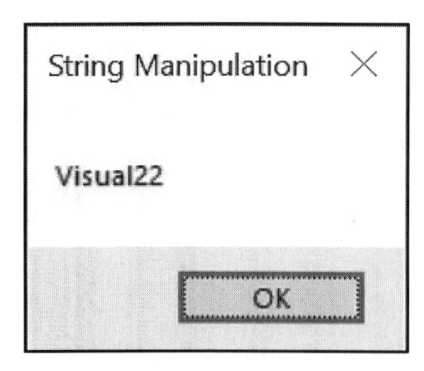

Figure 9.3

9.2 String Manipulation Using Built-in Functions

A function is like a normal procedure, but the main purpose of the function is to accept an input and return a value which is passed on to the main program to finish the execution. There is numerous string manipulation functions that are built into Visual Basic 2019.

9.2 (a) The Len Function

The Len function returns an integer value which is the length of a phrase or a sentence, including the empty spaces. The syntax is

```
Len("Phrase")
```

Example 9.3

```
Private Sub BtnShow_Click(ByVal sender As System.Object,
ByVal e As EventArgs) Handles BtnShow.Click
Dim MyText As String
MyText="Visual Basic 2019"
MsgBox(Len(MyText))
End Sub
```

The output is shown in Figure 9.4

```
String Manipulation  X

17


      OK
```

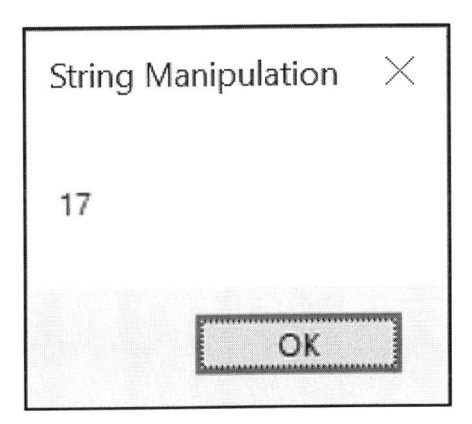

Figure 9.4

9.2(b) The Right Function

The Right function extracts the right portion of a phrase. The syntax is

Microsoft.VisualBasic.Right("Phrase",n)

Example 9.4

```
Private Sub BtnShow_Click(ByVal sender As Object,
 ByVal e As EventArgs) Handles BtnShow.Click
Dim MyText As String
MyText = "Visual Basic"
MsgBox(Microsoft.VisualBasic.Right(MyText, 4))
End Sub
```

Executing the above code returns four right most characters of the phrase entered the text box.

The Output is as shown in Figure 9.5

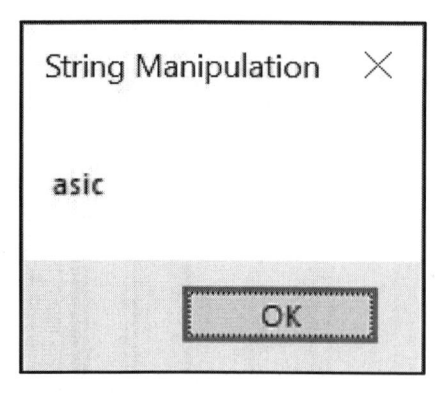

Figure 9.5

9.2(c) The Left Function

The Left function extracts the left portion of a phrase. The syntax is

Microsoft.VisualBasic.Left("Phrase",n)

n is the starting position from the left of the phase where the portion of the phrase will be extracted. For example,

Microsoft.VisualBasic.Left ("Visual Basic", 4) = Visu

9.2 (d) The Mid Function

The Mid function is used to retrieve a part of text from a given phrase. The syntax of the Mid Function is

Mid(phrase, position,n)

In the above function, phrase is the string from which a part of text is to be retrieved , position is the starting position of the phrase from which the retrieving process begins and n is the number of characters to retrieve.

Example 9.5

```
Private Sub BtnShow_Click(sender As Object, e As EventArgs)
Handles BtnShow.Click
Dim myPhrase As String
myPhrase = InputBox("Enter your phrase")
LblPhrase.Text = myPhrase
blExtract.Text = Mid(myPhrase, 2, 6)
End Sub
```

* In this example, when the user clicks the button, an input box will pop up prompting the user to enter a phrase. After a phrase is entered and the OK button is pressed, the label will show the extracted text starting from position 2 of the phrase and the number of characters extracted is 6. For example, if you entered the phrase "Visual Basic 2019", the extracted text is isual.

Example 9.6

You can also let the user decide the starting position of the text to be extracted as well as the number of characters to be extracted, as shown in the following code:

```
Private Sub BtnExtract_Click(sender As Object, e As EventArgs)
Handles BtnExtract.Click
    Dim myPhrase As String
    Dim pos, n As Integer
    myPhrase = TxtPhrase.Text
    pos = TxtPos.Text
    n = TxtNumber.Text
```

```
    LblExtract.Text = Mid(myPhrase, pos, n)
  End Sub
```

The runtime interface is as follows:

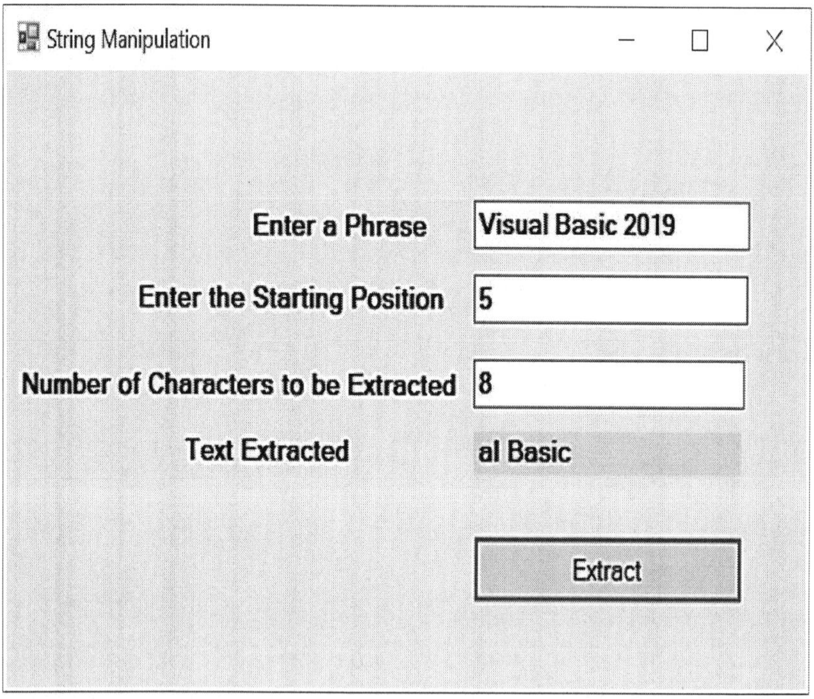

Figure 9.6

9.2(e) Trim Function

The Trim function trims the empty spaces on both sides of the phrase. The syntax is

Trim("Phrase")

For example, Trim (" Visual Basic ") = Visual Basic

Example 9.7

```
Private Sub Button1_Click(ByVal sender As Object,
ByVal e As EventArgs) Handles Button1.Click
Dim myPhrase As String
myPhrase = InputBox("Enter your phrase")
Label1.Text = Trim(myPhrase)
End Sub
```

9.2(f) Ltrim Function

The Ltrim function trims the empty spaces of the left portion of the phrase. The syntax is

Ltrim("Phrase")

For example,

Ltrim("Visual Basic 2019") = Visual basic 2019

9.2(g) The Rtrim Function

The Rtrim function trims the empty spaces of the right portion of the phrase. The syntax is

Rtrim("Phrase")

For example,

Rtrim("Visual Basic 2019") = Visual Basic 2019

9.2(h) The InStr function

The InStr function looks for a phrase that is embedded within the original phrase and returns the starting position of the embedded phrase. The syntax is

Instr(n, original phase, embedded phrase)

Where n is the position where the Instr function will begin to look for the embedded phrase. For example

Instr(1, "Visual Basic 2019 ","Basic")=8

9.2(i) The Ucase and the Lcase Functions

The Ucase function converts all the characters of a string to capital letters. On the other hand, the Lcase function converts all the characters of a string to small letters.

The syntaxes are

Microsoft.VisualBasic.UCase(Phrase)
Microsoft.VisualBasic.LCase(Phrase)

For example,

Microsoft.VisualBasic.Ucase("Visual Basic") = VISUAL BASIC
Microsoft.VisualBasic.Lcase("Visual Basic") = visual basic

9.2(j) The Chr and the Asc functions

The Chr function returns the string that corresponds to an ASCII code while the Asc function converts an ASCII character or symbol to the corresponding ASCII code. ASCII stands for "American Standard Code for Information Interchange". Altogether there are 255 ASCII codes and as many ASCII characters. Some of the characters may not be displayed as they may represent some actions such as the pressing of a key or produce a beep sound. The syntax of the Chr function is

Chr(charcode)

and the syntax of the Asc function is

Asc(Character)

The followings are some examples:

Chr(65)=A, Chr(122)=z, Chr(37)=% , Asc("B")=66, Asc("&")=38

Summary

- In section 9.1, you have learned how to manipulate string using the & and + signs
- In section 9.2, you have learned how to manipulate string using various built-in functions

Chapter 10 Using If...Then...Else

In the preceding chapters, we have learned how to write code that accepts input from the user and displays the output without controlling the program flow. In this lesson, we shall learn how to write Visual Basic 2019 code that can make decisions and control the program flow in the process.

The decision-making process is an important part of programming in Visual Basic 2019 because it can solve problems in a smart way and provide useful output or feedback to the user. For example, we can write a Visual Basic 2019 program that can ask the computer to perform certain task until a certain condition is met, or a program that will reject non-numeric data. In order to control the program flow and to make decisions, we need to use the conditional operators and the logical operators together with the `If...Then...Else`. control structure.

10.1 Conditional Operators

The conditional operators are powerful tools that resemble mathematical operators. These operators allow a Visual Basic 2019 program to compare data values and then decide what actions to take, whether to execute a program or terminate the program and more. They are also known as numerical comparison operators which are used to compare two values to see whether they are equal, or one value is greater or less than the other value. The comparison will return a true or a false result. These operators are shown in Table 10.1.

Table 10.1: Conditional Operators

Operators	Description
=	Equal to
>	Greater than
<	Less than
>=	More than and equal to
<=	Less than and equal to
<>	Not equal to

10.2 Logical Operators

Sometimes we might need to make more than one comparison before a decision can be made and an action taken. In this case, using numerical comparison operators alone is not enough, we need to use additional operators, and they are the logical operators. The logical operators are shown in the following table 10.2

Table 10.2: Logical Operators

Operators	Description
And	Both sides must be true
Or	One side or the other must be true
Xor	One side or the other must be true but not both
Not	Negates true

The above operators can be used to compare numerical data as well as non-numeric data such as text (string). In making strings comparison, there are certain rules to follow: Upper case letters are less than lowercase letters, "A"<"B"<"C"<"D".......<"Z" and number are less than letters.

10.3 Using If ...Then...Else

To effectively control the Visual Basic 2019 program flow, we shall use the If control structure together with the conditional operators and logical operators. There are basically three types of If control structures, namely If...Then statement, If...Then...Else statement and If...Then...ElseIf statement.

10.3(a) If...Then Statement

This is the simplest control structure which instructs the computer to perform a certain action specified by the Visual Basic 2019 expression if the condition is true. However, when the condition is false, no action will be performed. The syntax for the If...Then statement is

If condition Then
Visual Basic 2019 expressions
End If

Example 10.1

```
Private Sub Button1_Click(ByVal sender As Object,
ByVal e As EventArgs) Handles Button1.Click
Dim myNumber As Integer
myNumber = TextBox1.Text
If myNumber > 100 Then
Label2.Text = " You win a lucky prize"
```

End If
End Sub

* When you run the program and enter a number that is greater than 100, you will see the "You win a lucky prize" message. On the other hand, if the number entered is less than or equal to 100, you don't see any message.

10.3(b) If...Then...Else Statement

Using only `If...Then` statement is not especially useful in programming and it does not provide choices for the users. To provide a choice, we can use the `If...Then...Else` Statement. This control structure will ask the computer to perform a certain action specified by the Visual Basic 2019 expression if the condition is met. And when the condition is false, an alternative action will be executed. The syntax for the `If...Then...Else` statement is

Example 10.2

In this example, we create a lucky draw simulation program. We use the `Rnd()` function to generate a random number between 0 and 1. In addition, using the `Int()` function in the formula `Int(Rnd() * 10) + 1` will generate a random integer from 1 and 10. Next, we use the `If...Then...Else` statement to determine the condition for striking a lucky draw. Besides that, we insert two labels, one of them is to display the generated number and the other one is to display the message of the lucky draw outcome. In addition, we insert a button and rename it as BtnDraw then click it and enter the following code:

Public Sub BtnBet_Click(sender As Object, e As EventArgs)

```
Handles BtnBet.Click
    Dim myNum As Integer
    myNum = InputBox("Enter your lucky number and click OK")
    If myNum > LuckyNum Then
        MsgBox("Your number is too big")
    ElseIf myNum < LuckyNum Then
        MsgBox("Your number is too small")
    Else
        MsgBox("Congratulations! You strike the lucky number")
    End If
End Sub
```

Executing the code will display the output UI , as shown in Figure 10.1

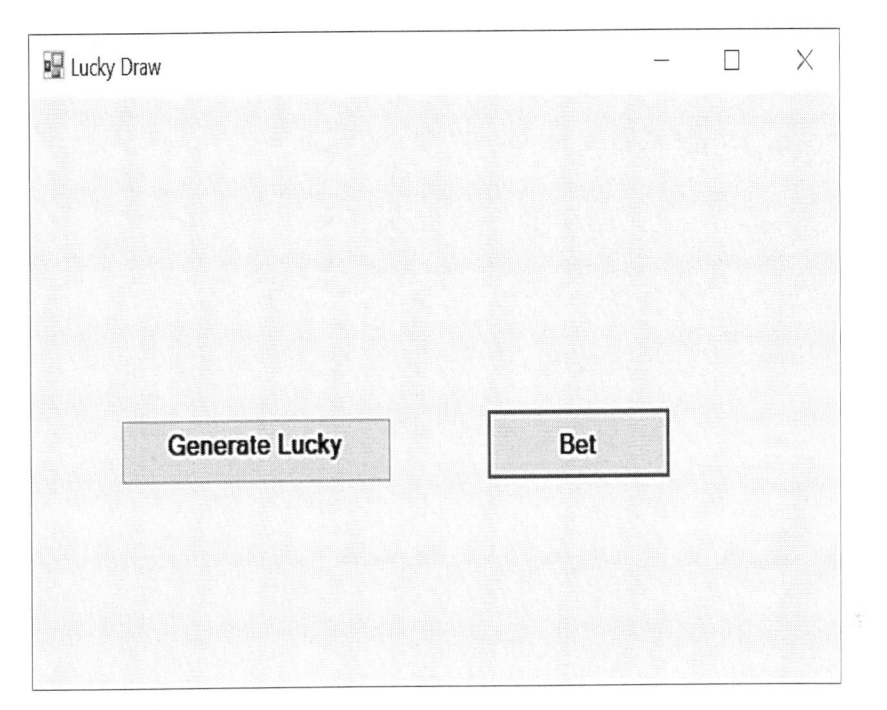

Figure 10.1

To start the lucky draw, click the 'Generate Lucky Number" button to generate the lucky number. Click the "Bet" button to bring up an input box, enter your lucky number and click OK, as shown in figure 10.2

Figure 10.2

If the generated number is greater than lucky number, the message "Your number is too big" will be displayed on a message box .If the generated number is smaller than lucky number, the message "Your number is too small" will be displayed on a message box. Otherwise, the message "Congratulations! You strike the lucky number" will be displayed on a message box. The outcomes are shown in Figure 10.3, 10.4 and 10.5.

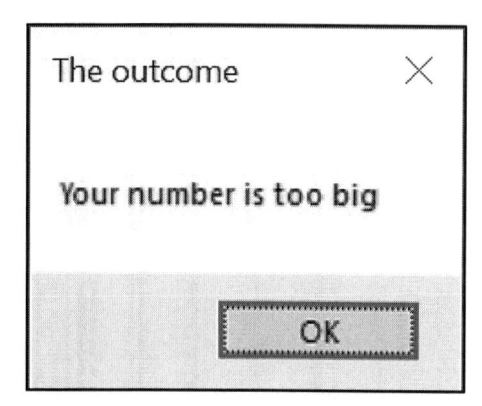

Figure 10.3

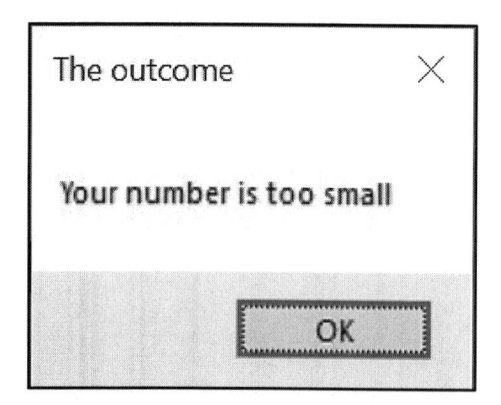

Figure 10.4

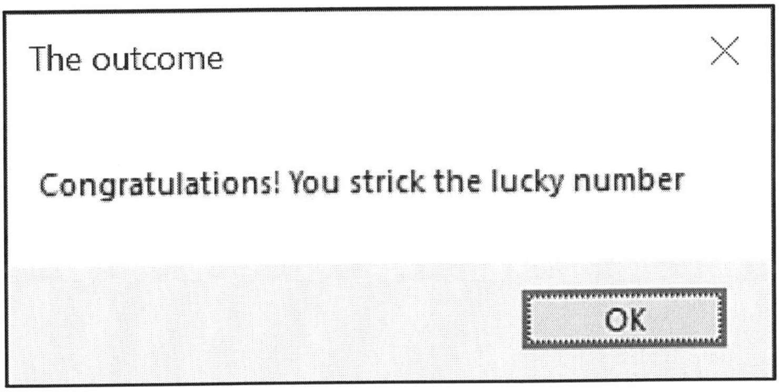

Figure 10.5

Example 10.3

Now we modify Example 10.2 and add in an additional constraint, age. In the program, we use the logical operator **And** beside the conditional operators. This means that both the conditions must be fulfilled for the conditions to be true, otherwise the second block of code will be executed. In this example, the lucky number must be more than 120 and the age must be more than 50 in order to win a lucky prize, any one of the above conditions not fulfilled will disqualify the user from winning a lucky prize. In addition, we make the program more interactive by adding name in the message. The code is as follows:

```
Public Class Form1

    Dim myAge As Integer

    Dim myName As String

Private Sub BtnDraw_Click(sender As Object, e As EventArgs) Handles BtnDraw.Click
    Dim myNumber As Integer
```

```
myAge = TxtAge.Text
myName = TxtName.Text
myNumber = Int(Rnd() * 200) + 1
LblNum.Text = myNumber

 If myNumber > 120 And myAge > 50 Then
LblMsg.Text = " Congratulation " & myName &
",You won a lucky prize!"
 Else
LblMsg.Text = " Sorry " & myName & ", you did not win any prize"
 End If
End Sub
End Class
```

The outcomes are shown in Figure 10.6 and Figure 10.7

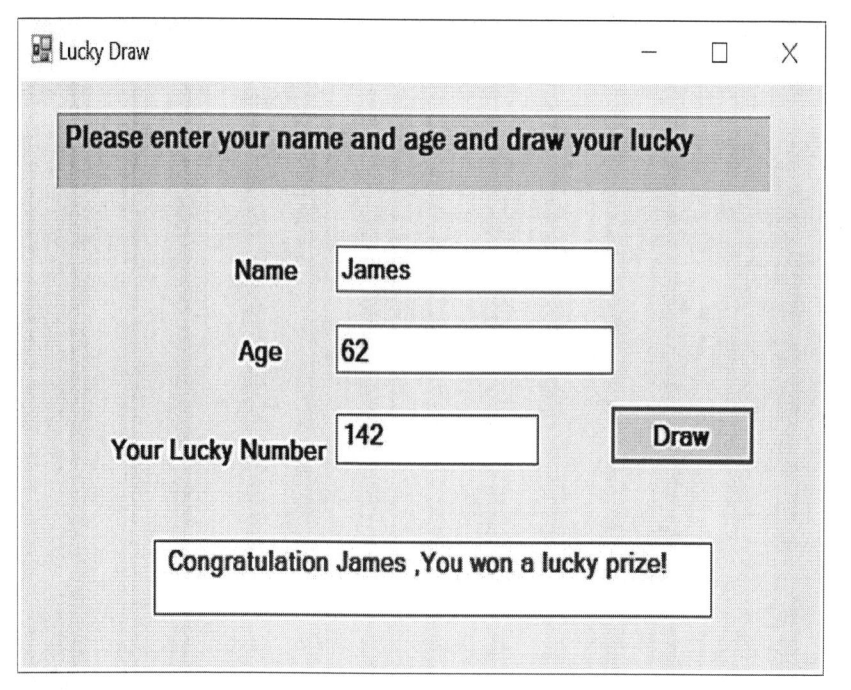

Figure 10.6

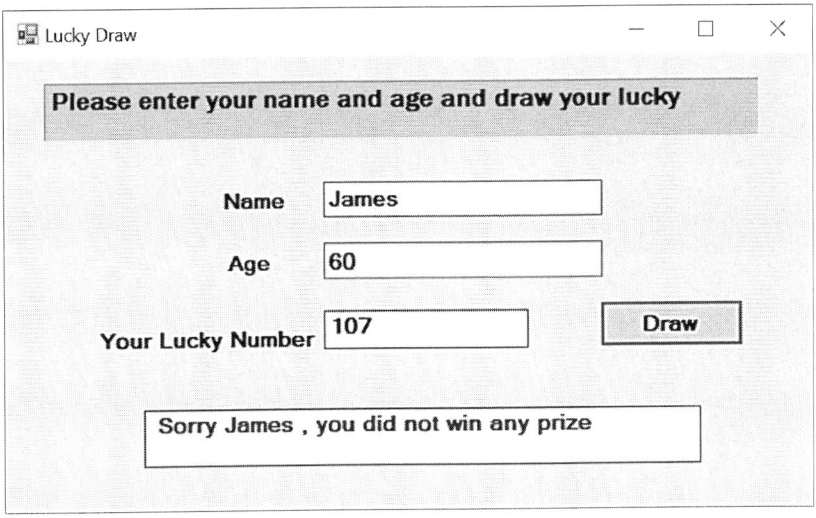

Figure 10.7

10.3(c) If...Then...ElseIf Statement

If there are more than two alternative choices, using just `If...Then...Else` statement will not be enough. To provide more choices, we can use the `If...Then...ElseIf` Statement. The structure of `If...Then...ElseIf` statement is

If condition Then
Visual Basic 2019 expression
ElseIf condition 1 Then
Visual Basic 2019 expression
ElseIf condition 2 Then
Visual Basic 2019 expression
Else
Visual Basic 2019 expression
End If

Example 10.4 Grade Generator

This program uses the **If... ElseIf** structure and the **And** logical operator to compute the grade for a certain mark.

```
Private Sub BtnCompute_Click(ByVal sender As Object, ByVal_
e As EventArgs)Handles Button1.Click
Dim Mark As Integer
Dim Grade As String
Mark = Val(TxtMark.Text)
If Mark>=80 Then
Grade="A"
ElseIf Mark>=60 And Mark<80 Then
Grade="B"

ElseIf Mark>=50 And Mark<60 Then

Grade="C"
Else
Grade="D"
End If
MsgBox("You grade is " & Grade)

End Sub
```

Running the program and will produce a form when the user can enter the mark. After entering the mark and clicking the 'Compute Grade' button, the grade will be displayed in a message box, as shown in Figure 10.8

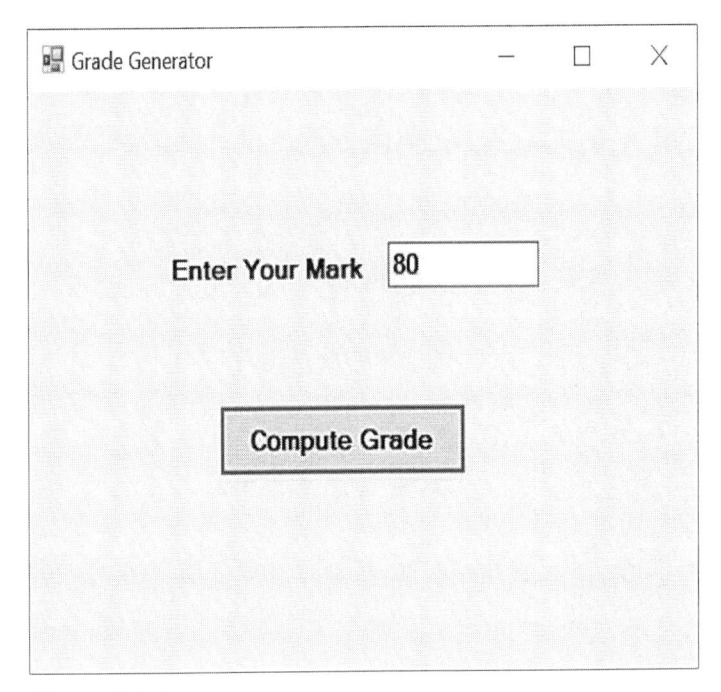

Figure 10.8

Clicking the OK produces a message box that shows the grade, as shown in Figure 10.9.

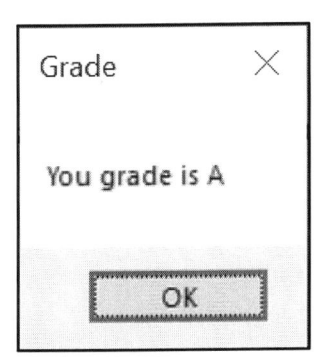

Figure 10.9

Summary

- In section 10.1, you have learned about the conditional operators
- In section 10.2, you have learned about the logical operators

- In section 10.3, you have learned how to write code involving If....Then...Else

Chapter 11 Using Select Case

In the preceding chapter, we have learned how to control the program flow using the `If...ElseIf` control structure. In this lesson, you will learn how to use the `Select Case` structure to control the program flow. The `Select Case` control structure is slightly different from the `If...ElseIf` structure. The difference is that the `Select Case` control structure only make decision on one expression or dimension (for example the examination grade) while the `If...ElseIf` statement control structure may evaluate only one expression, each `If...ElseIf` statement may also compute entirely different dimensions. `Select Case` is preferred when there exist multiple conditions.

11.1 The Select Case...End Select Structure

The structure of the Select Case control structure in Visual Basic 2019 is as follows:

Select Case test expression
Case expression list 1
Block of one or more Visual Basic 2019 statements
Case expression list 2
Block of one or more Visual Basic 2019 Statements
.
.
Case Else

Block of one or more Visual Basic 2019 Statements
End Select

11.2 The usage of Select Case

Example 11.1: Examination Grades

This example displays the examination results based on the grade obtained. The test expression here is grade. In this program, we insert a textbox for entering the grade, rename it as txtGrade. Next, insert a label for display the result, rename it as LblResult. Lastly, we insert a button, rename it as BtnCompute then enter the following code:

```
Private Sub BtnCompute_Click(ByVal sender As Object,
ByVal e As EventArgs) Handles BtnCompute.Click
Dim grade As String
grade=txtGrade.Text
Select Case grade
Case "A"
   LblResult.Text="High Distinction"
Case "A-"
   LblResult.Text="Distinction"
Case "B"
   LblResult.Text="Credit"
Case "C"
   LblResult.Text="Pass"
Case Else
   LblResult.Text="Fail"
```

End Select
End Sub

When the user runs the program, enters grade and clicks the 'Compute' button, the output is as shown in Figure 11.1

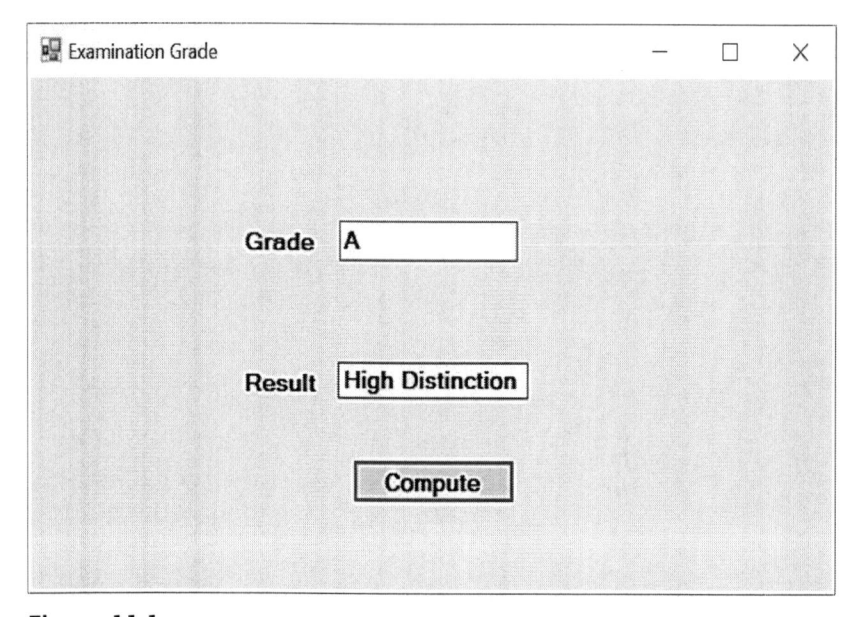

Figure 11.1

Example 11.2

This example is like the previous example, but we use the **Case IS** keyword and the conditional operator >= to compute the results.

```
Private Sub BtnCompute_Click(ByVal sender As Object, ByVal e As EventArgs) Handles BtnCompute.Click
Dim mark As integer
mark = TxtMark.Text
Select Case mark
  Case Is >= 85
```

```
        LblRemark.Text= "Excellence"
          Case Is >= 70
        LblRemark.Text= "Good"
          Case Is >= 60
        LblRemark.Text = "Above Average"
          Case Is >= 50
        LblRemark.Text= "Average"
          Case Else
        LblRemark.Text = "Need to work harder"
        End Select
        End Sub
```

The output is shown in Figure 11.2

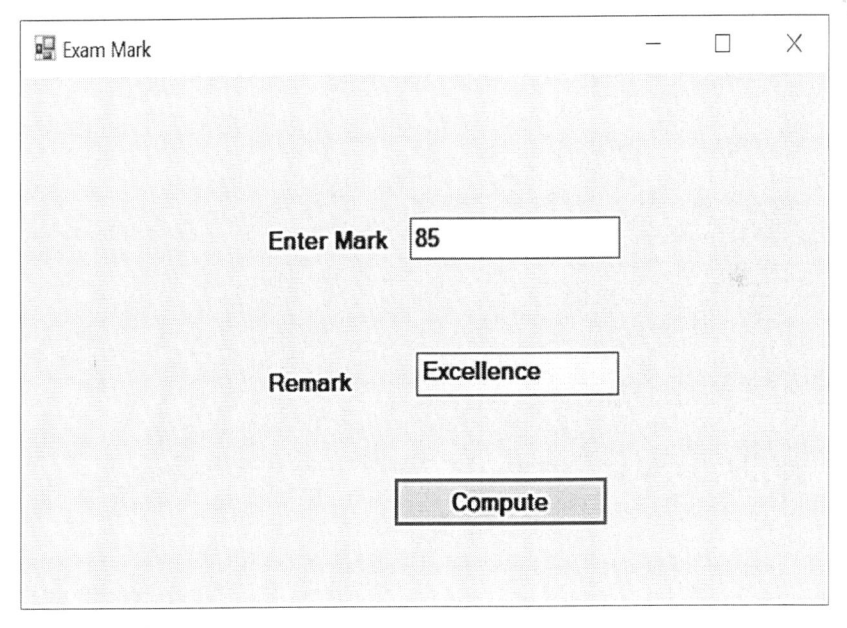

Figure 11.2

Example 11.3

Example 11.2 can be rewritten as follows:

```
Private Sub BtnCompute_Click(ByVal sender As Object,
```

```
ByVal e As EventArgs) Handles BtnCompute.Click
'Examination Marks
Dim mark As Single
mark = TxtMark.Text
Select Case mark
Case 0 to 49
  LblRemark.Text = "Need to work harder"
Case 50 to 59
  LblRemark.Text = "Average"
Case 60 to 69
  LblRemark.Text= "Above Average"
Case 70 to 84
  LblRemark.Text = "Good"
Case 85 to 100
  LblRemark.Text= "Excellence"
Case Else
LblRemark.Text= "Wrong entry, please re-enter the mark"
End Select
End Sub
```

Example 11.4

Grades in high school are usually presented with a single capital letter such as A, B, C, D or E. The grades can be computed as follows:

```
Private Sub BtnCompute_Click(ByVal sender As Object, ByVal e
  As EventArgs) Handles BtnCompute.Click
'Examination Marks
Dim mark As Single
mark = TextBox1.Text
Select Case mark
```

```
Case 0 To 49
Label1.Text = "E"
Case 50 To 59
Label1.Text = "D"
Case 60 To 69
Label1.Text = "C"
Case 70 To 79
Label1.Text = "B"
Case 80 To 100
Label1.Text = "A"
Case Else
Label1.Text = "Error, please re-enter the mark"
End Select
End Sub
```

The output is as shown in Figure 11.3

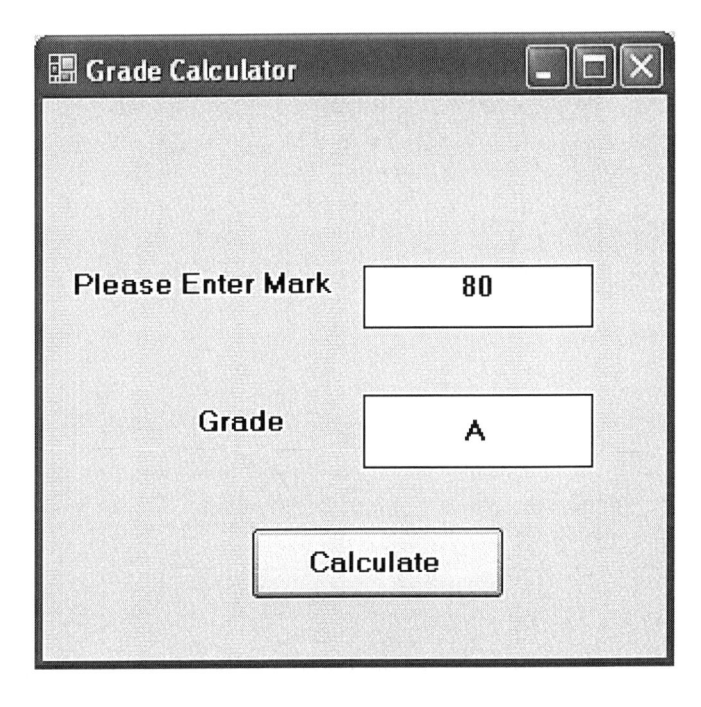

Figure 11.3
Summary

- In section 11.1, you have learned about the Select Case structure
- In section 11.2, you have learned how to write code using Select Case structure together with the conditional operators.

Chapter 12 Looping

In programming, we often need to write code that does a job repeatedly until a certain condition is met, this process is called looping. Looping allows a procedure to run repetitively as many times as long as the processor and memory could support. For example, we can design a program that adds a series of numbers until the sum exceeds a certain value, or a program that asks the user to enter data repeatedly until he or she enters the word 'Finish'. In Visual Basic 2019, there are three types of Loops, the **For...Next** loop, the **Do...loop** and the **While...End While** loop

12.1 For...Next Loop

The most common loop is the **For...Next** loop. The structure of a **For...Next** loop is as shown below:

For counter = startNumber to endNumber (Step increment)
One or more Visual Basic 2019 statements
Next

To exit a **For...Next** Loop, you can place the **Exit For** statement within the loop; and it is normally used together with the **If...Then** statement. For its application, you can refer to example 12.1 d.

Example 12.1 a

    Dim counter As Integer
    For counter=1 to 10
    ListBox1.Items.Add (counter)
    Next

* This loop will enter number 1 to 10 into the list box.

Example 12.1b

    Dim counter, sum As Integer
    For counter=1 to 100 step 10
    sum += counter
    ListBox1.Items.Add (sum)
    Next

* This loop will calculate the sum of the numbers as follows:

sum=0+10+20+30+40+......

Example 12.1c

    Dim counter, sum As Integer
    sum = 1000
    For counter = 100 To 5 Step -5
    sum - = counter

```
ListBox1.Items.Add(sum)
Next
```

*Notice that increment can be negative.

The program will compute the subtraction as follow:

1000-100 - 95 - 90 -..........

Example 12.1d

```
Dim n As Integer
For n=1 to 10
If n>6 then
Exit For
End If
Else
ListBox1.Items.Add (n)
End If
Next
```

The process will stop when n is greater than 6.

12.2 Do Loop

The **Do Loop** structures are

a)

```
Do While condition
Block of one or more Visual Basic 2019 statements
Loop
```

b)

Do

Block of one or more Visual Basic 2012 statements

Loop While condition

c)

Do Until condition

Block of one or more Visual Basic 2012 statements

Loop

d)

Do

Block of one or more Visual Basic 2012 statements

Loop Until condition

Sometimes we need exit to exit a loop prematurely because a certain condition is fulfilled. The syntax to use is Exit Do. Let us examine the following examples:

Example 12.2(a)

```
Do while counter <=1000
TextBox1.Text=counter
counter +=1
Loop
```

* The above example will keep on adding until counter >1000.

The above example can be rewritten as

```
Do
TextBox1.Text=counter
counter+=1
Loop until counter>1000
```

Example 12.2(b)

```
Private Sub BtnCompute_Click(ByVal sender As Object,
ByVal e As EventArgs) Handles BtnCompute.Click
Dim sum, n As Integer
MyListBox.Items.Add("n" & vbTab & "Sum")
MyListBox.Items.Add("---------------")
Do
n += 1
sum += n
MyListBox.Items.Add(n & vbTab & sum)
If n = 100 Then
Exit Do
End If
Loop
End Sub
```

* The loop in the above example can be replaced by the following loop:

```
Do Until n = 10
n += 1
sum += n
```

MyListBox.Items.Add(n & vbTab & sum)
Loop

The output is as shown in Figure 12.1

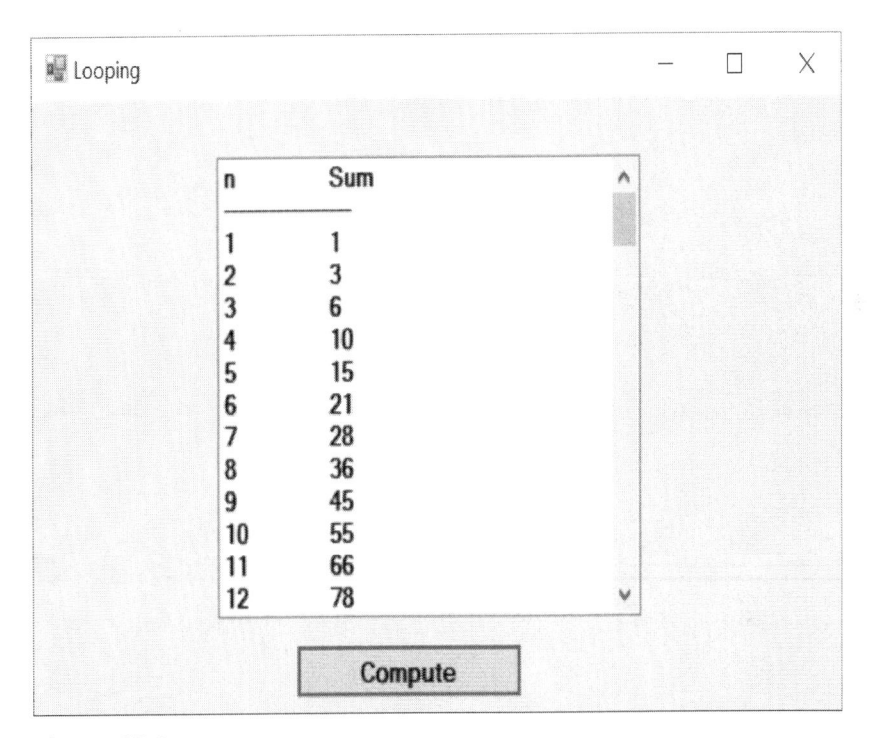

Figure 12.1

12.3 While...End While Loop

The structure of a While...End While Loop is very similar to the Do Loop, as shown below:

While conditions
Visual Basic 2019 statements
End While

The loop is illustrated in Example 12.3

Example 12.3

```
Private Sub BtnCompute_Click(ByVal sender As Object,
 ByVal e As EventArgs) Handles BtnCompute.Click
Dim sum, n As Integer
ListBox1.Items.Add("n" & vbTab & "sum")
ListBox1.Items.Add("---------------")
While n <> 10
n += 1
sum += n
ListBox1.Items.Add(n & vbTab & sum)
End While
End Sub
```

Summary

- In section 12.1, you have learned how to write code using the For...Next Loop
- In section 12.2, you have learned how to write code using the Do Loop
- In section 12.3. you have learned how to write code using the While...End While Loop

Chapter 13 Sub Procedures

13.1 What is a Sub Procedure

A sub procedure is a procedure that performs a specific task and to return values, but it does not return a value associated with its name. However, it can return a value through a variable name. Sub procedures are usually used to accept input from the user, display information, print information, manipulate properties, or perform some other tasks. It is a program code by itself and it is not an event procedure because it is not associated with a runtime procedure or a control such as a button. It is called by the main program whenever it is required to perform a certain task.

Sub procedures help to make programs smaller and easier to manage. A sub procedure begins with a Sub keyword and ends with an End Sub keyword. The main program can reference a procedure by using its name together with the arguments in parentheses. The program structure of a sub procedure is as follows:

Sub ProcedureName(arguments)
Statements
End Sub

13.2 Examples of Sub Procedure

Example 13.1

In this example, we create a sub procedure sum to add two values that are specified as the arguments. The Sub procedure adds two numbers a and b and display its sum on a Label which we named it as LblSum. Under the calculate procedure, we define two variables x and y and accept inputs from the users. The procedure calculates the sum of the values entered by the user by calling the sum subprocedure.

```
Private Sub BtnCompute(sender As Object, e As EventArgs) Handles
 MyBase.Load
Dim x, y As Single

x = Val(TxtX.Text)

y = Val(TxtY.Text)

sum(x, y)
End Sub



Sub sum(a As Single, b As Single)
Dim mySum As Single

   mySum = a + b

   LblSum.Text = mySum

End Sub
```

Executing the program produces a message box as shown in Figure 13.1

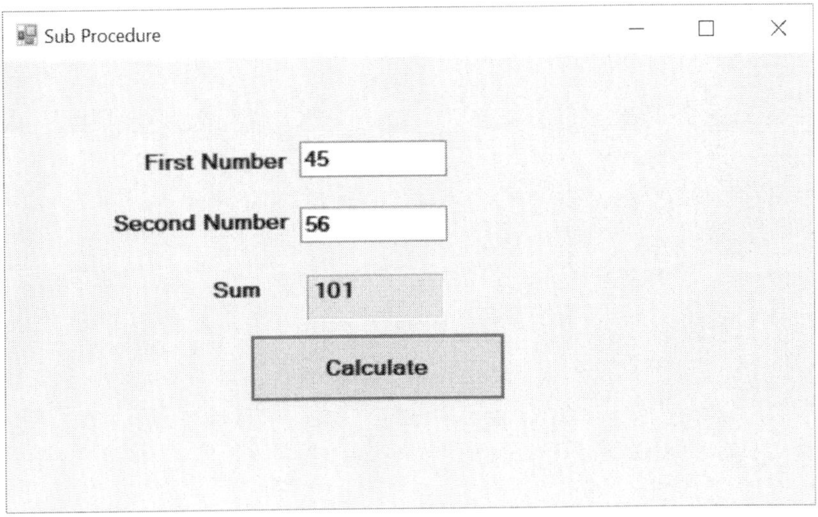

[Figure: Sub Procedure form with First Number 45, Second Number 56, Sum 101, and Calculate button]

Figure 13.1

Example 13.2: Password Cracker

This is a password cracking program that can generate possible passwords and then compares each of them with the actual password; and if the generated password found to be equal to the actual password, login will be successful. In this program, a timer is inserted into the form and it is used to do a repetitive job of generating the passwords.

We create a password generating procedure **generate** () and it is called by the `Timer1_Tick()` event so that the procedure is repeated after every interval. The interval of the timer can be set in its properties window where a value of 1 is 1 millisecond, so a value of 1000 is 1 second; the smaller the value, the shorter the interval. However, do not set the timer to zero because if you do that, the timer will not start. We shall set the Timer interval at 100 which is equivalent to 0.1 second. The `Timer1.Enabled` property is set to false so that the program will only start generating the passwords after you click on the Generate button. Rnd is a Visual Basic 2019 function that generates a random number between 0 and 1. Multiplying Rnd by 100 will obtain a number between 0 and 100. Int is a Visual Basic 2019 function that returns an integer by ignoring the decimal part of that number.

Therefore, `Int(Rnd*100)` will produce a random number between 0 and 99, and the value of `Int(Rnd*100)+100` will produce a random number between 100 and 199. Finally, the program uses `If...Then...Else` to check whether the generated password is equal the actual password or not; and if they are equal, the passwords generating process will be terminated by setting the `Timer1.Enabled` property to false. The code is as follows:

```
Dim password As Integer

Dim crackpass As Integer


Private Sub BtnGenerate_Click(sender As Object, e As EventArgs) Handles BtnGenerate.Click
Timer1.Enabled = True
End Sub


Private Sub Timer1_Tick(sender As Object, e As EventArgs) Handles Timer1.Tick
generate()
If crackpass = password Then
```

```
Timer1.Enabled = False
LblCrackPass.Text = crackpass
MsgBox("Password Cracked!Login Successful!")
Else Label1.Text = crackpass
LblMsg.Text = "Please wait..."
End If
End Sub


Sub generate()
crackpass = Int(Rnd() * 100) + 100
End Sub


Private Sub Form1_Load(sender As Object, e As EventArgs)
Handles MyBase.Load
password = 123
End Sub
```

Executing the program and clicking the Generate password will start generating the passwords until it gets the actual password. The output is as shown in Figure 13.2

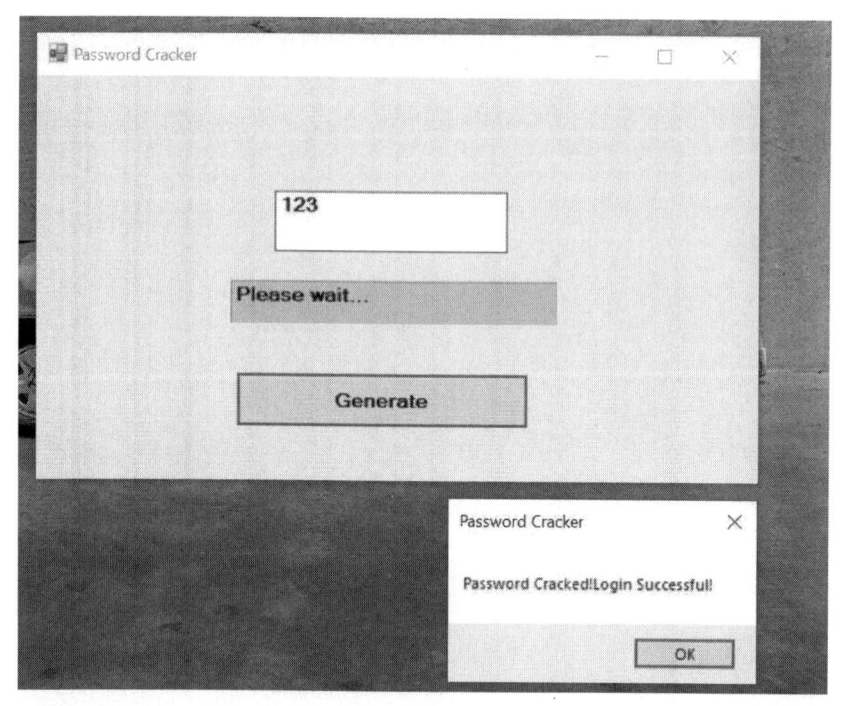

Figure 13.2

Summary

- In section 13.1, you have learned about the concept of a sub procedure
- In section 13.2, you have learned how to write code for a sub procedure

Chapter 14 Creating Functions

A function is similar to a sub procedure in the sense that both are called by the main procedure to fulfil certain tasks. However, there is one difference; a function returns a value whilst a sub procedure does not. There are two types of functions, the built-in functions (or internal functions) and the functions created by the programmers, or simply called user-defined functions.

14.1 Creating User-Defined Functions

To create a user defined function in Visual Basic 2019, you can type the function procedure directly into the code window as follows:

Public Function functionName (Argument As dataType,..........)
As dataType

or

Private Function functionName (Argument As dataType,..........)
As dataType

The keyword Public indicates that the function is applicable to the whole project and the keyword Private indicates that the function is only applicable to a certain module or procedure. Argument is a parameter that can pass a value back to the function. You can include as many arguments as you like.

Example 14.1: BMI Calculator

This BMI calculator is a Visual Basic 2019 program that can calculate the body mass index, or BMI of a person based on the body weight in kilograms and the body height in meters. BMI can be calculated using the formula weight/(height)^2, where weight is measured in kg and height in meters. If you only know your weight and height in lb and feet, then you need to convert them to the metric system. If your BMI is more than 30, you are considered obese

The Code

```
Private Function BMI(Height As Single, weight As Single) As Double
    BMI = weight / Height ^ 2
End Function


Private Sub BtnCal_Click(sender As Object, e As EventArgs) Handles BtnCal.Click

Dim h As Single, w As Single
h = Val(TxtHeight.Text)
w = Val(TxtWeight.Text)
LblBMI.Text = Format(BMI(h, w), "0.00")

End Sub
```

The output is as shown in Figure 14.1

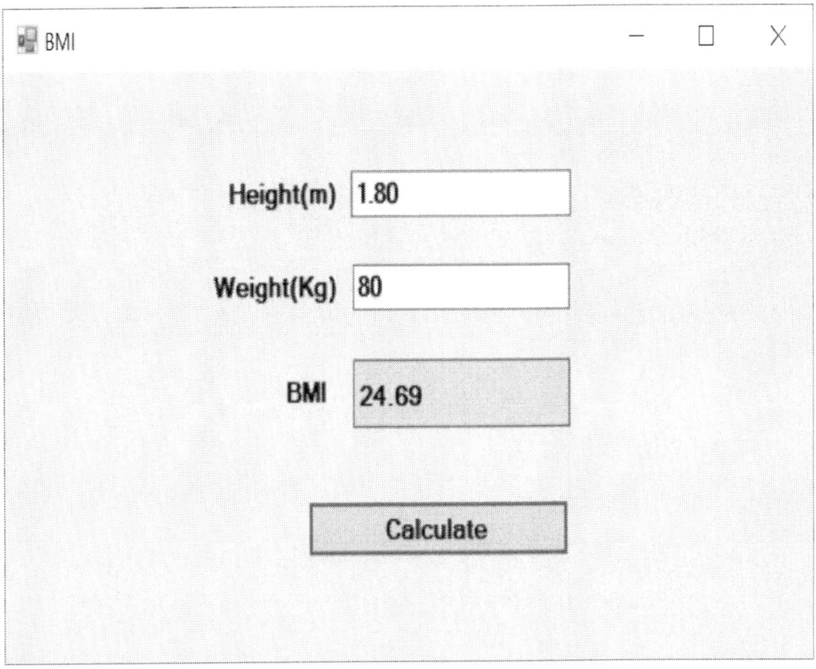

Figure 14.1

Example 14.2: Future Value Calculator

The concept of future value is related to time value of money. For example, if you deposit your money in a bank as a savings account or a fixed deposit account for a certain period of time, you will earn a certain amount of money based on the compound interest computed periodically, and this amount is added to the principal if you continue to keep the money in the bank. Interest for the following period is now computed based on the initial principal plus the interest (the amount which becomes your new principal). Subsequent interests are computed in the same way.

For example, let's say you deposited $1000 in a bank and the bank is paying you 5% compound interest annually. After the first year, you will earn an interest of $1000×0.05=$50 . Your new principal will be

$1000+$1000×0.05=$1000(1+0.05)=$1000(1.05)=$1050.

After the second year, your new principal is $1000(1.05) x1.05=$1000(1.05)2 =$1102.50. This new principal is called the future value.

Following the above calculation, the future value after n years will be

FV = PV * (1 + i / 100)^n

Where PV represents the present value, FV represents the future value, i is the interest rate and n is the number of periods (Normally months or years).

The Code

```
Private Function FV(pv As Single, i As Single, n As Integer) As Double
FV = pv * (1 + i / 100) ^ n
End Function


Private Sub BtnCal_Click(sender As Object, e As EventArgs)
Handles BtnCal.Click
Dim FutureVal As Single
Dim PresentVal As Single
Dim interest As Single
Dim period As Integer
PresentVal = TxtPV.Text
interest = TxtInt.Text
period = TxtN.Text
```

```
FutureVal = FV(PresentVal, interest, period)
LblFV.Text = Format(FutureVal, "$#,##0.00")
End Sub
```

The Output is shown in Figure 14.2

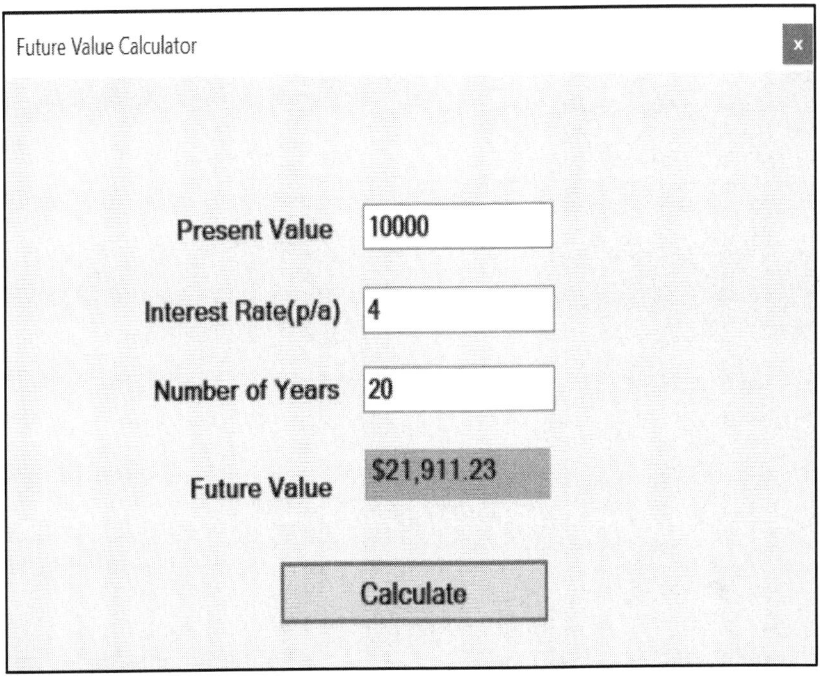

Figure 14.2

14.2 Passing Arguments by Value and by Reference

Functions can be called by value or called by reference. By default, the arguments in the function are passed by reference. If arguments are passed by reference, the original data will be modified and no longer preserved. On the one hand, if arguments are passed by value, the original data will be preserved. The keyword to pass arguments by reference is ByRef and the keyword to pass arguments by value is ByVal.

For example,

> Private Function FV(ByVal pv As Single,
> ByRef i As Single, n As Integer)
> As Double

The function FV receives pv by value, i by reference and n by reference. Notice that although ByRef is not used to pass n, by default it is passed by reference.

Example 14.2(a)

In this example, we create two functions that compute the square root of a number, the first uses the keyword ByRef and the second uses the keyword ByVal.

The Code

> Private Function sqroot(ByRef x As Single) As Double
> x = x ^ 0.5
> sqroot = x
> End Function

> Private Function sqroot1(ByVal y As Single) As Double
> y = y ^ 0.5
> sqroot1 = y
> End Function

```
Private Sub Button1_Click(sender As Object, e As EventArgs)
Handles Button1.Click
Dim u As Single
u = 9
MsgBox(3 * sqroot(u), , "ByRef")
MsgBox("Value of u is " & u, , "ByRef")
End Sub
Private Sub Button2_Click(sender As Object, e As EventArgs)
Handles Button2.Click
Dim u As Single
u = 9
MsgBox(3 * sqroot1(u), , "ByVal")
MsgBox("Value of u is " & u, , "ByVal")
End Sub
```

The Outputs

Case 1: Passing arguments using ByRef (As shown in Figure 14.3)

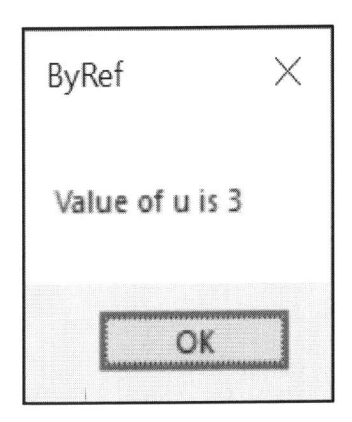

Figure 14.3

Notice that the value of u has been changed to 3

Case 2: Passing arguments using ByVal(as shown in Figure 14.4)

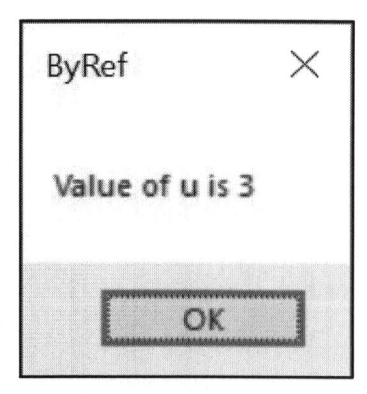

Figure 14.4
Notice that the value of u remains unchanged.

Summary

- In section 14.1, you have learned how to create a user-defined function
- In section 14.2, you have learned about the difference between passing arguments using ByVal and ByRef

Chapter 15 Mathematical Functions

In previous chapters, we have learned how to write codes in Visual Basic 2019 that perform mathematical operations using standard mathematical operators. However, for more complex mathematical calculations, we need to use the built-in math functions in Visual Basic 2019. There are numerous built-in mathematical functions in Visual Basic 2019 which we shall introduce them one by one in this lesson.

15.1 The Abs Function

The Abs function returns the absolute value of a given number. The syntax is

Math.Abs(number)

* The Math keyword here indicates that the Abs function belong to the Math class. However, not all mathematical functions belong to the Math class.

Example 15.1

In this example, we shall add a textbox control for the user to input his or her number and a label control to display the absolute value of the number. We need to use the Val function to convert text to numeric value. Rename the text box as TxtNum and the label as LblAbs.

The Code

```
Private Sub BtnComp_Click(sender As Object, e As EventArgs)
Handles BtnComp.Click
LblAbs.Text = Math.Abs(Val(TxtNum.Text))
End Sub
```

The output is shown in Figure 15.1

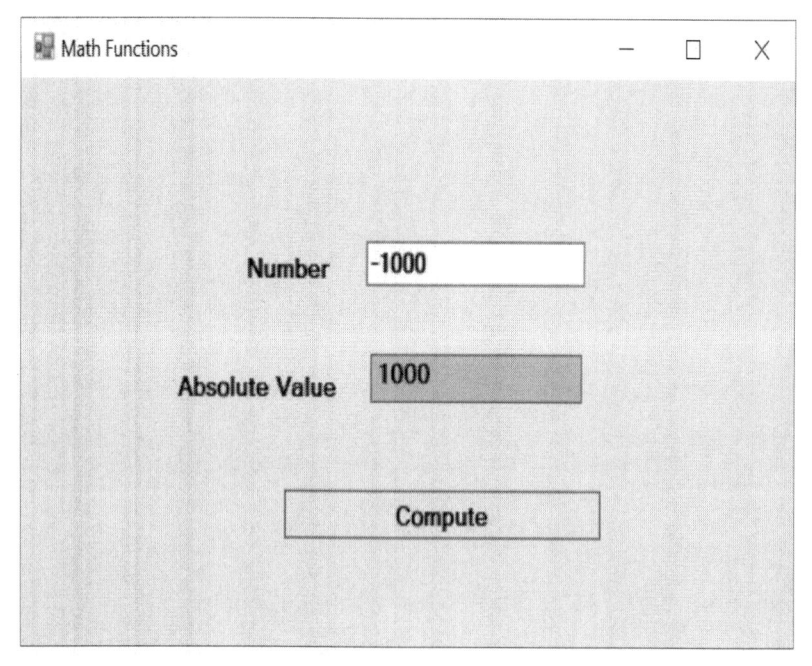

Figure 15.1

15.2 The Exp function

The Exp function returns the exponential value of a given number. For example, Exp(1)=e=2.71828182

The syntax is

Math.Exp(number)

Example 15.2

In this example, we shall add a textbox control for the user to input his or her number and a label control to display the exponential value of the number. Rename the text box as TxtNum and the label as LblAbs.

The Code

```
Private Sub BtnComp_Click(sender As Object, e As EventArgs)
Handles BtnComp.Click
LblExp.Text = Math.Exp(Val(TxtNum.Text))
End Sub
```

The Output is shown in Figure 15.2

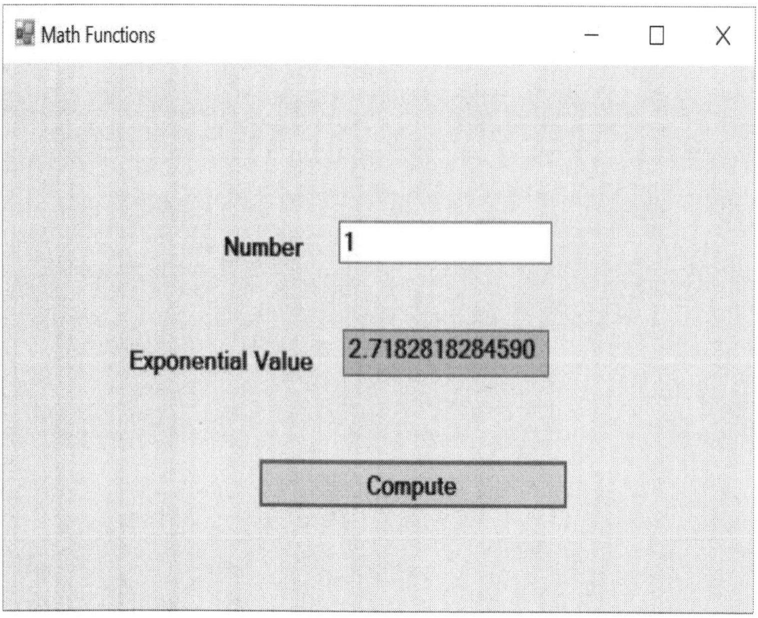

Figure 15.2

15.3 The Fix Function

The Fix function truncates the decimal part of a positive number and returns the largest integer smaller than the number. However, when the number is negative, it returns the smallest integer larger than the number. Fix does not belong to the Math class therefore we do not use the Math keyword.

Example 15.3

```
Private Sub BtnComp_Click(sender As Object, e As EventArgs)
 Handles BtnComp.Click
LblFixNum1.Text = Fix(Val(TxtPosNum.Text))
LblFixNum2.Text = Fix(Val(TxtNegNum.Text))
End Sub
```

The Output is shown in Figure 15.3

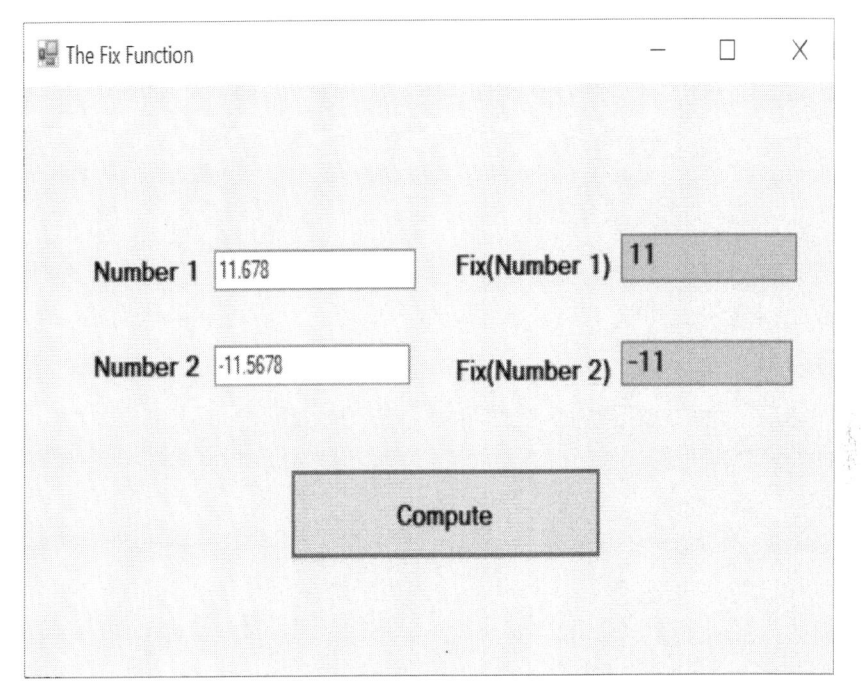

Figure 15.3

15.4 The Int Function

The Int is a function that converts a number into an integer by truncating its decimal part and the resulting integer is the largest integer that is smaller than the number. For example

Int(2.4)=2, Int(6.9)=6 , Int(-5.7)=-6, Int(-99.8)=-100

15.5 The Log Function

The Log function is the function that returns the natural logarithm of a number.

Example 15.4

Private Sub BtnComp_Click(sender As Object, e As EventArgs)
Handles BtnComp.Click
LblLog.Text = Math.Log(Val(TxtNum.Text))
End Sub

The Output is shown in Figure 15.4

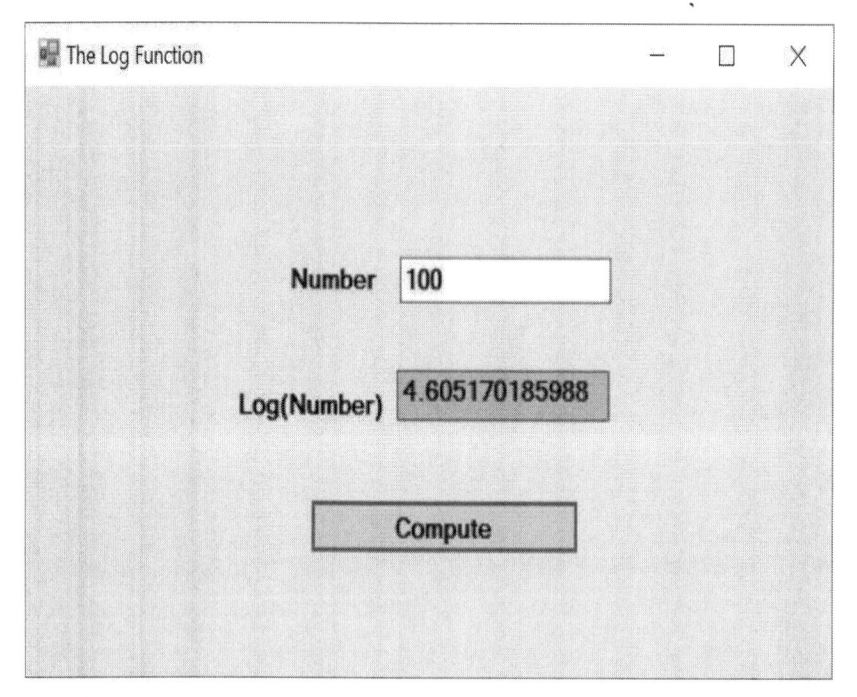

Figure 15.4

15.6 The Rnd( ) Function

We use the Rnd function to write code that involves chance and probability. The Rnd function returns a random value between 0 and 1. Random numbers in their original form are not very useful in programming until we convert them to integers. For example, if we need to obtain a random output of 6 integers ranging from 1 to 6, which makes the program behave like a virtual dice, we need to convert the random numbers to integers using the formula Int(Rnd*6)+1.

Example 15.5

```
Private Sub BtnGen_Click(sender As Object, e As EventArgs)
Handles BtnGen.Click
LblRnd.Text = Int(VBMath.Rnd() * 6) + 1
End Sub
```

Notice that the **Rnd()** function belongs to the **VBMath** class in Visual Basic 2019. This is different from Visual Basic 2012, where you can omit the VBMath keyword.

In this example, **Int(Rnd*6)** will generate a random integer between 0 and 5 because the function Int truncates the decimal part of the random number and returns an integer. After adding 1, you will get a random number between 1 and 6 every time you click the command button. For example, let's say the random number generated is 0.98, after multiplying it by 6, it becomes 5.88, and using the integer function Int(5.88) will convert the number to 5; and after adding 1 you will get 6.

The Output is shown in Figure 15.5

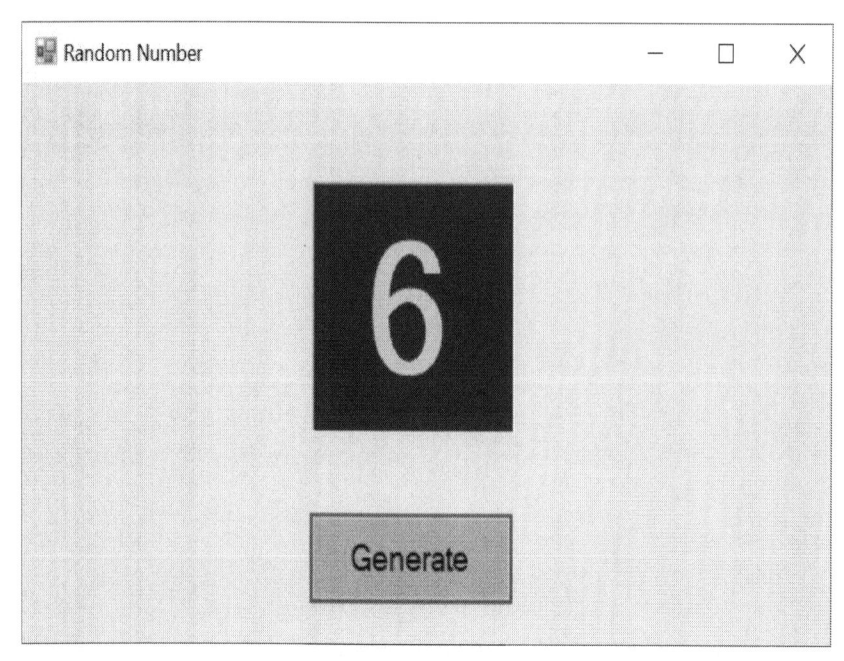

Figure 15.5

15.7 The Round Function

The Round function is the function that rounds up a number to a certain number of decimal places. The Format is Round (n, m) which means to round a number n to m decimal places. For example, Math.Round (7.2567, 2) =7.26

Example 15.6

    Private Sub Button1_Click(sender As Object, e As EventArgs)
    Handles Button1.Click
    Dim n As integer

    n=Txtn
    Label1.Text = Math.Round(Val(TextBox1.Text), n)
    End Sub

The Output is shown in Figure 15.6

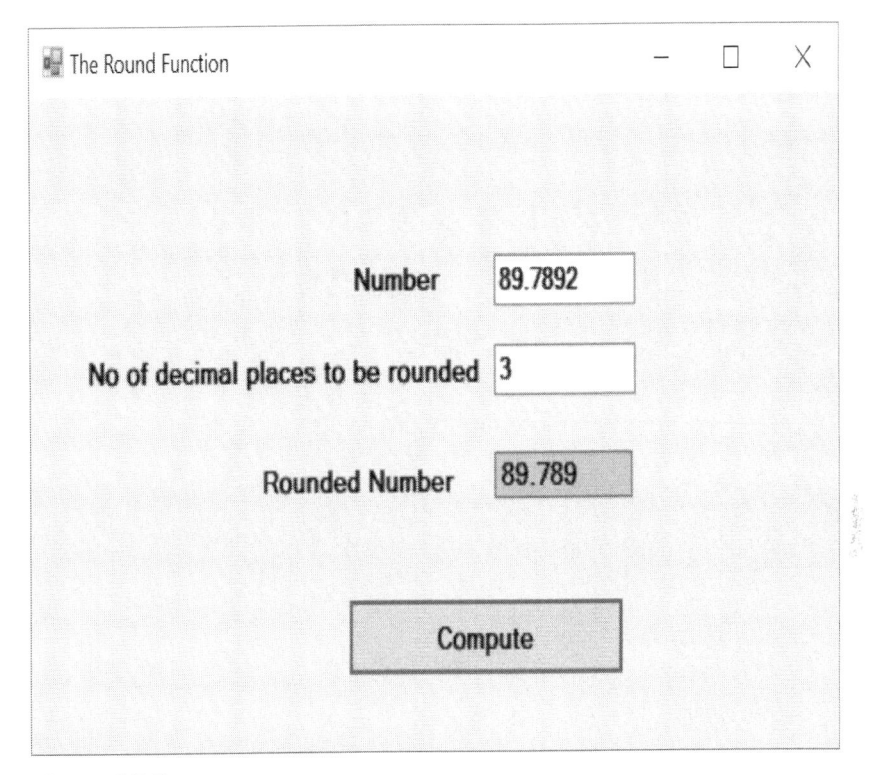

Figure 15.6

Summary

- In section 15.1, you have learned how to use the Abs function
- In section 15.2, you have learned how to use the Exp function
- In section 15.3, you have learned how to use the Fix function
- In section 15.4, you have learned how to use the Int function
- In section 15.5, you have learned how to use the Log function
- In section 15.6, you have learned how to use the Rnd function
- In section 15.7, you have learned how to use the Round function

Chapter 16 The Format Function

The Format function is used to display numbers as well as date and time in various formats.

16.1 Format Function for Numbers

There are two types of Format functions for numbers; one of them is the built-in or predefined format while another one can be defined by the user.

16.1(a) Built-in Format function for Numbers

The syntax of the built-in Format function is

Format(n, "style argument")

Where n is a number.

The list of style arguments is listed in Table 16.1

Table 16.1

Style Argument	Explanation	Example
General Number	To display the number without having separators between thousands.	Format(8972.234, "General Number")=8972.234
Fixed	To display the number without having separators between thousands and rounds it up to two decimal places.	Format(8972.2, "Fixed")=8972.23

Standard	To display the number with separators or separators between thousands and rounds it up to two decimal places.	Format(6648972.265, "Standard")= 6,648,972.27
Currency	To display the number with a dollar sign in front, has separators between thousands as well as rounding it up to two decimal places.	Format(6648972.265, "Currency")= $6,648,972.27
Percent	Converts the number to the percentage form and displays a % sign and rounds it up to two decimal places.	Format(0.56324, "Percent")=56.32 %

Example 16.1

Private Sub BtnFormat_Click(sender As Object, e As EventArgs)
Handles BtnFormat.Click
Label1.Text = Format(8972.234, "General Number")
Label2.Text = Format(8972.2, "Fixed")
Label3.Text = Format(6648972.265, "Standard")
Label4.Text = Format(6648972.265, "Currency")
Label5.Text = Format(0.56324, "Percent")
End Sub

The output is shown in Figure 16.1

Format Function

General Number	8972.234
Fixed Number	8972.20
Standard Number	6,648,972.27
Currency	RM6,648,972.27
Percentage	56.32%

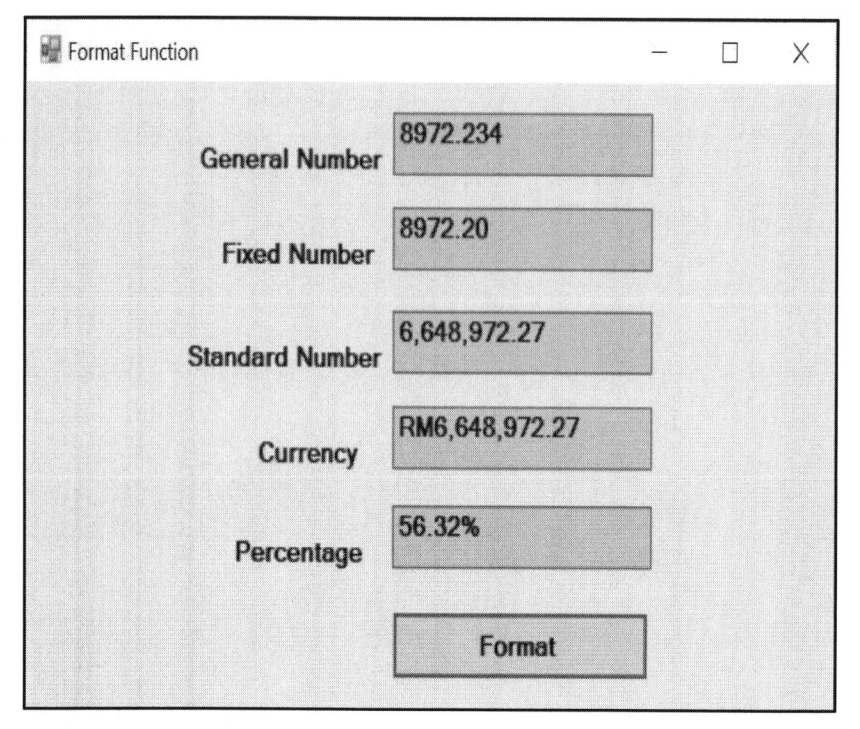

[Format]

Figure 16.1

16.1(b) User-Defined Format

The syntax of the user-defined Format function is

Format(n, "user's format")

Although it is known as user-defined format, we still need to follow certain formatting styles. Examples of user-defined formatting styles are listed in Table 16.2

Table 16.2

Format	Description	Output
Format(781234.576,"0")	Rounds to whole number without separators between thousands	781235
Format(781234.576,"0.0")	Rounds to 1 decimal place without separators between thousands	781234.6
Format(781234.576,"0.00")	Rounds to 2 decimal places without separators between thousands	781234.58
Format(781234.576,"#,##0.00")	Rounds to 2 decimal places with separators between thousands	781,234.58
Format(781234.576,"$#,##0.00")	Displays dollar sign and Rounds to 2 decimal places with separators between thousands	$781,234.58
Format(0.576,"0%")	Converts to percentage without decimal place	58%
Format(0.5768,"0%")	Converts to percentage form with two decimal places	57.68%

Example 16.2

```
Private Sub BtnFormat_Click(sender As Object, e As EventArgs)
Handles BtnFormat.Click
Label1.Text = Format(8972.234, "0.0")
Label2.Text = Format(8972.2345, "0.00")
Label3.Text = Format(6648972.265, "#,##0.00")
Label4.Text = Format(6648972.265, "$#,##0.00")
Label5.Text = Format(0.56324, "0%")
End Sub
```

The Output is shown in Figure 16.2

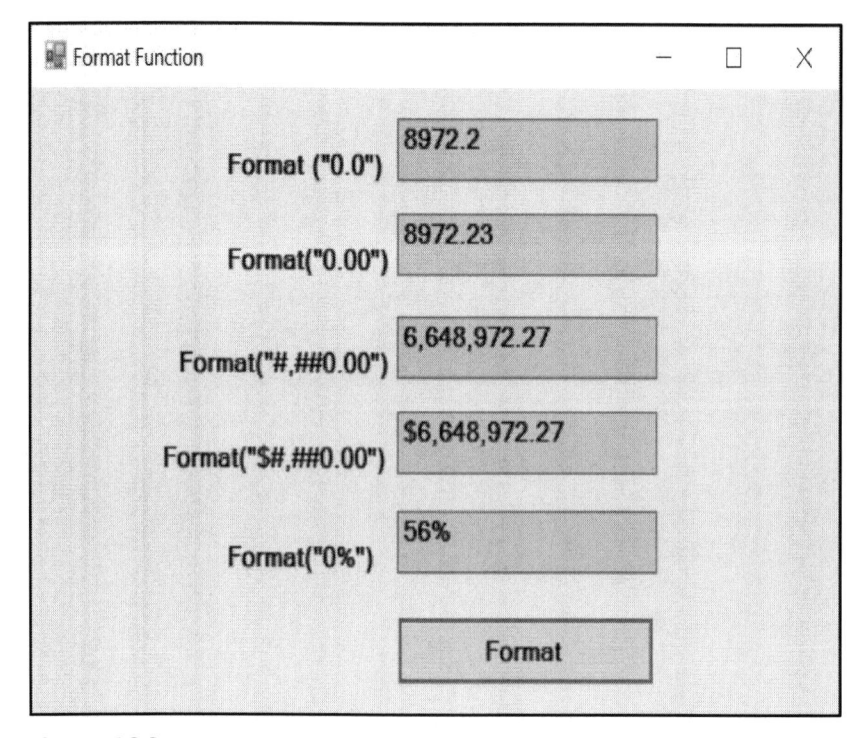

Figure 16.2

16.2 Formatting Date and Time

There are two types of Format functions for Date and time one of them is the built-in or predefined format while another one can be defined by the user.

16.2(a) Formatting Date and time using predefined formats

In Visual Basic 2019, we can format date and time using predefined formats or user-defined formats. The predefined formats of date and time are shown in Table 16.3

Table 16.3

Format	Description
Format(Now, "General Date")	Displays current date and time
Format(Now, "Long Date")	Displays current date in long format
Format (Now, "Short date")	Displays current date in short format
Format (Now, "Long Time")	Displays current time in long format.
Format (Now, "Short Time")	Displays current time in short format.

Example 16.3

Private Sub BtnDisplay_Click(sender As Object, e As EventArgs)
Handles BtnDisplay.Click
Label1.Text = Format(Now, "General Date")
Label2.Text = Format(Now, "Long Date")
Label3.Text = Format(Now, "short Date")
Label4.Text = Format(Now, "Long Time")
Label5.Text = Format(Now, "Short Time")
End Sub

The Output is shown in Figure 16.3

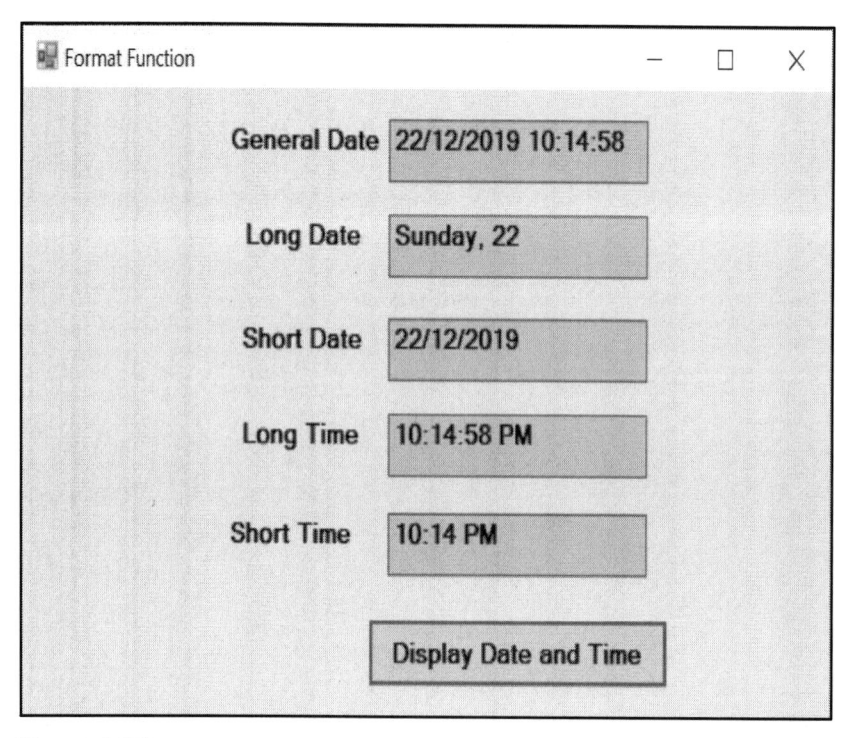

Figure 16.3

You can display dates and time in real-time using a timer and set its property Enabled to true and interval 100. The code is as follows:

```
Private Sub Timer1_Tick(sender As Object, e As EventArgs)
Handles Timer1.Tick
Label1.Text = Format(Now, "General Date")
Label2.Text = Format(Now, "Long Date")
Label3.Text = Format(Now, "short Date")
Label4.Text = Format(Now, "Long Time")
Label5.Text = Format(Now, "Short Time")
End Sub
```

16.2(b) Formatting Date and time using user-defined formats

Besides using the predefined formats, you can also use the user-defined formatting functions. The syntax of a user-defined format for date and time is

Format(expression,style)

Table 16.4

Format	Description
Format (Now, "m")	Displays current month and date
Format (Now, "mm")	Displays current month in double digits.
Format (Now, "mmm")	Displays abbreviated name of the current month
Format (Now, "mmmm")	Displays full name of the current month.
Format (Now, "dd/mm/yyyy")	Displays current date in the day/month/year format.
Format (Now, "mmm,d,yyyy")	Displays current date in the Month, Day, Year Format
Format (Now, "h:mm:ss tt")	Displays current time in hour:minute:second format and show am/pm
Format (Now, "MM/dd/yyyy h:mm:ss)	Displays current date and time in hour:minute:second format

Example 16.4

Private Sub Timer1_Tick(sender As Object, e As EventArgs) Handles Timer1.Tick

Label1.Text = Format(Now, "m")

Label2.Text = Format(Now, "mm")

Label3.Text = Format(Now, "mmm")

Label4.Text = Format(Now, "mmmm")

Label5.Text = Format(Now, "dd/mm/yyyy")

```
Label6.Text = Format(Now, "mmm,d,yyyy")
Label7.Text = Format(Now, "h:mm:ss tt")
Label8.Text = Format(Now, "MM/dd/yyyy h:mm:ss tt")
End Sub
```

The output is shown in Figure 16.4

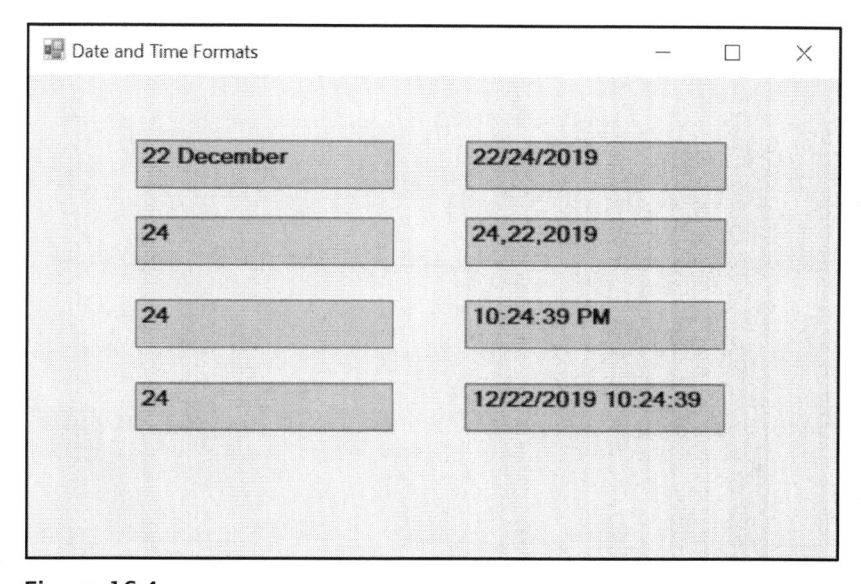

Figure 16.4

Summary

- In section 16.1(a), you have learned how to use the built-in format function
- In section 16.1(b), you have learned how to use the user-defined format function
- In section 16.2(a), you have learned how to format date and time using predefined formats

- In section 16.2(b), you have learned how to format date and time using user-defined formats

Chapter 17 Using Checkbox and Radio Button

We have learned how to use some of the controls in Visual Basic 2019 in chapter 4 and chapter 5. In this chapter, we shall learn how to use two very useful controls in, checkbox and radio button.

17.1 Check Box

A Check box allows the user to select one or more items by checking the checkbox or check boxes concerned. For example, in the Font dialog box of any Microsoft Text editor like FrontPage, there are many checkboxes under the Effects section such as that shown in the diagram below. The user can choose underline, subscript, small caps, superscript, blink etc. In VB 2019, you may create a shopping cart where the user can click on checkboxes that correspond to the items they intend to buy, and the total payment can be computed at the same time.

Example 17.1: Shopping Mall

In this example, we add a few labels, two buttons and six checkboxes. We declare the price of each item using the Const keyword. If a checkbox is being ticked, its state is True else its state is False. To calculate the total amount of purchase, we use the mathematical operator +=. For example, sum+=Iphone is sum=sum+Iphone. Finally, we use the ToString method to display the amount in currency. The code is shown overleaf

The Code

```vb
Private Sub BtnCal_Click(sender As Object, e As EventArgs)
Handles BtnCal.Click
    Const Iphone As Integer = 5000
    Const Samsung As Integer = 4500
    Const Huawei As Integer = 3500
    Const Xiaomi As Integer = 2500
    Const Vivo As Integer = 3000
    Const Oppo As Integer = 3399
    Dim sum As Integer
    If CheckBox1.Checked = True Then
        sum += Iphone
    End If
    If CheckBox2.Checked = True Then
        sum += Samsung

    End If
    If CheckBox3.Checked = True Then
        sum += Huawei
    End If
    If CheckBox4.Checked = True Then
        sum += Xiaomi

    End If
    If CheckBox5.Checked = True Then
        sum += Vivo

    End If
    If CheckBox6.Checked = True Then
        sum += Oppo
    End If
    LblTotal.Text = sum.ToString("c")
```

End Sub
Private Sub BtnReset_Click(sender As Object, e As EventArgs)
Handles BtnReset.Click
CheckBox1.Checked = False
CheckBox2.Checked = False
CheckBox3.Checked = False
CheckBox4.Checked = False
CheckBox5.Checked = False
CheckBox6.Checked = False
End Sub

The Runtime Interface is shown in Figure 17.1

Figure 17.1: Shopping Mall

Example 17.2

```
Private Sub Button1_Click(sender As System.Object,
e As EventArgs)
Handles Button1.Click
Const large As Integer = 10.0
Const medium As Integer = 8
Const small As Integer = 5
Dim sum As Integer
If CheckBox1.Checked = True Then
sum += large
End If

If CheckBox2.Checked = True Then
sum += medium
End If
If CheckBox3.Checked = True Then
sum += small
End If
Label5.Text = sum.ToString("c")
End Sub
```

Example 17.3

In this example, the text on the label can be formatting using the three check boxes that represent bold, italic and underline.

The Code

```
Private Sub ChkBold_CheckedChanged(sender As Object,
e As EventArgs)Handles ChkBold.CheckedChanged
If ChkBold.Checked Then
LblDisplay.Font = New Font(LblDisplay.Font, LblDisplay.Font.Style
Or FontStyle.Bold)
Else
LblDisplay.Font = New Font(LblDisplay.Font, LblDisplay.Font.Style
And Not FontStyle.Bold)
End If
End Sub


Private Sub ChkItalic_CheckedChanged(sender As Object, e
As EventArgs) Handles ChkItalic.CheckedChanged


If ChkItalic.Checked Then
LblDisplay.Font = New Font(LblDisplay.Font, LblDisplay.Font.Style
Or FontStyle.Italic)
Else
LblDisplay.Font = New Font(LblDisplay.Font, LblDisplay.Font.Style
And Not FontStyle.Italic)
End If
End Sub


Private Sub ChkUnder_CheckedChanged(sender As Object, e
As EventArgs) Handles ChkUnder.CheckedChanged


If ChkUnder.Checked Then
LblDisplay.Font = New Font(LblDisplay.Font, LblDisplay.Font.Style
 Or FontStyle.Underline)
Else
LblDisplay.Font = New Font(LblDisplay.Font, LblDisplay.Font.Style
```

    And Not **FontStyle.Underline**)
    End If
    End Sub

* The above program uses the CheckedChanged event to respond to the user selection by checking a particular checkbox; it is similar to the click event. The statement

    LblDisplay.Font = New Font(LblDisplay.Font, LblDisplay.Font.Style
    Or **FontStyle.Italic**)

will retain the original font type but change it to italic font style.

    LblDisplay.Font = New Font(LblDisplay.Font, LblDisplay.Font.Style
    And Not **FontStyle.Italic**)

will also retain the original font type but change it to regular font style. (The other statements employ the same logic)

The Output interface is shown in Figure 17.2

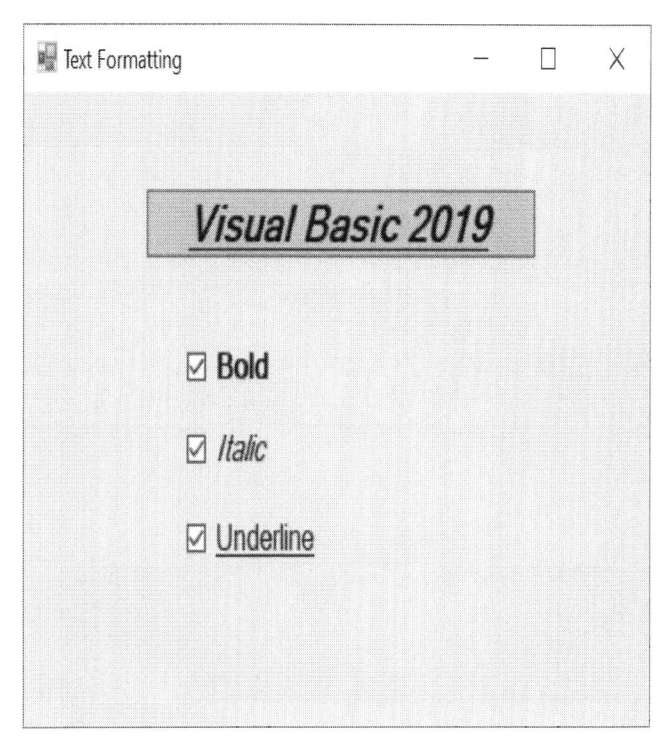

Figure 17.2

17.2 Radio Button

We have learned how to use the checkbox control in section 17.1. Radio buttons operate differently from the check boxes. While the check boxes work independently and allow the user to select one or more items, radio buttons are mutually exclusive, which means the user can only choose one item only out of several choices.

Example 17.4

In this example, the user can only choose one T-shirt color. To design the interface, add three radio buttons and name them as RadioRed, RadioGreen and RadioYellow respectively. Besides that, add a button to confirm the chosen color and a label control to display the chosen colour. Name the button as BtnConfirm and the label as LblDisplay.

We use the **If...Then...Else** decision making structure to construct the program. The state of the radio button is indicated by its checked property.

The code

```
Private Sub BtnConfirm_Click(sender As Object, e As EventArgs)
Handles BtnConfirm.Click
Dim Tcolor As String
If RadioRed.Checked Then
Tcolor = "Red Color"
LblDisplay.ForeColor = Color.Red
ElseIf RadioGreen.Checked Then
Tcolor = "Green Color"
LblDisplay.ForeColor = Color.Green
ElseIf RadioBlue.Checked Then
Tcolor = "Blue Color"
LblDisplay.ForeColor = Color.Blue

ElseIf RadioPink.Checked Then
Tcolor = "Pink Color"
LblDisplay.ForeColor = Color.Pink

ElseIf RadioOrange.Checked Then
Tcolor = "Orange Color"
LblDisplay.ForeColor = Color.Orange
Else
Tcolor = "Yellow Color"
LblDisplay.ForeColor = Color.Yellow
End If
LblDisplay.Text = Tcolor
End Sub
```

The Runtime Interface is shown in Figure 17.3

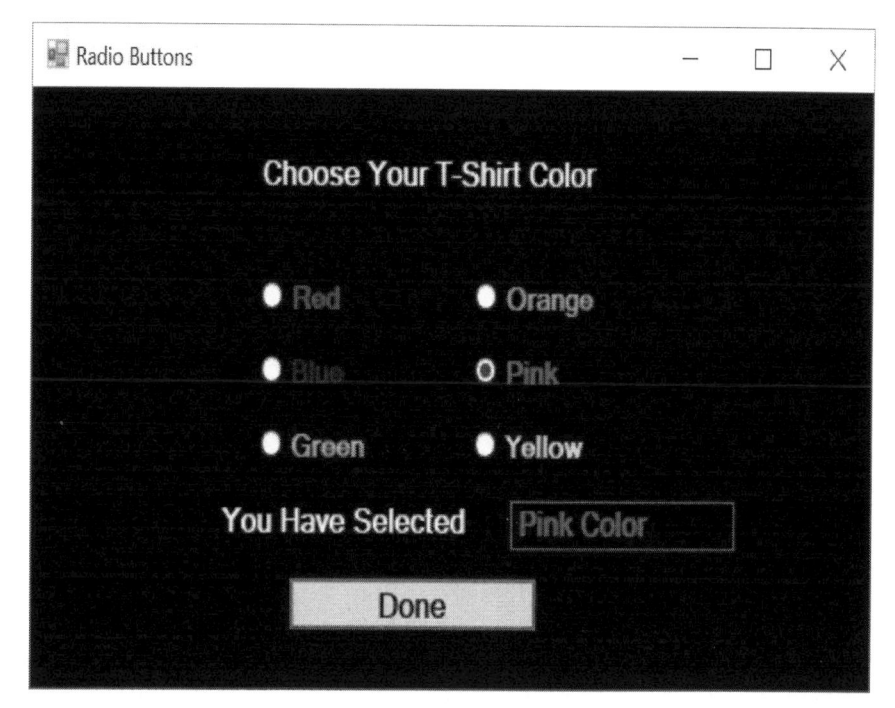

Figure 17.3

Example 17.5

Although radio buttons only allow the user to select one item at a time, he/she may make more than one selection if those items belong to different categories. For example, the user wishes to choose T-shirt size and color, he needs to select one color and one size, which mean one selection in each category. In this case, we need to group the radio buttons together according to the categories. This is easily achieved in using the Groupbox control under the container's categories.

In the Visual Basic 2019 IDE, after inserting the Groupbox from the toolbox into the form, you can proceed to insert the radio buttons into the Groupbox. Only the radio buttons inside the Groupbox are mutually exclusive, they are not mutually exclusive with the radio buttons outside the Groupbox. In this example, the user can select one color and one size of the T-shirt. To design the interface, insert two group boxes. In the first group box, add four radio buttons and name them as RadioXL, RadioL, RadioM and Radio S respectively. In the second group box, add three radio buttons and name them RadioRed, RadioBlue and RadioBeige respectively. Besides that, insert two label controls to display the chosen size and color, name them LblSize and LblColor respectively. Finally, add a button and name it as BtnConfirm. In the code, we shall declare the variable TSize to indicate the T-shirt size. We also write code to change the background color of LblColor correspond to the selected color.

The Code

```
Private Sub BtnConfirm_Click(sender As Object, e As EventArgs)
 Handles BtnConfirm.Click
Dim TSize, TColor As String
If RadioXL.Checked Then
TSize = "XL"
ElseIf RadioL.Checked Then
TSize = "L"
ElseIf RadioM.Checked Then
TSize = "M"
Else : TSize = "S"
End If


If RadioRed.Checked Then

    LblColor.BackColor = Color.DarkRed

ElseIf RadioBlue.Checked Then

    LblColor.BackColor = Color.Blue
```

ElseIf RadioGreen.Checked Then

    LblColor.BackColor = Color.Green

ElseIf RadioPink.Checked Then

    LblColor.BackColor = Color.DeepPink

ElseIf RadioOrange.Checked Then

    LblColor.BackColor = Color.DarkOrange

Else : LblColor.BackColor = Color.Yellow

LblSize.Text = TSize

End Sub

The Runtime Interface is shown in Figure 17.5

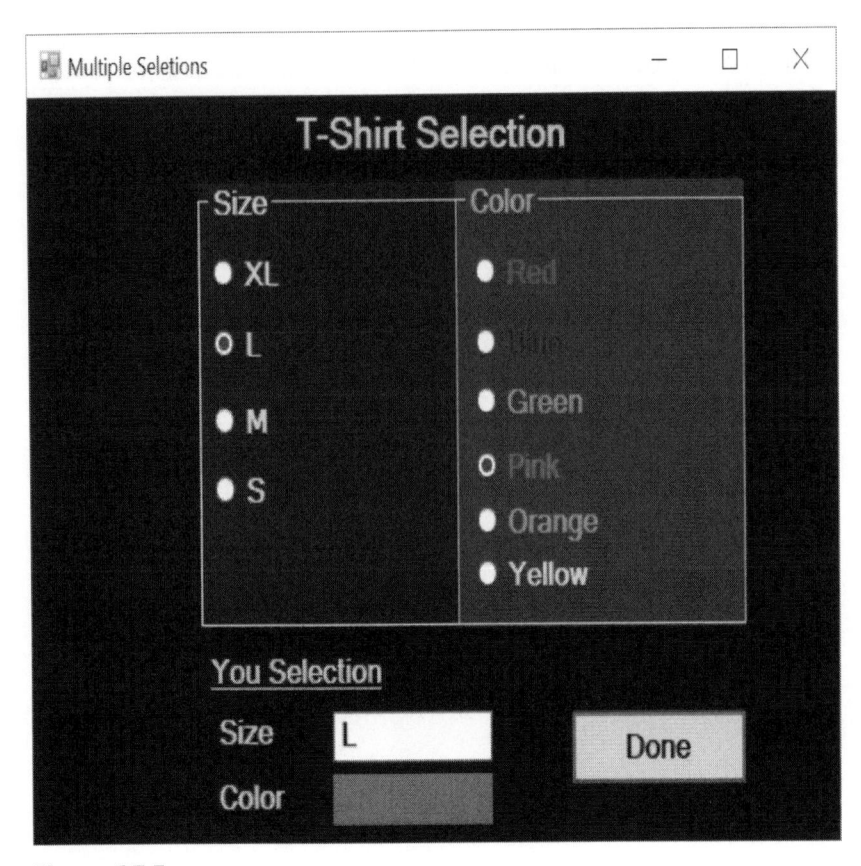

Figure 17.5

Summary

- In section 17.1, you have learned how to use the check box
- In section 17.2, you have learned how to use the radio button

Chapter 18 Errors Handling

18.1 Introduction to Object Oriented Programming

Error handling is an essential procedure in Visual Basic 2019 programming because it helps make a program error-free. Error-free code not only enables the program to run smoothly and efficiently, it can also prevent all sorts of problems from happening like program crashes or system hangs.

Errors often occur due to incorrect input from the user. For example, the user might make the mistake of attempting to enter text (string) to a box that is designed to handle only numeric values such as the weight of a person, the computer will not be able to perform arithmetic calculation for text therefore will create an error. These errors are known as synchronous errors.

Therefore, a good programmer should be more alert to the parts of program that could trigger errors and should write errors handling code to help the user in managing the errors. Writing errors handling code is a good practice for Visual Basic 2019 programmers, so do not try to finish a program fast by omitting the errors handling code. However, there should not be too many errors handling code in the program as it creates problems for the programmer to maintain and troubleshoot the program later. Visual Basic 2019 has improved a lot in its built-in errors handling capabilities compared to Visual Basic 6. For example, when the user attempts to divide a number by zero, Visual Basic 2019 will not return an error message but gives the 'infinity' as the answer (although this is mathematically incorrect, because it should be undefined)

18.2 Using On Error GoTo Syntax

Visual Basic 2019 still supports the VB6 errors handling syntax that is the On Error GoTo program_label structure. The syntax for error handling is

On Error GoTo program_label

* program_label is the section of code that is designed by the programmer to handle the error committed by the user. Once an error is detected, the program will jump to the program_label section for error handling.

Example 18.1: Division Errors

In this example, we will deal with the error of entering non-numeric data into the text boxes that are supposed to hold numeric values. The program_label here is error_handler. when the user enters a non-numeric value into the text boxes, the error message will display the text" One or both of the entries is/are non-numeric!". If no error occurs, it will display the correct answer. Try it out yourself.

The Code

```
Private Sub BtnCal_Click(sender As Object, e As EventArgs)
Handles BtnCal.Click
Lbl_ErrMsg.Visible = False
Dim firstNum, secondNum As Double
On Error GoTo error_handler
firstNum = TxtNum1.Text
secondNum = TxtNum2.Text
Lbl_Answer.Text = firstNum / secondNum
```

Exit Sub 'To prevent error handling even the inputs are valid
error_handler:
Lbl_Answer.Text = "Error"
Lbl_ErrMsg.Visible = True
Lbl_ErrMsg.Text =
"One or both of the entries is/are non-numeric! Try again!"
End Sub

The runtime interface is shown in Figure 18.1

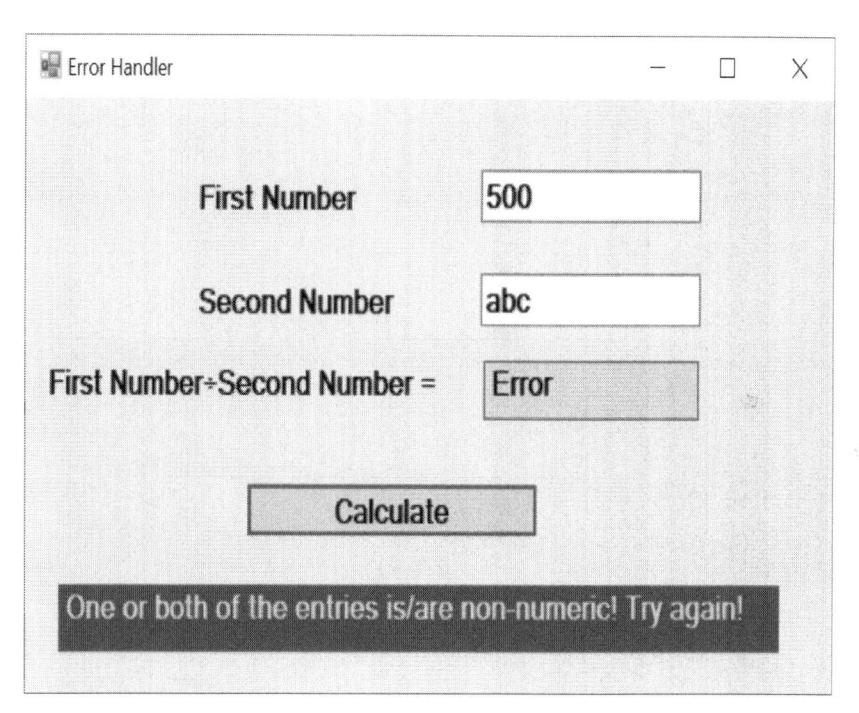

Figure 18.1
*Please note that division by zero in Visual Basic 2019 no longer gives an error message, but it displays the answer as Infinity(∞).

18.3 Errors Handling with Try...Catch ...End Try Structure

Visual Basic 2019 has adopted a new approach in handling errors, or rather exceptions handling. It is supposed to be more efficient than the old On Error Goto method, where it can handle various types of errors within the Try...Catch...End Try structure. The structure is as follows:

```
Try
statements
Catch exception_variable As Exception
statements to deal with exceptions
End Try
```

The Code

```
Private Sub BtnCal_Click(sender As Object, e As EventArgs)
Handles BtnCal.Click
Lbl_ErrMsg.Visible = False
Dim firstNum, secondNum, answer As Double
Try
firstNum = TxtNum1.Text
secondNum = TxtNum2.Text
answer = firstNum / secondNum
LblAnswer.Text = answer
Catch ex As Exception
LblAnswer.Text = "Error"
Lbl_ErrMsg.Visible = True
Lbl_ErrMsg.Text =
```

" One or both of the entries is/are non-numeric! Try again!"
End Try
End Sub

The runtime interface is shown in Figure 18.2

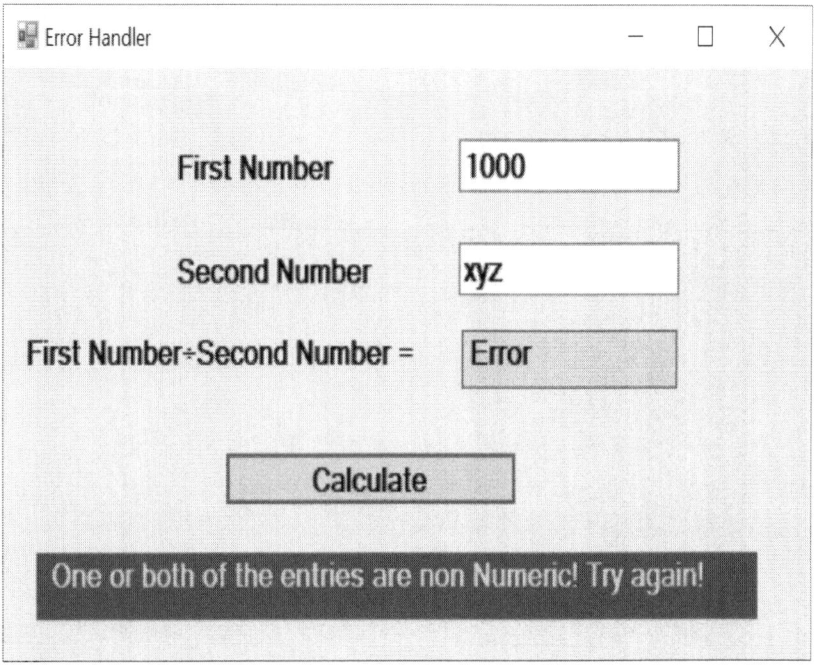

Figure 18.2

Summary

- In section 18.1, you have learned the concept of errors handling
- In section 18.2, you have learned how to handle errors using On Error Goto Syntax
- In section 18.3, you have learned how to handle errors using Try...Catch...End Try Structure

Chapter 19 Object Oriented Programming

19.1 Concepts of Object-Oriented Programming

In all the preceding chapters, you have learned how to write the program code in Visual Basic 2019 but we have not discussed the concepts of object oriented programming that forms the foundation of Visual Basic 2019. Now, let us get down to learning the basic concepts of object-oriented programming.

For a programming language to qualify as an object oriented programming language, it must have three core technologies namely encapsulation, inheritance and polymorphism. These three terms are explained below:

(a) Encapsulation

Encapsulation refers to the creation of self-contained modules that bind processing functions to the data. These user-defined data types are called classes. Each class contains data as well as a set of methods which manipulate the data. The data components of a class are called instance variables and one instance of a class is an object. For example, in a library system, a class could be a member, and John and Sharon could be two instances (two objects) of the library class.

(b) Inheritance

Classes are created according to hierarchies, and inheritance allows the structure and methods in one class to be passed down the hierarchy. That means less programming is required when adding functions to complex systems. If a step is added at the bottom of a hierarchy, then only the processing and data associated with that unique step needs to be added. Everything else about that step is inherited.

(c) Polymorphism

Object-oriented programming allows procedures about objects to be created whose exact type is not known until runtime. For example, a screen cursor may change its shape from an arrow to a line depending on the program mode. The routine to move the cursor on screen in response to mouse movement would be written for "cursor," and polymorphism allows that cursor to take on whatever shape is required at runtime. It also allows new shapes to be easily integrated.

19.2 Creating Class

Visual Basic 2019 allows users to write programs that break down into modules. These modules represent the real-world objects and are known as classes or types. An object can be created out of a class and it is known as an instance of the class. A class can also comprise subclass. For example, an apple tree is a subclass of the plant class and the apple in your backyard is an instance of the apple tree class. Another example is a student class is a subclass of the human class while your son John is an instance of the student class. A class consists of data members as well as methods. In Visual Basic 2019, the program structure to define a Human class can be written as follows:

Public Class Human
'Data Members
Private Name As String

```
    Private Birthdate As String
    Private Gender As String
    Private Age As Integer
    'Methods
    Overridable Sub ShowInfo()
    MessageBox.Show(Name)
    MessageBox.Show(Birthdate)
    MessageBox.Show(Gender)
    MessageBox.Show(Age)
    End Sub
    End Class
```

Another Example:

```
    Public Class Car
    'Data Members
    Private Brand As String
    Private Model As String
    Private Year Made As String
    Private Capacity As Integer
    'Methods
    Overridable Sub ShowInfo()
    MessageBox.Show(Brand)
    MessageBox.Show(Model)
    MessageBox.Show(Year Made)
    MessageBox.Show(Capacity)
    End Sub
    End Class
```

Let us look at one example on how to create a class. The following example shows you how to create a class that can calculate your BMI (Body Mass Index).

To create class, start Visual Basic 2019 as usual and choose Windows Applications. In the Visual Basic 2019 IDE, click on Project on the menu bar and select Add Class, the Add New Item dialog appears, as shown in Figure 19.1

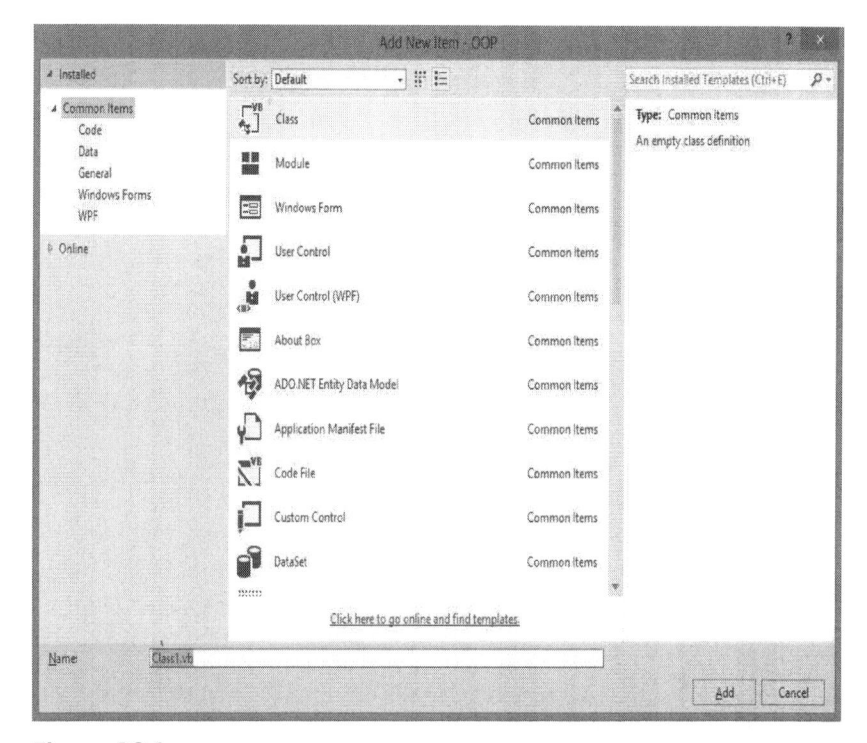

Figure 19.1

The default class Class1.vb will appear as a new tab with a code window. Rename the class as MyClass.vb. Rename the form as MyFirstClass.vb.

Now, in the MyClass.vb window, create a new class MyClass1 and enter the following code

```
Public Class MyClass1
Public Function BMI(ByVal height As Single, ByVal weight As Single)
BMI = Format((weight) / (height ^ 2), "0.00")
End Function
End Class
```

Now you have created a class (an object) called MyClass1 with a method known as BMI.

In order to use the BMI class, insert a button into the form and click on the button to enter the following code:

```
Private Sub BtnBMI_Click(sender As Object, e As EventArgs)
Handles BtnBMI.Click
Dim MyObject As Object
Dim h, w As Single
MyObject = New MyClass1()
h = InputBox("What is your height in meter")
w = InputBox("What is your weight in kg")
MessageBox.Show(MyObject.BMI(h, w))
End Sub
```

When you run this program and click the button, the user will be presented with two input boxes to enter his or her height and weight subsequently and the value of BMI will be shown in a pop-up message box, as shown in the figures below:

Figure 19.2

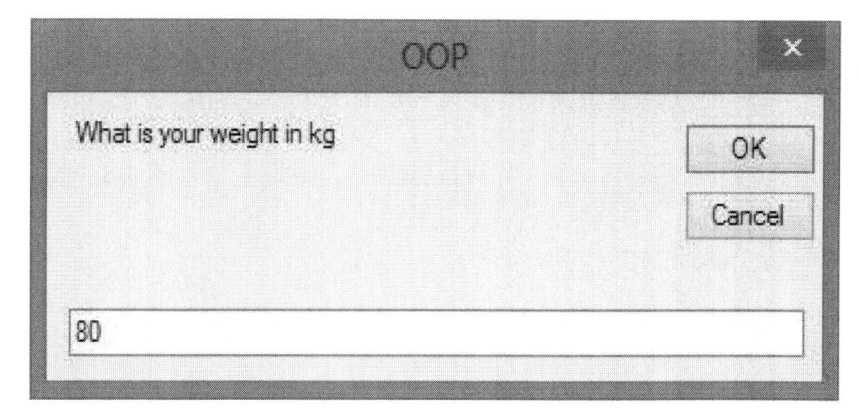

Figure 19.3

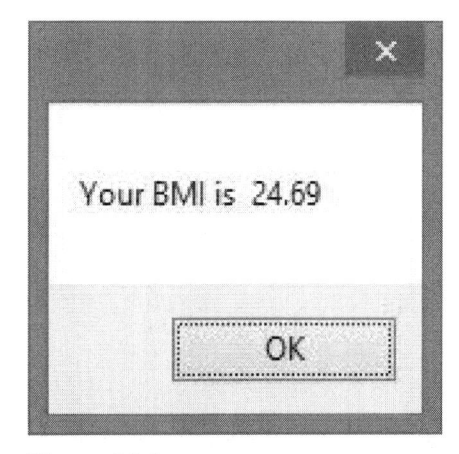

Figure 19.4

Summary

- In section 19.1, you have learned the concepts of object oriented programming
- In section 19.2, you have learned how to create a class

Chapter 20 Creating Graphics

20.1 Introduction to Graphics Creation

Creating graphics is easy in earlier versions of Visual Basic because they have built-in drawing tools. For example, In Visual Basic 6, the drawing tools are included in the toolbox where the programmer just need to drag the shape controls into the form to create a rectangle, square, ellipse, circle and more. However, its simplicity has the shortcomings; you do not have many choices in creating customized graphics.

Since Visual Basic evolved into an object oriented programming language under the VB.net framework, shape controls are no longer available. Now the programmer needs to write code to create various shapes and drawings. Even though the learning curve is steeper, the programmer can write powerful code to create all kinds of graphics. You can even design your own controls

Visual Basic 2019 offers various graphics capabilities that enable programmers to write code that can create all kinds of shapes and even fonts. In this lesson, you will learn how to write code to draw lines and shapes on the Visual Basic 2019 IDE.

20.2 Creating the Graphics Object

Before you can draw anything on a form, you need to create the Graphics object in Visual Basic 2019. A graphics object is created using the CreateGraphics() method. You can create a graphics object that draw to the form itself or a control.

To draw graphics on the default form, you can use the following statement:

Dim myGraphics As Graphics = me.CreateGraphics

To draw a picture box, you can use the following statement:

Dim myGraphics As Graphics = PictureBox1.CreateGraphics

You can also use the text box as a drawing surface, the statement is:

Dim myGraphics As Graphics = TextBox1.CreateGraphics

The Graphics object that is created does not draw anything on the screen until you call the methods of the Graphics object. In addition, you need to create the Pen object as the drawing tool. We shall examine the code that can create a pen in the following section.

20.3 Creating the Pen Object

A Pen can be created using the following code:

myPen = New Pen(Brushes.Color, LineWidth)

myPen is a Pen variable. You can use any variable name instead of myPen. The first argument of the pen object defines the colour of the drawing line and the second argument defines the width of the drawing line. For example, the following code created a pen that can draw a dark magenta line and the width of the line is 10 pixels:

myPen = New Pen(Brushes.DarkMagenta, 10)

You can also create a Pen using the following statement:

```
Dim myPen As Pen

myPen = New Pen(Drawing.Color.Blue, 5)
```

Where the first argument defines the color (here is blue, you can change that to red or whatever colour you want) and the second argument is the width of the drawing line.

Having created the Graphics and the Pen objects, you are now ready to draw graphics on the screen.

20.4 Drawing a Line

In this section, we will show you how to draw a straight line on the Form.

First, launch Visual basic 2019. In the startup page, drag a button into the form. Double click on the button and key in the following code.

```
Private Sub BtnDraw_Click(sender As Object, e As EventArgs)
Handles BtnDraw.Click
Dim myGraphics As Graphics = Me.CreateGraphics
Dim myPen As Pen
myPen = New Pen(Brushes.DarkMagenta, 20)
myGraphics.DrawLine(myPen, 60, 180, 220, 50)
End Sub
```

The second line of the code creates the Graphics object and the third and fourth line create the Pen object. The fifth draw a line on the Form using the DrawLine method. The first argument use the Pen object created by you, the second argument and the third arguments define the coordinate the starting point of the line, the fourth and the last arguments define the ending coordinate of the line. The syntax of the Drawline argument is

object.DrawLine(Pen, x1, y1, x2, y2)

For the above example, the starting coordinate is (60,80) and the ending coordinate is (220,50). Figure 20.1 shows the line created by the program.

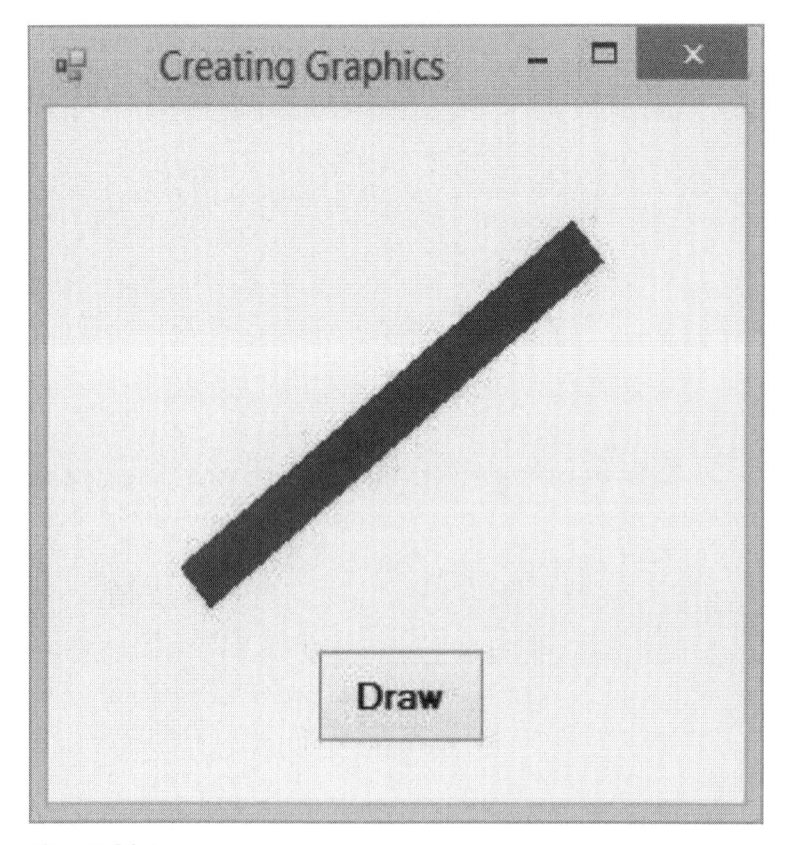

Figure 20.1

20.5 Drawing Lines that Connect Multiple Points

In section 20.4, we have learned to draw a straight line that connects two points. Now we shall learn how to draw lines that connect multiple points. The method is Drawlines and the syntax is

Graphics.DrawLines(Pen, Point())

Notice that the method to draw a straight line is DrawLine whilst the method to draw multiple lines is Drawlines, by adding an extra s. The points can be defined using the Point() array with the following syntax:

Point() = {point1, point2, point3, point4,.............}

We need to declare the array using the Dim keyword, as follows:

Dim MyPoints As Point() = {point1, point2, point3, point4,.....}

In addition, each point need to declare using the Dim keyword, as follows:

Dim point1 As New Point (x1,y1)
Dim point2 As New Point (x2,y2)
Dim point3 As New Point (x3,y3)

Let us examine the following example.

Example 20.1

Private Sub BtnDrawLine_Click(sender As Object, e As EventArgs)
Handles BtnDrawLine.Click
Dim point1 As New Point(30, 30)

```
        Dim point2 As New Point(70, 15)
        Dim point3 As New Point(100, 5)
        Dim point4 As New Point(200, 70)
        Dim point5 As New Point(350, 90)
        Dim point6 As New Point(300, 150)
        Dim point7 As New Point(20, 200)
        Dim myPoints As Point() = {point1, point2, point3,
         point4, point5, point6, point7}
        Dim myGraphics As Graphics = Me.CreateGraphics
        Dim myPen As Pen
            myPen = New Pen(Brushes.OrangeRed, 2)
            myGraphics.DrawLines(myPen, myPoints)
        End Sub
```

The output interface is as shown in Figure 20.2

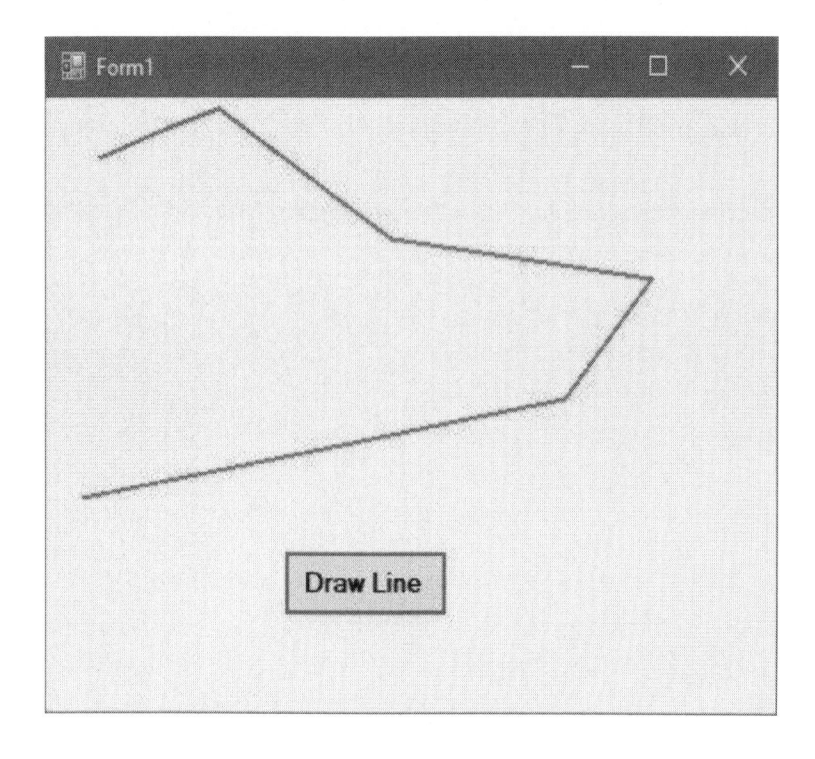

Figure 20.2

20.6 Drawing a curve that Connect Multiple Points

We have learned how to draw straight lines that connect multiple points. Now, we shall learn how to draw a curve that connects multiple points. To draw a curve, we use the DrawCurve() method and the syntax is

Graphics.DrawCurve(Pen, Point())

The points can be defined using the Point() array with the following syntax:

Point() = {point1, point2, point3, point4,............}

We need to declare the array using the Dim keyword, as follows:

Dim MyPoints As Point() = {point1, point2, point3, point4,.....}

In addition, each point needs to declare using the Dim keyword, as follows:

Dim point1 As New Point (x1,y1)
Dim point2 As New Point (x2,y2)
Dim point1 As New Point (x3,y3)

Example 20.2

Private Sub BtnDrawCurve_Click(sender As Object, e As EventArgs)

```vb
Handles BtnDrawCurve.Click
Dim point1 As New Point(30, 30)
Dim point2 As New Point(70, 15)
Dim point3 As New Point(100, 5)
Dim point4 As New Point(200, 70)
Dim point5 As New Point(350, 90)
Dim point6 As New Point(300, 150)
Dim point7 As New Point(20, 200)
Dim myPoints As Point() = {point1, point2, point3, point4, point5, point6, point7}
Dim myGraphics As Graphics = Me.CreateGraphics
Dim myPen As Pen
    myPen = New Pen(Brushes.DarkMagenta, 2)
    myGraphics.DrawCurve(myPen, myPoints)
End Sub
```

The output interface is as shown in Figure 20.3

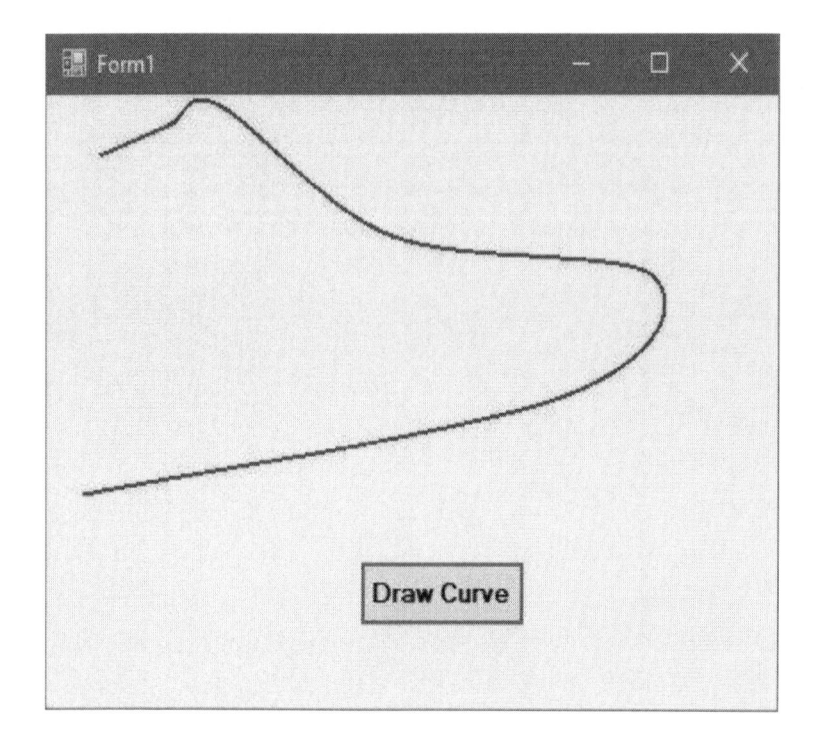

Figure 20.3
20.7 Drawing a Quadratic Curve

In this section, we shall learn how to draw a quadratic curve. However, we need to adjust the coordinate system of the drawing surface. The default origin of the drawing surface of the VB2019 object such as the form or the PictureBox is at the upper left corner. We can move its origin to another point using the **TranslateTransform** method of the Graphics class, the syntax is as follows:

MyGraphics.TranslateTransform(dx:=x1, dy:=y1)

where (x1,y1) is the new origin.

Example 20.3
In this example, we want to draw a quadratic graph for the following quadratic function:

$y=x^2-3x+1$

First, we insert a PictureBox as a drawing canvas. Set its size to 500, 300 which means its width=500 pixels and height=300 pixels. We wish to move the origin to the middle of x-axis and close to x-axis, so we set its origin using the following syntax:

myGraphics.TranslateTransform(dx:=250, dy:=295)

Next, we need to declare a point array so that we can use the For...Next loop to generate points for the quadratic equation. After generating the points, we can use the DrawCurve method to draw the curve.

The equation x = i - 250 is to make sure the point start from -250 and end at 250. The equation y =300 - (x ^ 2 - 3 * x + 1) is to ensure the point start from the bottom instead of the top of the drawing canvas. We divide it by 200 to reduce the values of the y-coordinates so that it will not go out of bounds.

The Code

```
Private p(500) As Point
Private Sub BtnDrawCurve_Click(sender As Object, e As EventArgs) Handles BtnDrawCurve.Click
    Dim x, y, i As Double
    For i = 0 To 500
        x = i - 250
        y = (300 - (x ^ 2 - 3 * x + 1)) / 200
        p(i) = New Point(x, y)
    Next
    Dim myGraphics As Graphics = MyCanvas.CreateGraphics
    Dim myPen As Pen
    myGraphics.TranslateTransform(dx:=250, dy:=295)
    myPen = New Pen(Brushes.DarkMagenta, 2)
    myGraphics.DrawCurve(myPen, p)
    myGraphics.Dispose()
End Sub
```

The output is as shown in Figure 20.4.

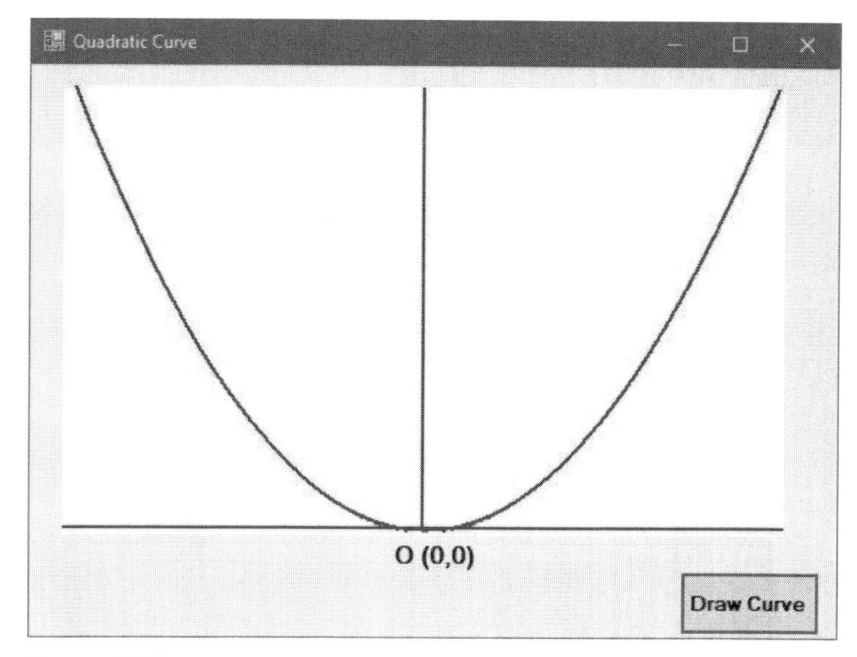

Figure 20.4

20.8 Drawing a Sine Curve

The Sin function returns the sine value of an angle. We need to convert the angle to radian as Visual Basic 2019 cannot deal with an angle in degrees. The conversion is based on the following equation:

π radian= 180°

so 1°=π/180 radian

The issue is how to get the exact value of π? We can use π=3.14159 but it will not be accurate. To get the exact value of π, we use the arc sine function, i.e. is Asin. Using the equation sin(π/2)=1, so Asin(1)=π/2, therefore, π=2Asin(1). Therefore, The syntax of the Sin function in Visual Basic 2019 is

Math.Sin(Angle in radian)

Example 20.4

In this example, we insert a picture box and fix its size as 600, 300 which means its width is 600 and its height is 300. Based as the same principle as in Example 20.3, we shift the origin to (300, 180) using the TranslateTransform method. The sine function in VB2019 is

y = -(Math.Sin((pi * x) / 180)) * 80

We use the negative to accommodate to the new coordinate system. We multiply it by 80 so that the value is big enough for the coordinate y to be visible on the drawing canvas.

The Code

```
Private p(600) As Point
Private Sub BtnDrawCurve_Click(sender As Object, e As EventArgs) Handles BtnDrawCurve.Click
    Dim x, y, i As Double
    Dim pi As Single
    pi = 2 * Math.Asin(1)
    For i = 0 To 600
       x = i - 300
       y = -(Math.Sin((pi * x) / 180)) * 80
       p(i) = New Point(x, y)
    Next
    Dim myGraphics As Graphics = MyCanvas.CreateGraphics
    Dim myPen As Pen
    myGraphics.TranslateTransform(dx:=300, dy:=180)
    myPen = New Pen(Brushes.DarkMagenta, 2)
```

```
myGraphics.DrawLine(myPen, 0, 100, 0, -200)
myGraphics.DrawLine(myPen, -300, 0, 300, 0)
myGraphics.DrawCurve(myPen, p)
myGraphics.Dispose()

End Sub
```

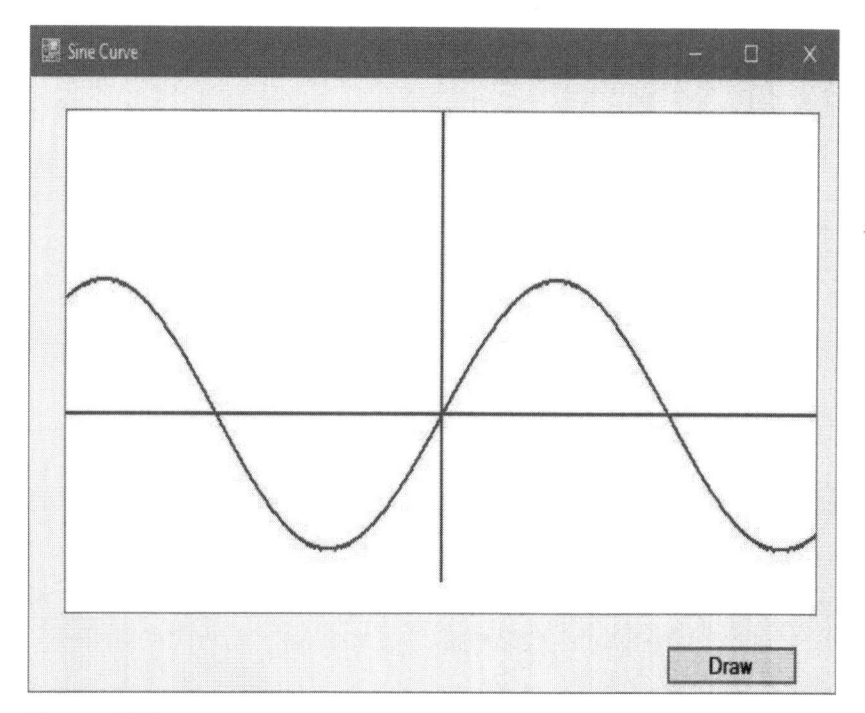

Figure 20.5

20.9 Drawing a Rectangle

To draw a rectangle on the default form in Visual Basic 2019, there are two ways:

(i)The first is to draw a rectangle directly using the **DrawRectangle** method by specifying its upper-left corner coordinates and it width and height. You also need to create a Graphics and a Pen object to handle the actual drawing. The method of the Graphics object to draw the rectangle is DrawRectangle .

The syntax is:

myGrapphics.DrawRectangle(myPen, X, Y, width, height)

Where **myGraphics** is the variable name of the **Graphics** object and myPen is the variable name of the Pen object created by you. You can use any valid and meaningful variable names. X, Y is the coordinate of the upper left corner of the rectangle while width and height are self-explanatory, i.e., the width and height of the rectangle.

The code is as follows:

```
Dim myPen As Pen
myPen = New Pen(Drawing.Color.Blue, 5)
Dim myGraphics As Graphics = Me.CreateGraphics
myGraphics.DrawRectangle(myPen, 0, 0, 100, 50)
```

(ii) The second way is to create a rectangle object first and then draw this triangle using the **DrawRectangle** method. The syntax is as shown below:

myGraphics.DrawRectangle(myPen,myRectangle)

where **myRectangle** is the rectangle object created by you, the user.

The code to create a rectangle object is as shown below:

```
Dim myRectangle As New Rectangle
myRect.X = 10
```

```
myRect.Y = 10
myRect.Width = 100
myRect.Height = 50
```

You can also create a rectangle object using a one-line code as follows:

```
Dim myRectangle As New Rectangle(X,Y,width, height)
```

The code to draw the above rectangle is

```
myGraphics.DrawRectangle(myPen, myRectangle)
```

20.10 Customizing Line Style of the Pen Object

The shape we draw so far are drawn with solid line, we can customize the line style of the Pen object so that we have dotted line, line consisting of dashes and more. For example, the syntax to draw with dotted line is shown below.

```
myPen.DashStyle=Drawing.Drawing2D.DashStyle.Dot
```

The last argument Dot specifies a particular line DashStyle value, a line that makes up of dots. Other DashStyles values are `Dash`, `DashDot`, `DashDotDot` and `Solid`. The following code draws a rectangle with blue dotted line, as shown in Figure 20.6.

Example 20.5

```
Private Sub Button1_Click(sender As Object, e As EventArgs)
Handles Button1.Click
Dim myPen As Pen
myPen = New Pen(Drawing.Color.Blue, 5)
```

```
Dim myGraphics As Graphics = Me.CreateGraphics
myPen.DashStyle = Drawing.Drawing2D.DashStyle.Dot
myGraphics.DrawRectangle(myPen, 10, 10, 100, 50)
End Sub
```

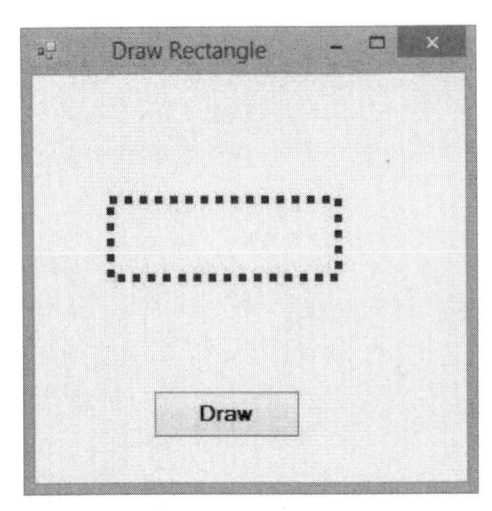

Figure 20.6

If you change the DashStyle value to DashDotDot, you will get the rectangle as shown in Figure 20.7

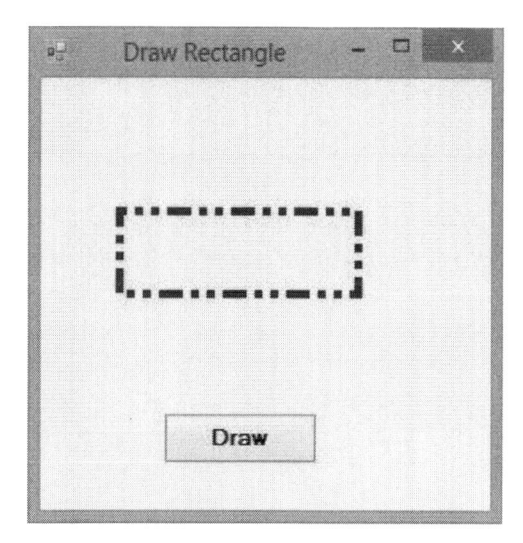

Figure 20.7

20.11 Drawing an Ellipse

We have learned how to draw rectangles with various line styles in Visual Basic 2019 in the previous section. Now we shall learn how to draw ellipse and circle. First of all, we need to understand the principle behind drawing an ellipse in Visual Basic 2019. The basic structure of most shapes is a rectangle, ellipse is no exception. Ellipse is an oval shape that is bounded by a rectangle, as shown in Figure 20.7

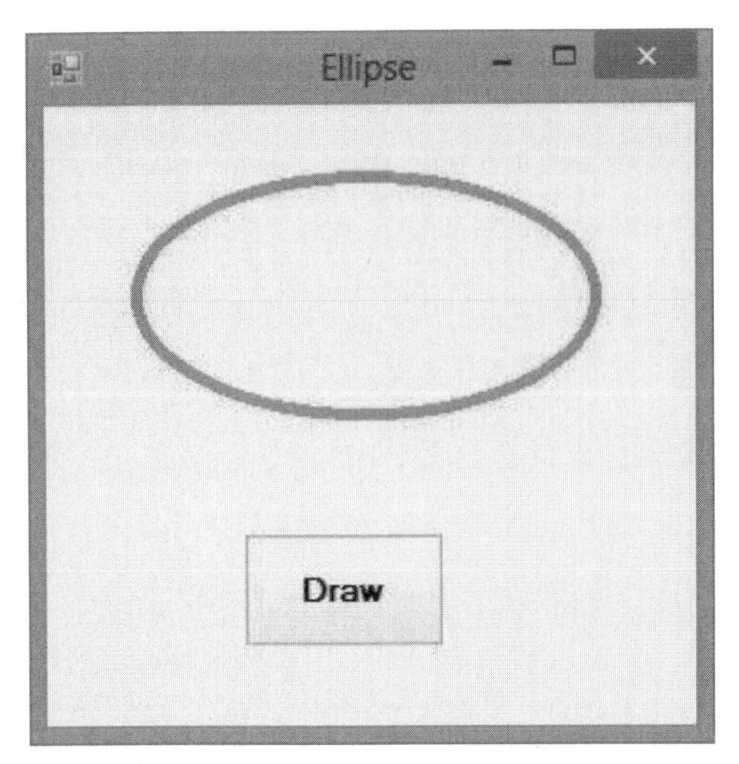

Figure 20.8

Therefore, we need to create a Rectangle object before we can draw an ellipse. This rectangle serves as a bounding rectangle for the ellipse. However, you still need to use the **DrawEllipse** method to finish the job. On the other hand, we can also draw an ellipse with the **DrawEllipse** method without first creating a rectangle. We shall show you both ways. In the first method, let's say you have created a rectangle object known as **myRectangle** and a pen object as myPen, then you can draw an ellipse using the following statement:

myGraphics.DrawEllipse(myPen, myRectangle)

* Assume you have already created the Graphics object **myGraphics**.

Example 20.6

```
Private Sub BtnDraw_Click(sender As Object, e As EventArgs)
Handles BtnDraw.Click
Dim myPen As Pen
myPen = New Pen(Drawing.Color.DarkTurquoise, 5)
myGraphics As Graphics = Me.CreateGraphics
Dim myRectangle As New Rectangle
myRectangle.X = 40
myRectangle.Y = 30
myRectangle.Width = 200
myRectangle.Height = 100
myGraphics.DrawEllipse(myPen, myRectangle)
End Sub
```

The output image is shown in Figure 20.9

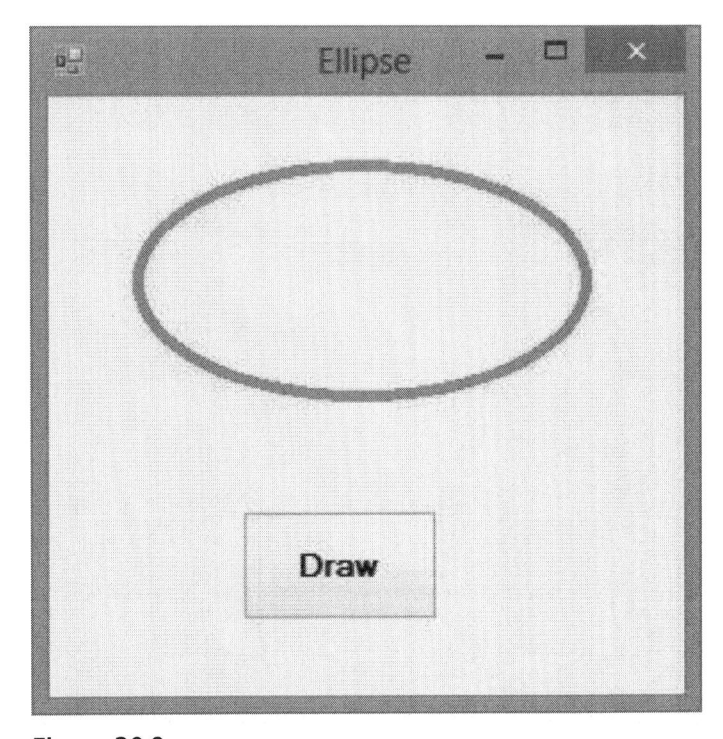

Figure 20.9

The second method is using the **DrawEllipse** method without creating a rectangle object. Of course, you still must create the Graphics and the Pen objects. The syntax is:

myGraphics.DrawEllipse(myPen, X,Y,Width, Height)

Where (X,Y) are the coordinates of the upper left corner of the bounding rectangle, width is the width of the ellipse and height is the height of the ellipse.

Example 20.7

Private Sub BtnDraw_Click(sender As Object, e As EventArgs)

Handles BtnDraw.Click
Dim myPen As Pen
myPen = New Pen(Drawing.Color.DarkTurquoise, 5)
Dim myGraphics As Graphics = Me.CreateGraphics
myGraphics.DrawEllipse(myPen, 40, 30, 200, 100)
End Sub

20.12 Drawing a Circle

After you have learned how to draw an ellipse, drawing a circle becomes quite simple. We use the same methods used in the preceding section but modify the width and height so that they are of the same values. The following examples draw the same circle.

Example 20.8

```
Dim myPen As Pen
myPen = New Pen(Drawing.Color.DarkTurquoise, 5)
Dim myGraphics As Graphics = Me.CreateGraphics
Dim myRectangle As New Rectangle
myRectangle.X = 90
myRectangle.Y = 30
myRectangle.Width = 100
myRectangle.Height = 100
myGraphics.DrawEllipse(myPen, myRectangle)
```

Example 20.9

```
Dim myPen As Pen
myPen = New Pen(Drawing.Color.DarkTurquoise, 5)
Dim myGraphics As Graphics = Me.CreateGraphics
myGraphics.DrawEllipse(myPen, 90, 30, 100, 100)
```

The output image is shown in Figure 20.10

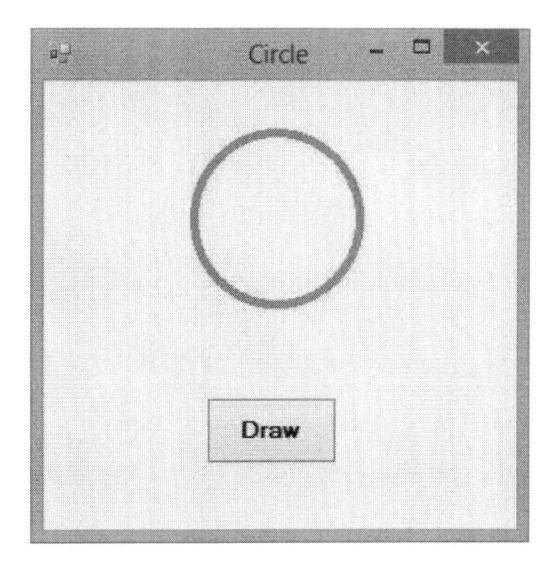

Figure 20.10

20.13 Drawing Text

To draw text on the screen, we can use the DrawString method. The format is as follows:

   myGraphics.DrawString(myText, myFont, mybrush, X , Y)

Where **myGraphics** is the Graphics object, myText is the text you wish to display on the screen, myFont is the font object created by you, myBrush is the brush style created by you and X, Y are the coordinates of upper left corner of the Text.

You can create the Font object in visual basic 2019 using the following statement:

   myFont = New System.Drawing.Font("Verdana", 20)

Where the first argument of the font is the font typeface, and the second argument is the font size. You can add a third argument as font style, bold, italic, underline. Here are the examples:

   myFont = New System.Drawing.Font("Verdana", 20, FontStyle.Bold)

   myFont = New System.Drawing.Font("Verdana", 20, FontStyle.Underline)
   myFont = New System.Drawing.Font("Verdana", 20, FontStyle.Italic)
   myFont = New System.Drawing.Font("Verdana", 20, FontStyle.Regular)

To create your Brush object, you can use the following statement:

   Dim myBrush As Brush
   myBrush = New Drawing.SolidBrush(Color.BrushColor)

Besides the seven colours, some of the common Brush colours are AliceBlue, AquaMarine Beige, DarkMagenta, DrarkOliveGreen, SkyBlue and more. You don't have to remember the names of all the colours, the intelliSense will let you browse through the colours in a drop-down menu once you type the dot after the word Color.

Now we shall proceed to draw the font using the sample code in Example 20.8, as follows:

Example 20.10

```
Private Sub BtnDraw_Click(sender As Object, e As EventArgs)
Handles BtnDraw.Click
Dim myGraphics As Graphics = Me.CreateGraphics
Dim myFont As Font
Dim myBrush As Brush
myBrush = New Drawing.SolidBrush(Color.DarkOrchid)
myFont = New System.Drawing.Font("Verdana", 20,
FontStyle.Underline)
myGraphics.DrawString("Visual Basic 2019",
myFont, myBrush, 10, 10)
End Sub
```

The runtime interface is as shown in Figure 20.11

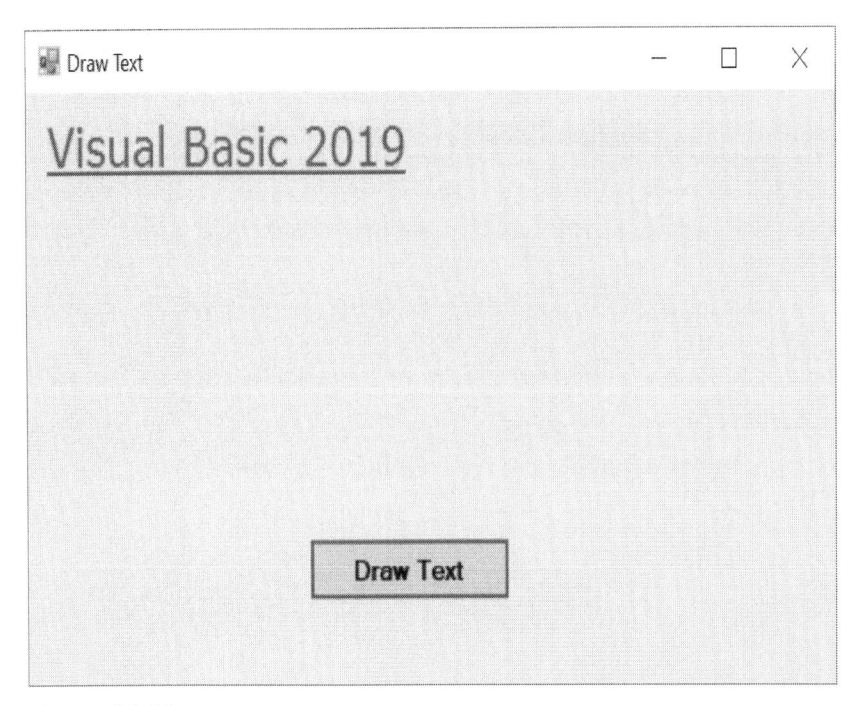

Figure 20.11

The preceding example can be modified if you don't want to create the Font and the Brush objects. You can use the font of an existing object such as the Form and the System Colors. Replace the last line in the preceding example with this line (you need to delete the lines that create the Brush and Font objects as well)

myGraphics.DrawString("Visual Basic 2019", me.Font, System.Drawing.Brushes.DarkOrchid, 10, 10)

You can also add an InputBox which let the user enter his or her message then display the message on the screen. Besides that, you can insert a picture box and draw text on it instead of drawing on the form. In this example, insert a picture box and rename it as MyPicBox. Now, when you declare the Graphics object, you use the object MyPicBox instead of Me (the Form object)

The Code is as shown in Example 20.10

Example 20.11

```
Private Sub BtnDrawText_Click(sender As Object,
e As EventArgs)
Handles BtnDrawText.Click
Dim myGraphics As Graphics = MyPicBox.CreateGraphics
Dim myFont As Font
Dim myBrush As Brush
Dim userMsg As String
userMsg = InputBox("What is your message?",
"Message Entry Form",
"Enter your message here", 100, 200)
myBrush = New Drawing.SolidBrush(Color.DarkOrchid)
myFont = New System.Drawing.Font("Verdana", 20,
FontStyle.Underline)
myGraphics.DrawString(userMsg, myFont, myBrush, 10, 10)
End Sub
```

The runtime interfaces are shown in Figure 20.12 and 20.13

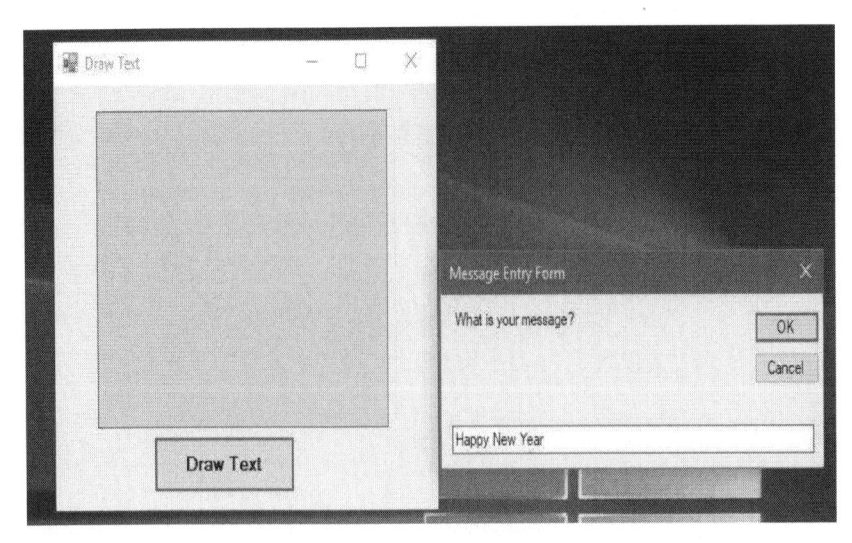

Figure 20.12

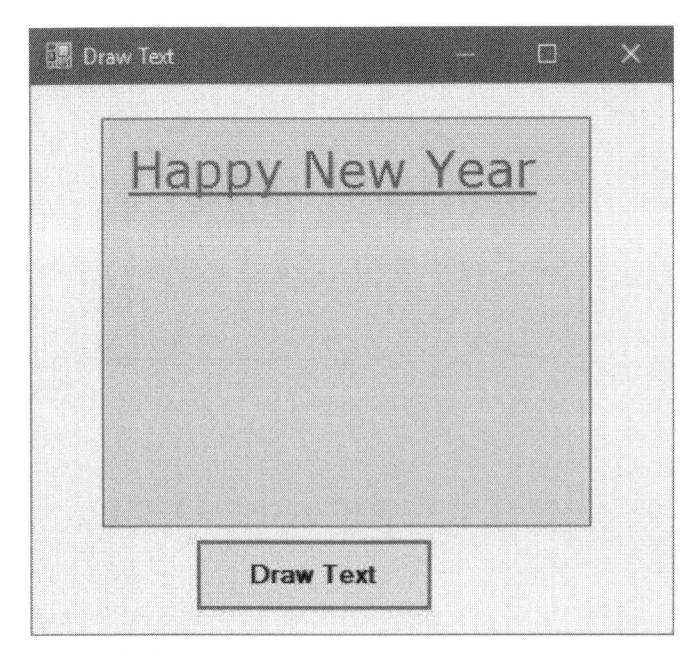

Figure 20.13

20.14 Drawing Polygons

Polygon is a closed plane figure bounded by three or more straight sides. To draw a polygon on the screen, we need to define the coordinates of all the points (also known as vertices) that joined up to form the polygon. The syntax to define the points of a polygon with vertices A1,A2,A3,A4...An is as follows;

```
Dim A1 As New Point(X1,Y1)
Dim A2 As New Point(X2,Y2)
Dim A3 As New Point(X3,Y3)
Dim A4 As New Point(X4,Y4)
.
.
Dim An As New Point(Xn,Yn)
```

After declaring the points, we need to define a point structure that group all the points together using the following syntax:

```
Dim myPoints As Point() = {A1, A2, A3,....,An}
```

Finally, create the graphics object and use the *DrawPolygon* method to draw the polygon using the following syntax:

```
Dim myGraphics As Graphics = Me.CreateGraphics
myGraphics.DrawPolygon(myPen, myPoints)
```

where myPen is the Pen object created using the following syntax:

```
myPen = New Pen(Drawing.Color.Blue, 5)
```

A triangle is a polygon with three vertices. Let us examine Example 20.10

Example 20.12 Drawing a Triangle

```
Private Sub BtnDraw_Click(sender As Object, e As EventArgs)
```

```
Handles BtnDraw.Click
Dim myPen As Pen
Dim A As New Point(10, 10)
Dim B As New Point(100, 50)
Dim C As New Point(60, 150)
Dim myPoints As Point() = {A, B, C}
myPen = New Pen(Drawing.Color.Blue, 5)
Dim myGraphics As Graphics = Me.CreateGraphics
myGraphics.DrawPolygon(myPen, myPoints)
End Sub
```

Running the program produces the image as shown in Figure 20.14

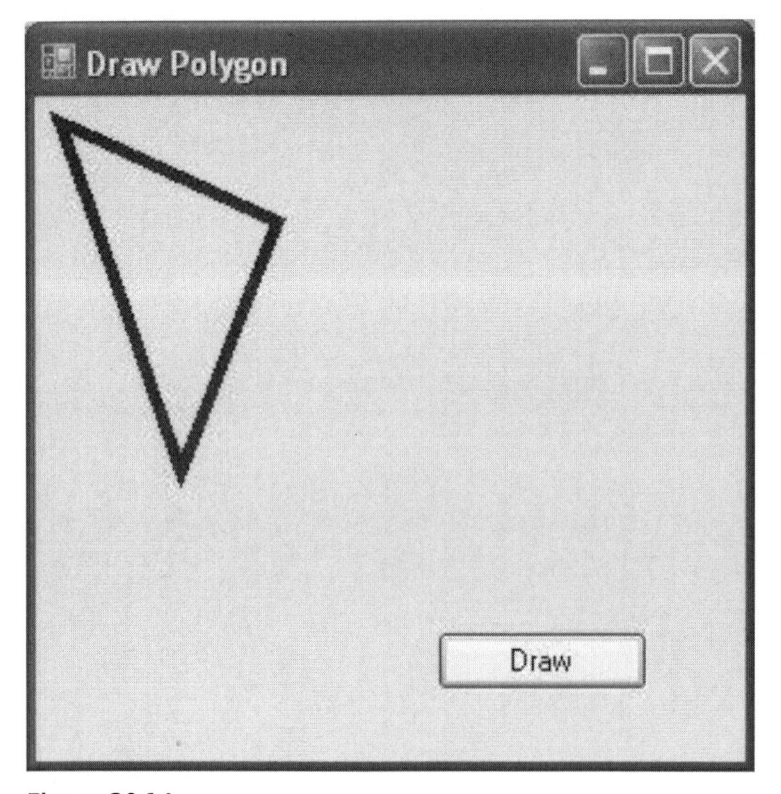

Figure 20.14

Example 20.13 Drawing a Quadrilateral

A quadrilateral is a polygon consists of four sides, so you need to define four vertices.

The Code

```
Private Sub BtnDraw_Click(sender As Object, e As EventArgs)
 Handles BtnDraw.Click
Dim myPen As Pen
Dim A As New Point(10, 10)
Dim B As New Point(100, 50)
Dim C As New Point(120, 150)
Dim D As New Point(60, 200)
Dim myPoints As Point() = {A, B, C, D}
        myPen = New Pen(Drawing.Color.Blue, 5)
Dim myGraphics As Graphics = Me.CreateGraphics
        myGraphics.DrawPolygon(myPen, myPoints)
End Sub
```

The output image is as shown in Figure 20.15

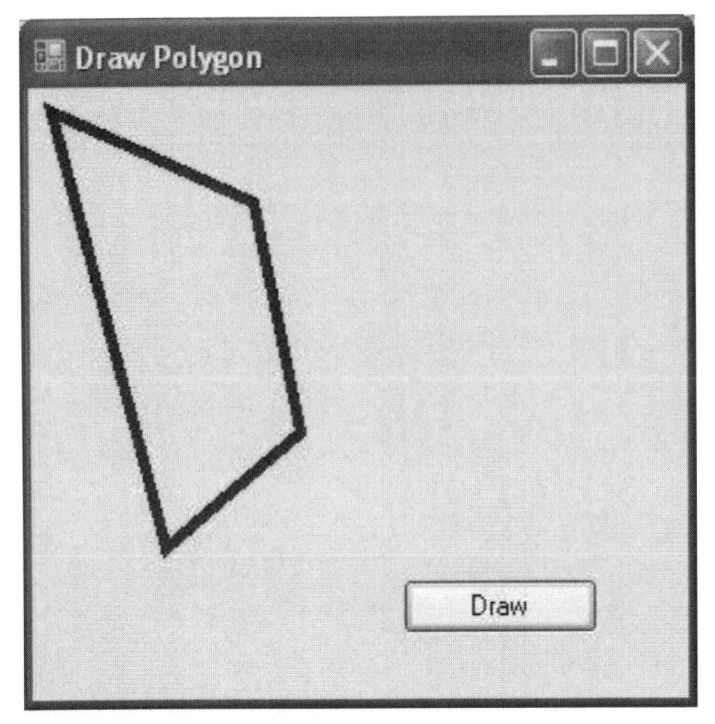

Figure 20.15

20.15 Drawing a Pie

In order to draw a pie, you can use the DrawPie method of the graphics object. As usual, you need to create the Graphics and the Pen objects. The syntax for drawing a pie is:

myGraphics.DrawPie(myPen, X, Y, width,height, StartAngle, SweepAngle)

Where X and Y are the coordinates the bounding rectangle, other arguments are self-explanatory. Both StartAngle and SweepAngle are measured in degree. SweepAngle can take possible or negative values. If the value is positive, it sweeps through clockwise direction while negative means it sweeps through anticlockwise direction.

Example 20.14 Drawing a pie that sweeps clockwise through 60 degrees.

```
Private Sub BtnDraw_Click(sender As Object, e As EventArgs)
 Handles BtnDraw.Click
 Dim myPen As Pen myPen = New Pen(Drawing.Color.Blue, 5)
 Dim myGraphics As Graphics = Me.CreateGraphics
        myGraphics.DrawPie(myPen, 50,50, 150,150,0,60)
 End Sub
```

The output image is as shown in Figure 20.16

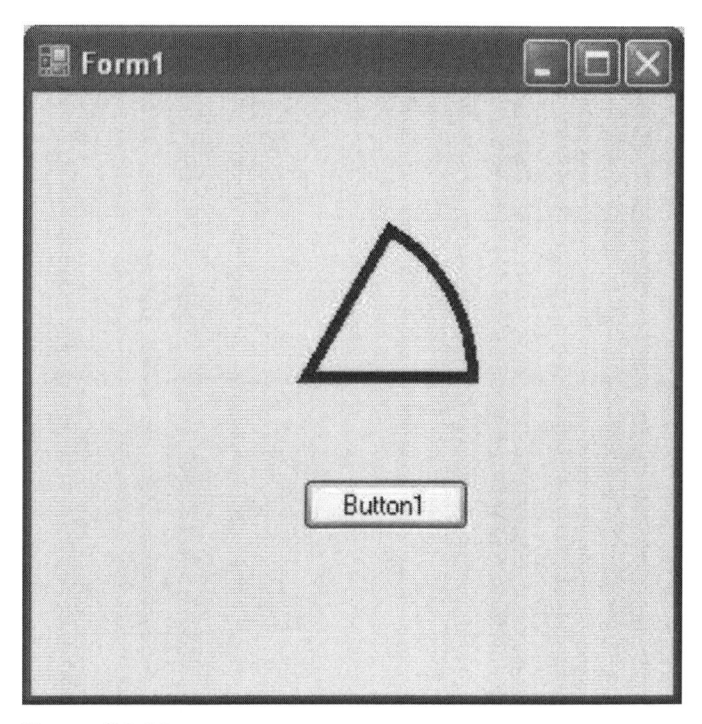

Figure 20.16

20.16 Filling Shapes with Color

In preceding lessons, we have learned how to draw a rectangle, ellipse, circle, polygon, and pie with outlines only. In this lesson, we will show you how to fill the shapes with color, or simply solid shapes in Visual Basic 2103. Three methods that are used to fill shapes are **FillRectangle, FillEllipse, FillPolygon** and **FillPie**.

In order to fill the above shapes with color, we need to create the Brush object using the following syntax:

myBrush = New SolidBrush(Color.myColor)

myColor can be any color such as red, blue, yellow and more. You do not have to worry about the names of the colors because the intellisense will display the colors and enter the period after the Color keyword.

20.16(a) Drawing and Filling a Rectangle with Color

In Visual Basic 2019, the syntax to fill a rectangle with the color defined by the brush object is:

myGraphics.FillRectangle (myBrush, 0, 0, 150, 150)

Example 20.15

```
Private Sub BtnDraw_Click(sender As Object, e As EventArgs)
Handles BtnDraw.Click
Dim myPen As Pen
Dim myBrush As Brush
Dim myGraphics As Graphics = Me.CreateGraphics
myPen = New Pen(Drawing.Color.Blue, 5)
myBrush = New SolidBrush(Color.Coral)
myGraphics.DrawRectangle(myPen, 65, 50, 150, 150)
myGraphics.FillRectangle(myBrush, 65, 50, 150, 150)
End Sub
```

The output is as shown in Figure 20.17

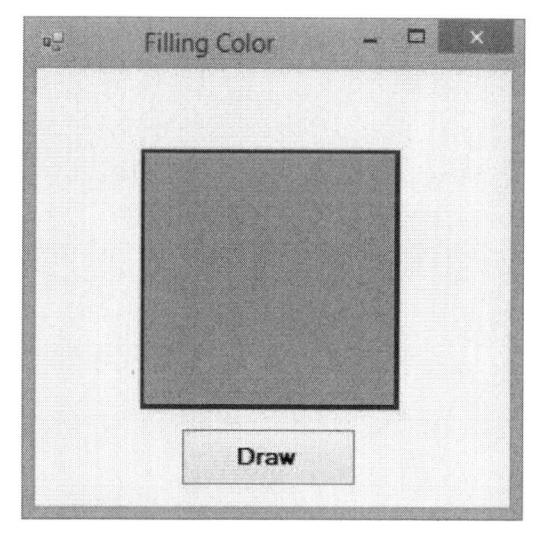

Figure 20.17

*Note that if you omit the line myGraphics.DrawRectangle(myPen, 65, 50, 150, 150), you will get a solid rectangle without outline, as shown in Figure 20.18

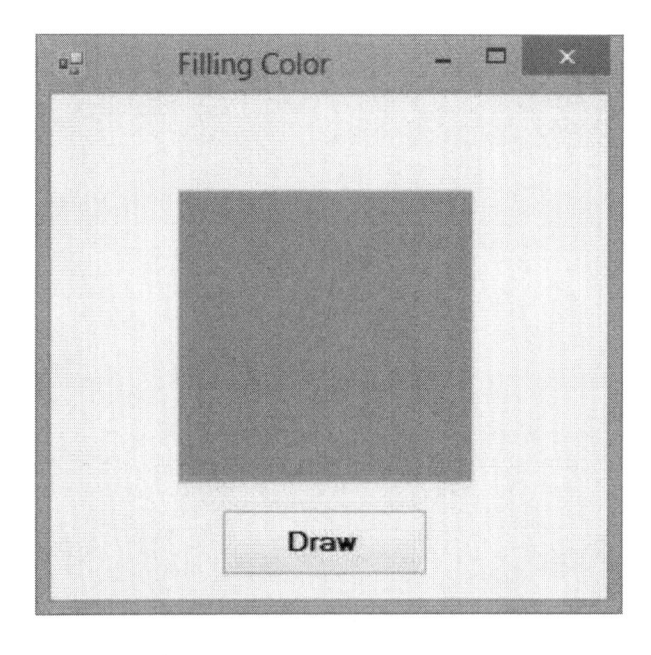

Figure 20.18

20.16(b) Drawing and Filling an Ellipse with Color

The syntax to fill an ellipse with the color defined by the brush object is:

myGraphics.FillEllipse (myBrush, 0, 0, 150, 150)

Example 20.16

Private Sub BtnDraw_Click(sender As Object, e As EventArgs)
Handles BtnDraw.Click
Dim myPen As Pen
Dim myBrush As Brush
Dim myGraphics As Graphics = Me.CreateGraphics
myPen = New Pen(Drawing.Color.Blue, 5)
myBrush = New SolidBrush(Color.Coral)
myGraphics.DrawEllipse(myPen, 50, 50, 180, 100)
myGraphics.FillEllipse(myBrush, 50, 50, 180, 100)
End Sub

The output interface is as shown in Figure 20.19

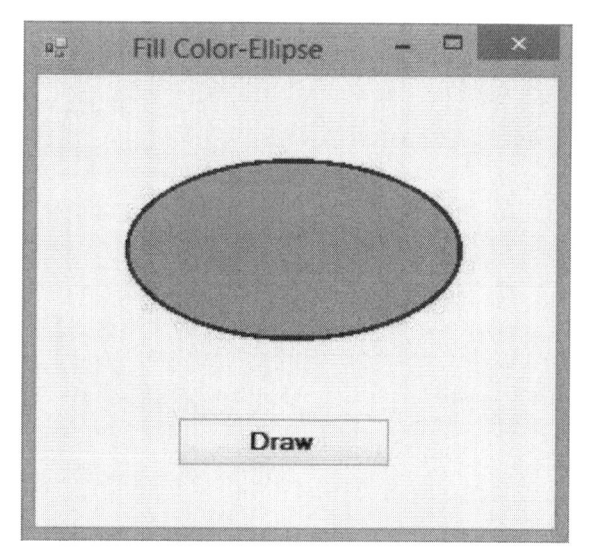

Figure 20.19

*If you omit the line myGraphics.DrawEllipse(myPen, 50, 50, 180, 100), you will get a solid ellipse without outline.

20.16(c) Drawing and Filling a Polygon with Color

The syntax to fill a polygon with the colour defined by the brush object is:

myGraphics.FillPolygon(myBrush, myPoints)

Example 20.17

Private Sub BtnDraw_Click(sender As Object, e As EventArgs)
Handles BtnDraw.Click
Dim myPen As Pen
Dim myBrush As Brush
Dim A As New Point(70, 10)
Dim B As New Point(170, 50)
Dim C As New Point(200, 150)

```
Dim D As New Point(140, 200)
Dim myPoints As Point() = {A, B, C, D}
myPen = New Pen(Drawing.Color.Blue, 5)
myBrush = New SolidBrush(Color.Coral)
Dim myGraphics As Graphics = Me.CreateGraphics
myGraphics.DrawPolygon(myPen, myPoints)
myGraphics.FillPolygon(myBrush, myPoints)
End Sub
```

The output interface is as shown in Figure 20.20

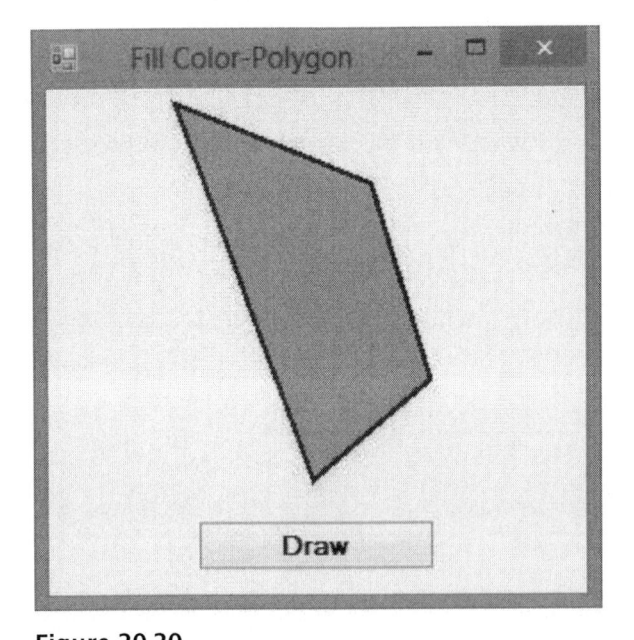

Figure 20.20

* If you omit myGraphics the line DrawPolygon(myPen, myPoints), you will get a polygon without outline

20.16(d) Drawing and Filling a Pie

The syntax to fill a pie with the color defined by the brush object is:

```
myGraphics.FillPie(myBrush, X, Y, width, height,
   StartAngle, SweepAngle)
```

Example 20.18

```
Private Sub BtnDraw_Click(sender As Object, e As EventArgs)
Handles BtnDraw.Click
Dim myPen As Pen
Dim myBrush As Brush
Dim myGraphics As Graphics = Me.CreateGraphics
 myPen = New Pen(Drawing.Color.Blue, 5)
myBrush = New SolidBrush(Color.Coral)
myGraphics.DrawPie(myPen, 30, 40, 150, 150, 0, 60)
myGraphics.FillPie(myBrush, 30, 40, 150, 150, 0, 60)
End Sub
```

The output is as shown in Figure 20.21

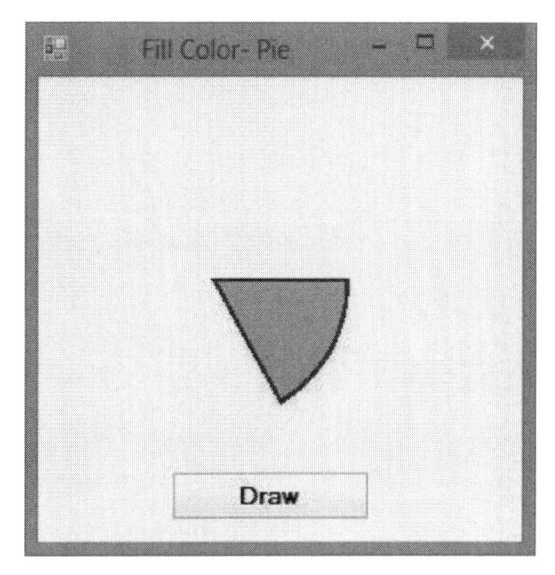

Figure 20.21

Summary

- In section 20.1, you have understood the concept of graphics creation
- In section 20.2, you have learned how to create the Graphics object

- In section 20.3, you have learned how to create the Pen object
- In section 20.4, you have learned how to draw a line
- In section 20.5, you have learned how to draw a rectangle
- In section 20.6, you have learned how to customize line style
- In section 20.7, you have learned how to draw an ellipse
- In section 20.8, you have learned how to draw a circle
- In section 20.9, you have learned how to draw a polygon
- In section 20.10, you have learned how to draw a pie
- In section 20.12, you have learned how to fill shapes with colours

Chapter 21 Using Timer

Timer is a useful control in Visual Basic 2019. It can be used to program events that are time related. For example, you need the timer to create a clock, a stopwatch, a dice, animation and more. Timer is a hidden control at runtime, like the engine of an automobile. We shall illustrate the usage of timer through a few examples.

21.1 Creating a Digital Clock

To create the clock, first, start a new project in Visual Basic 2019 and select a new Windows Application. You can give the project any name you wish, but we will name it MyClock. Change the text of Form1 to MyClock in the properties window. Now add the Timer control to the form by double-clicking it in the ToolBox. Next, insert a label control into the form. Change the Font size of the label to any size you wish and set the Font alignment to be middle centre. Before we forget, you shall also set the Interval property of the Timer control to 1000, which reflects a one second interval (1 unit is 1 millisecond). Remember to set the MaximizeBox property of Form1 to false so that the user cannot enlarge the clock. You also need to ensure that the Enabled property of the Timer control is set to True so that the clock starts running as soon as it is loaded.

Now, you are ready for the coding. Actually, you would be surprised at what you need to create a clock is only a one-line code, that is:

  Label1.Text = TimeOfDay

*TimeOfDay() is a Visual Basic 2019 function that returns the current time today based on your computer system's time.

Click on the Timer control and enter the code as shown below:

```
Private Sub Timer1_Tick(sender As Object,  e As EventArgs)
 Handles Timer1.Tick
LblClock.Text = TimeOfDay
End Sub
```

The digital clock is as shown in Figure 21.1

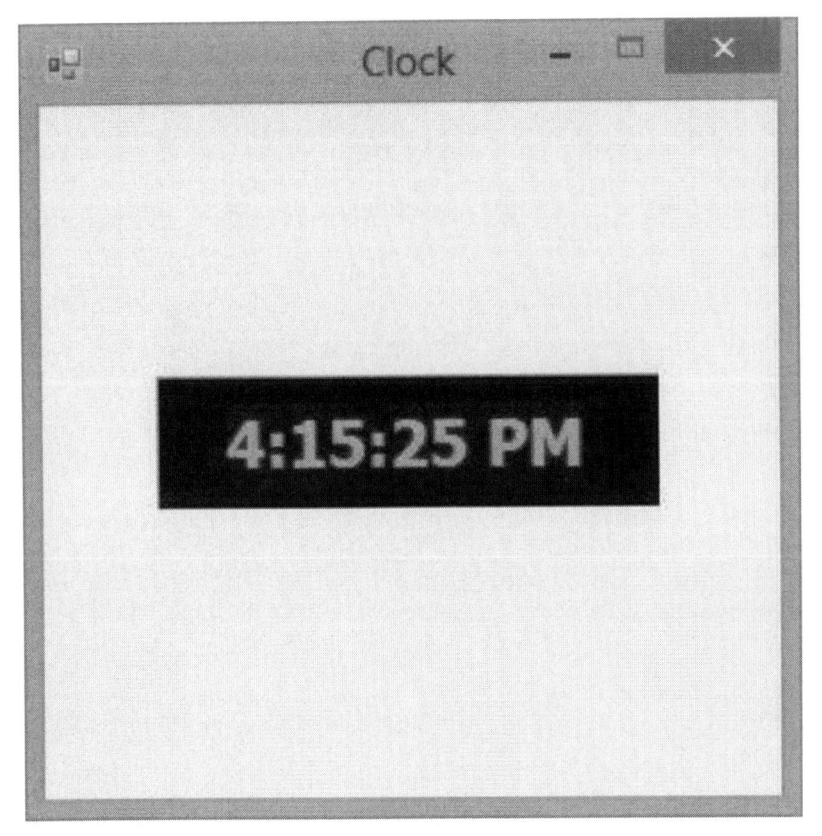

Figure 21.1

21.2 Creating a Stopwatch

We can create a stopwatch using the Timer control. Start a new project and name it stopwatch. Change the Form1 caption to Stopwatch. Insert the Timer control into the form and set its interval to 1000 which is equal to one second. Besides that, set the timer Enabled property to False so that it will not start ticking when the program is started. Insert three buttons and change their names to BtnStart, BtnStop and BtnReset respectively. Change their text to "Start", "Stop" and "Reset" accordingly. Now, enter the code as follows:

```vb
Private Sub BtnStart_Click(sender As Object, e As EventArgs)
Handles BtnStart.Click
Timer1.Enabled = True
End Sub
Private Sub Timer1_Tick(sender As Object, e As EventArgs)
Handles Timer1.Tick
LblPanel.Text = Val(LblPanel.Text) + 1
End Sub
Private Sub BtnStop_Click(sender As Object, e As EventArgs)
Handles BtnStop.Click
Timer1.Enabled = False
End Sub
Private Sub BtnReset_Click(sender As Object, e As EventArgs)
Handles BtnReset.Click
LblPanel.Text = 0
End Sub
```

The Interface of the Stopwatch is as shown in Figure 21.2

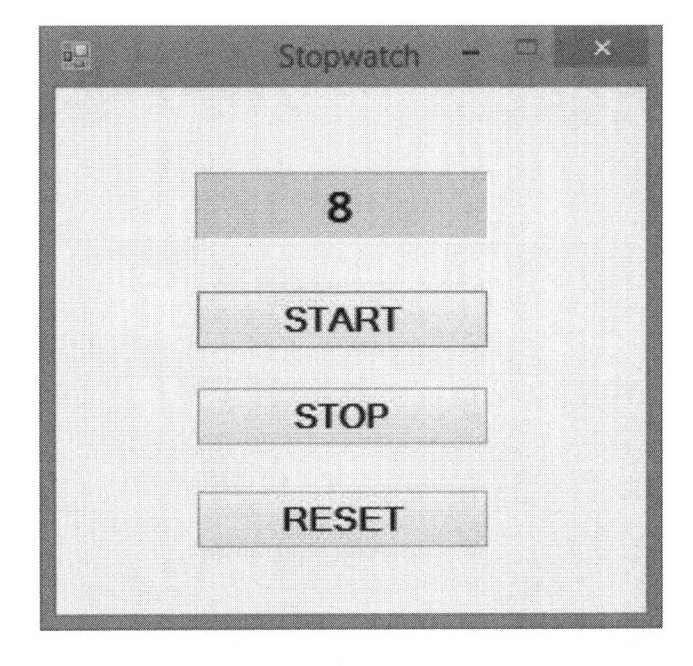

Figure 21.2

21.3 Creating a Digital Dice

We can create a digital dice easily using the Timer Control. To create a dice, you need to generate random numbers using the Rnd function. The Rnd function generates numbers between 0 and 1. However, you need to use the Int function to obtain random integers. The following statement generates random integers from 1 to 6 is as follows:

```
n = Int(1 + Rnd() * 6)
```

In the code, we introduce the variable m to control the length of time of the rolling process. If m is more than 1000, then the rolling process will stop by setting the timer enabled property to False. Set the timer interval to 10 so that the number changes every 0.01 second.

The Code

```
Dim n, m As Integer
Private Sub Timer1_Tick(sender As Object, e As EventArgs)
Handles Timer1.Tick
m = m + 10
If m < 1000 Then
n = Int(1 + Rnd() * 6)
LblDice.Text = n
```

```
Else
Timer1.Enabled = False
m = 0
End If
End Sub
Private Sub BtnRoll_Click(sender As Object, e As EventArgs)
 Handles BtnRoll.Click
Timer1.Enabled = True
End Sub
```

Running the program produces a dice with fast changing numbers which stops at a certain number. The interface is as shown in Figure 21.3

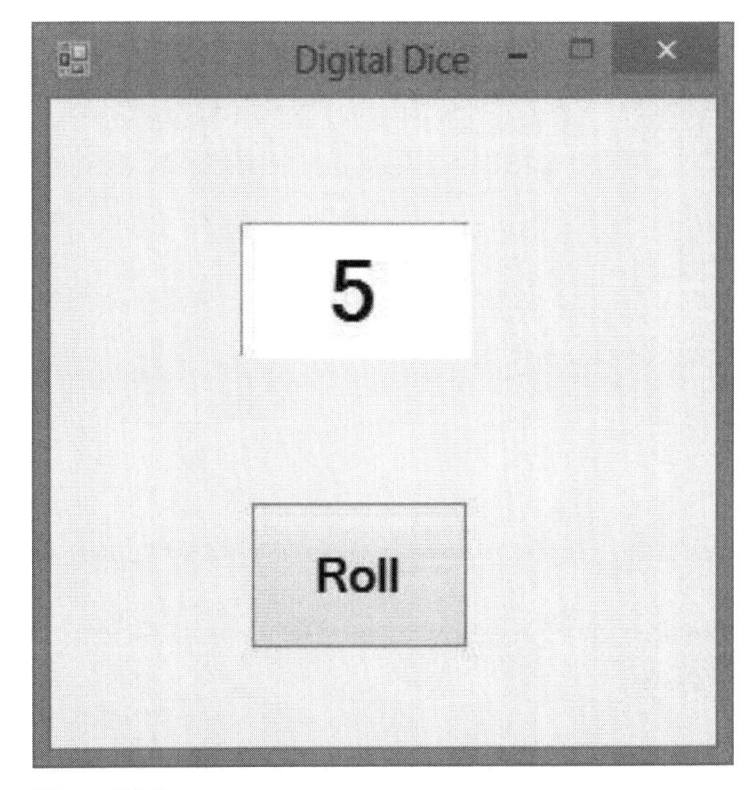

Figure 21.3

Summary

- In section 21.1, you have learned how to create a digital clock
- In section 21.2, you have learned how to create a digital stopwatch
- In section 21.3, you have learned how to create a digital dice

Chapter 22 Creating Animation

Although Visual Basic 2019 is a programming language designed for creating business and other industrial applications and not for creating animation, it can be used to create animation. In the preceding lesson, we have learned how to create animation using timer. In fact, the programs we have created in the previous chapter such as the stopwatch and the digital dice are animated programs. In this lesson, we shall show you more advanced animated programs.

22.1 Creating Motion

We can create a continuously moving object using timer. The motion can be from left to right or from top to bottom motion or diagonal.

First, insert a picture box into the form. In the picture box properties window, select the image property and click to import an image file from your storage devices such as your hard drive, your pen drive or DVD drive. We have inserted an image of a bunch of grapes. Next, insert a Timer control into the form and set its interval property to 100, which is equivalent to 0.1 second. Finally, add two buttons to the form, name one of them as `AnimateBtn` and the other one as `StopBtn`, and change to caption to Animate and Stop respectively.

We make use of the Left property of the picture box to create the motion. PictureBox.Left means the distance of the PictureBox from the left border of the Form. Now click on the Timer control and type in the following code:

```
Private Sub Timer1_Tick(sender As Object, e As EventArgs)
 Handles Timer1.Tick
If PictureBox1.Left < Me.Width Then
PictureBox1.Left = PictureBox1.Left + 10
Else
PictureBox1.Left = 0
End If
End Sub
```

In the code above, Me.Width represents the width of the Form. If the distance of the PictureBox from the left is less than the width of the Form, a value of 10 is added to the distance of the PictureBox from the left border each time the Timer tick, or every 0.1 second in this example. When the distance of the PictureBox from the left border is equal to the width of the form, the distance from the left border is set to 0, which move the PictureBox object to the left border and then move left again, thus creates an oscillating motion from left to right. We need to insert a button to stop the motion. The code is:

```
Timer1.Enabled = False
```

To animate the PictureBox object, we insert a button and enter the following code:

```
Timer1.Enabled = True
```

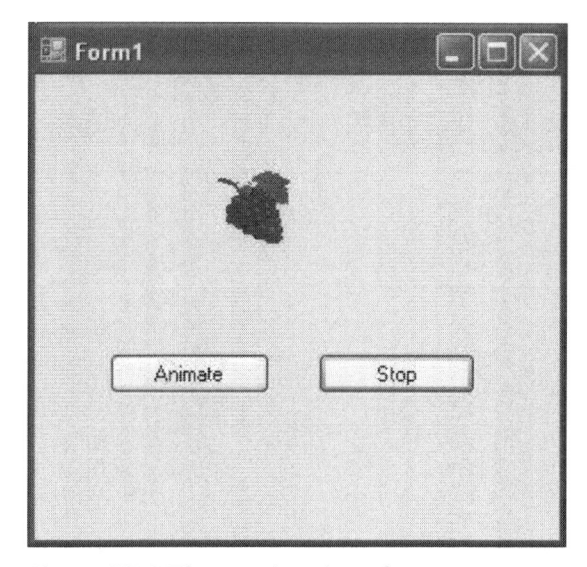

Figure 22.1 The runtime interface

22.2 Creating a Graphical Dice

In preceding lessons, we have learned how to create graphics and draw objects on the form. Now we shall use the previous knowledge to create an animated graphical dice using timer.

In this program, we need to insert a timer and set its interval to 100, which means the drawings will refresh every 0.1 second. Next, insert a picture box which is used as the surface of a dice. Finally, add a button and change its text to Roll. Under the Timer sub procedure, we create the Graphics object and the Pen object following the procedures we have learned in preceding lessons. Next, we use a **Do loop** and the Select Case structure to cycle through all six surfaces of the dice. To create six random cases, we use the syntax **n = Int(6 * Rnd()) + 1**. We can stop the loop by introducing a variable t and the loop until condition. The condition we set here is t >1000, you can use any figure you wish.

The code

```vb
Private Sub BtnRoll_Click(sender As Object, e As EventArgs)
 Handles BtnRoll.Click
Timer1.Enabled = True
End Sub
Private Sub Timer1_Tick(sender As Object, e As EventArgs)
Handles Timer1.Tick
Dim t As Integer
t = 0
Do
MyPicBox.Refresh()
Dim n As Integer
Dim myPen As Pen
myPen = New Pen(Drawing.Color.DarkTurquoise, 10)
Dim myGraphics As Graphics = MyPicBox.CreateGraphics
n = Int(6 * Rnd()) + 1
Select Case n
Case 1
myGraphics.DrawEllipse(myPen, 80, 80, 10, 10)

Case 2
myGraphics.DrawEllipse(myPen, 40, 40, 10, 10)
myGraphics.DrawEllipse(myPen, 120, 120, 10, 10)
Case 3
myGraphics.DrawEllipse(myPen, 40, 40, 10, 10)
myGraphics.DrawEllipse(myPen, 80, 80, 10, 10)
myGraphics.DrawEllipse(myPen, 120, 120, 10, 10)
Case 4
myGraphics.DrawEllipse(myPen, 40, 40, 10, 10)
myGraphics.DrawEllipse(myPen, 120, 40, 10, 10)
```

myGraphics.DrawEllipse(myPen, 40, 120, 10, 10)
myGraphics.DrawEllipse(myPen, 120, 120, 10, 10)
Case 5
myGraphics.DrawEllipse(myPen, 40, 40, 10, 10)
myGraphics.DrawEllipse(myPen, 120, 40, 10, 10)
myGraphics.DrawEllipse(myPen, 80, 80, 10, 10)
myGraphics.DrawEllipse(myPen, 40, 120, 10, 10)
myGraphics.DrawEllipse(myPen, 120, 120, 10, 10)
Case 6
myGraphics.DrawEllipse(myPen, 40, 40, 10, 10)
myGraphics.DrawEllipse(myPen, 120, 40, 10, 10)
myGraphics.DrawEllipse(myPen, 40, 80, 10, 10)
myGraphics.DrawEllipse(myPen, 120, 80, 10, 10)
myGraphics.DrawEllipse(myPen, 40, 120, 10, 10)
myGraphics.DrawEllipse(myPen, 120, 120, 10, 10)
End Select
t = t + 1
Loop Until t > 1000
Timer1.Enabled = False
End Sub

The runtime interface is as shown in Figure 22.2

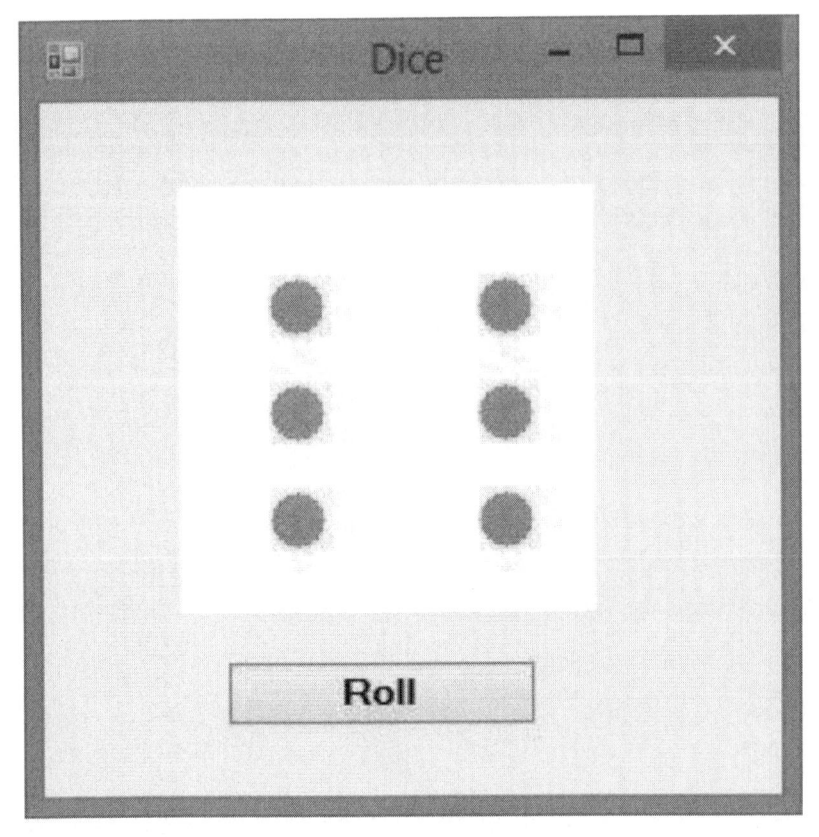

Figure 22.2

22.3 Creating a Slot Machine

You can also create a slot machine using timer. In this program, we add three picture boxes, a timer, a button and a label. Set the timer interval to 10, which means the images will refresh every 0.01 second. In the code, we shall introduce four variables m,a, b and c, where m is used to stop the timer and a,b,c are used to generate random images using the syntax Int(1 + Rnd() * 3). To load the images, we use the following syntax:

PictureBox.Image = Image.FromFile(Path of the image file)

We employ the If…Then structure to control the timer and the Select Case…..End Select structure to generate the random images. The label is used to display the message of the outcomes.

The Code

```
Dim m, a, b, c As Integer
Private Sub BtnSpin_Click(sender As Object, e As EventArgs)
 Handles BtnSpin.Click
Timer1.Enabled = True
End Sub
Private Sub Timer1_Tick(sender As Object, e As EventArgs)
 Handles Timer1.Tick
m = m + 10
If m < 1000 Then
a = Int(1 + Rnd() * 3)

b = Int(1 + Rnd() * 3)

c = Int(1 + Rnd() * 3)
Select Case a
Case 1
PictureBox1.Image = Image.FromFile("C:\Image\apple.gif")
Case 2
PictureBox1.Image = Image.FromFile("C:\Image\grape.gif")
Case 3
PictureBox1.Image = Image.FromFile("C:\Image\strawberry.gif")
End Select
Select Case b
Case 1
PictureBox2.Image = Image.FromFile("C:\Image\apple.gif")
```

```
Case 2
    PictureBox2.Image = Image.FromFile("C:\Image\grape.gif")
Case 3
    PictureBox2.Image = Image.FromFile("C:\Image\strawberry.gif")
End Select
Select Case c
Case 1
    PictureBox3.Image = Image.FromFile("C:\Image\apple.gif")
Case 2
    PictureBox3.Image = Image.FromFile("C:\Image\grape.gif")
Case 3
    PictureBox3.Image = Image.FromFile("C:\Image\strawberry.gif")
End Select
Else
Timer1.Enabled = False
m = 0
If a = b And b = c Then
LblMsg.Text = "Jackpot! You won $1,000,000"

Else
LblMsg.Text = "No luck, try again"
End If
End If
End Sub
```

The runtime interface is shown in Figure 32.3

Figure 32.3

Summary

- In section 22.1, you have learned how to create motion
- In section 22.2, you have learned how to create a graphical dice
- In section 22.3, you have learned how to create a slot machine

Chapter 23 Working with Databases

23.1 Introduction to Database

In our daily life, we deal with many types of information or data such as names, addresses, money, date, stock quotes, statistics and more. If you are in business or working as a professional, you must handle even more data. For example, a doctor needs to keep track of patients' personal and medical information such as names, addresses, phone numbers as well as blood pressure readings, blood sugar readings, surgical history, medicines prescribed in the past and more. On the other hand, businesses usually must manage large amount of data pertaining to products and customers. All these data need to be organized into a database for ease of data management.

In the past, people usually deal with data manually like using cards and folders. However, in the present day fast paced global environment and Information age, it is no longer feasible to manage data manually. Most data are now managed using computer-based database management systems. Computer-based Database management systems can handle data much faster, more accurate and more efficient than human beings do. With the advent of the network and the Internet technologies, data can now be managed locally and remotely. Companies usually invest heavily in database management systems to run the organizations efficiently and effectively. Database management systems are usually used in running payroll system, inventory system, accounting system, payment system, order handling system, customer relationship management system (CRM) and more. Some of the commercial database management systems (DBMS) are Oracle, Microsoft SQL server and Microsoft Access

23.2 Creating a Database Application

A database management system typically deals with storing, modifying, and extracting information from a database. It can also add, edit and delete records from the database. However, a DBMS can be very difficult to handle by ordinary people or businessmen who have no technological backgrounds. Fortunately, we can create user friendly database applications to handle the jobs with the DBMS running in the background. One of the best programs that can create such database application is none other than Visual Basic 2019.

Visual Basic 2019 uses ADO.NET to handle databases. ADO.NET is Microsoft's latest database technology which can work with many other advanced database management systems such as Microsoft SQL server. In this lesson, we will develop codes that make use of SQL Server 2019; therefore you need to have Microsoft SQL Server 2019 installed in your PC, you can download Microsoft SQL Server 2019 Express for free from

https://www.microsoft.com/en-us/sql-server/sql-server-downloads

To begin building the database project in Visual Basic 2019, launch Visual Basic 2019. You can name your project as Database Project 1 or whatever name you wish to call it. Next, change the default form's Text property to Contacts as we will be building a database of contact list. There are a few objects in ADO.NET that are required to build the database. There are:

- SqlConnection- to connect to a data source in SQL Server
- DataTable -to store data for navigation and manipulation
- DataAdapter- to populate a DataReader

The objects belong to the System.Data and System.Xml namespace. Therefore, we need to reference them in the beginning before we can work with them. To reference the ADO.NET object, choose project from the menu then select Database Project 1 properties to display the project properties. Next click the References tab to show the active references for the project, as shown in Figure 23.1

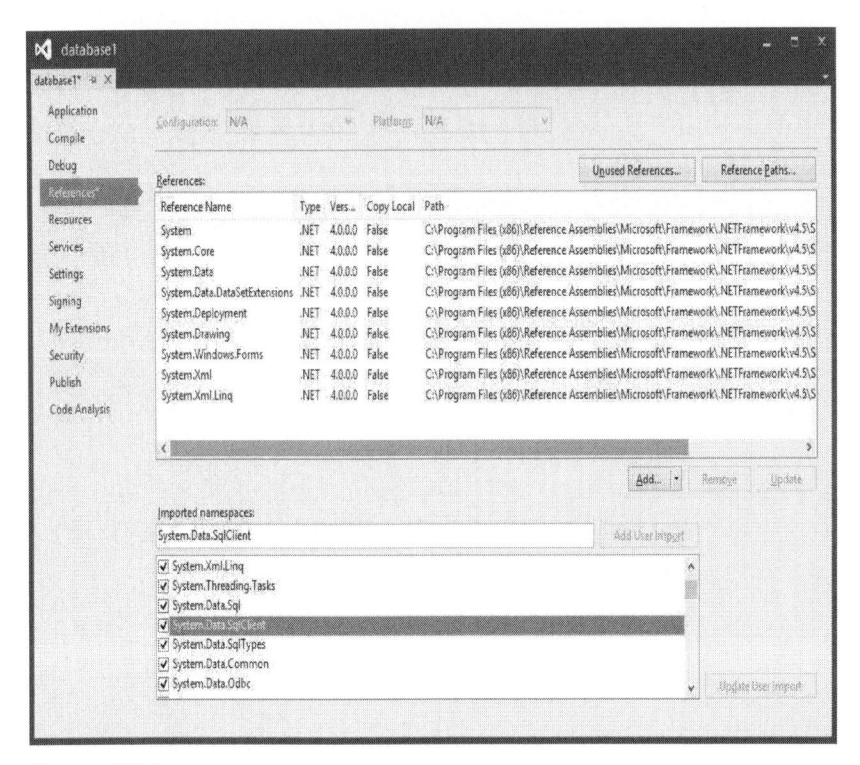

Figure 23.1

Under imported namespaces, make sure system.data, System.Data.Sqlclient are selected, otherwise check them. Having done that you need to click the Save All button on the toolbar and then return to the Visual Basic 2019 IDE.

23.3 Creating a Connection to a Database using ADO.NET

In Visual Basic 2019, we need to create a connection to a database before we can access its data. Before we begin, let's create a new database. Since we are using SQL Server 2019 as the database engine, we will use **SQL Server Management Studio** to create a database file with the mdf extension. You can download **SQL Server Management Studio (SSMS)** for free.

from the link below:

https://docs.microsoft.com/en-us/sql/ssms/download-sql-server-management-studio-ssms

We suggest you download the latest SSMS, SQL Server Management Studio 17.4. Upon launching SSMS, the initial dialog will ask you to connect it to the SQL server, as shown in Figure 23.2.

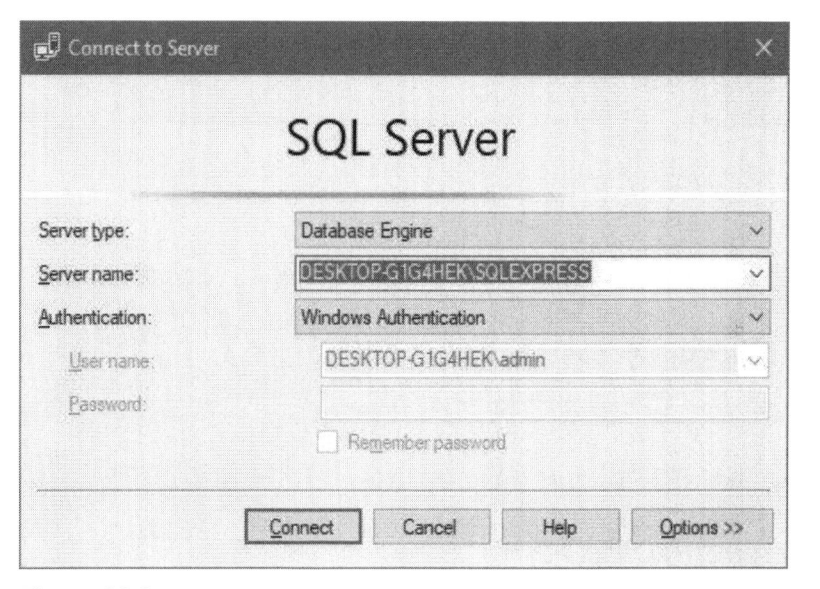

Figure 23.2

After clicking the 'Connect' button, SSMS wil be connected to SQL server, as shown in Figure 23.3

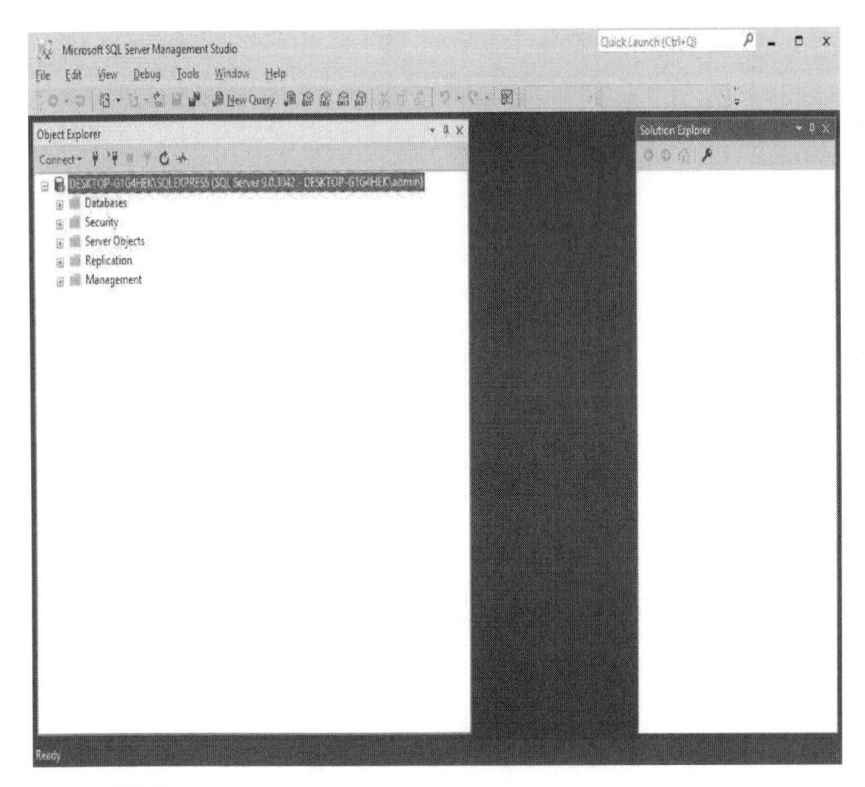

Figure 23.3

You can also disconnect from the SQL server anytime you wish. Next, we will create a database file. To create a new database, right-click on databases and select New Database, as shown in Figure 23.4

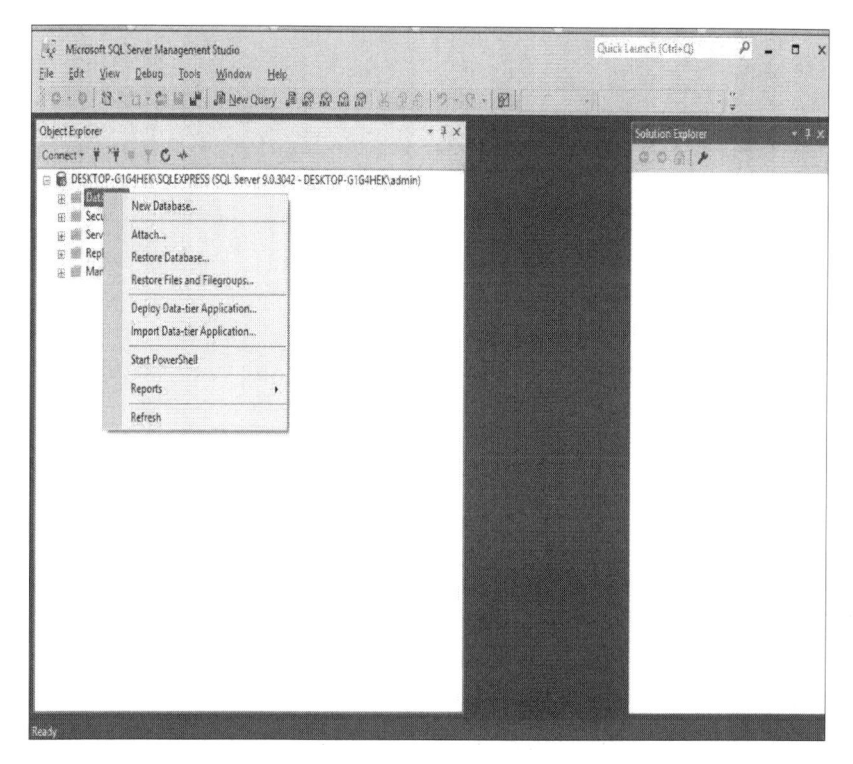

Figure 23.4

Clicking on New Database will bring out the New Database window, where you can create a new database by entering the database name as well as initial number of rows, as shown in Figure 23.5. In our example, we will create a database name known as **customer**, the database file is **customer.mdf**. After creating the database file, it will appear in SSMS, as shown in Figure 23.6

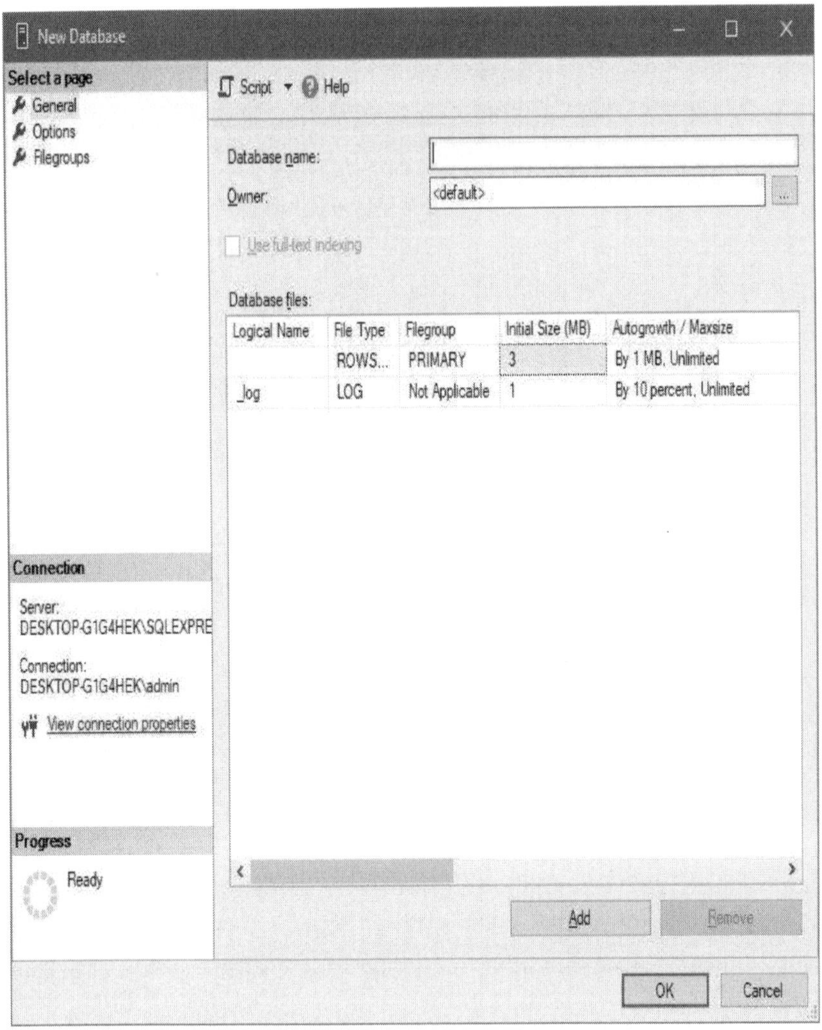
New Database
Select a page
General
Options
Filegroups
Script
Help
Database name:
Owner:
<default>
Use full-text indexing
Database files:
Logical Name
File Type
Filegroup
Initial Size (MB)
Autogrowth / Maxsize
ROWS...
PRIMARY
3
By 1 MB, Unlimited
_log
LOG
Not Applicable
1
By 10 percent, Unlimited
Connection
Server:
DESKTOP-G1G4HEK\SQLEXPRE
Connection:
DESKTOP-G1G4HEK\admin
View connection properties
Progress
Ready
Add
Remove
OK
Cancel

Figure 23.5

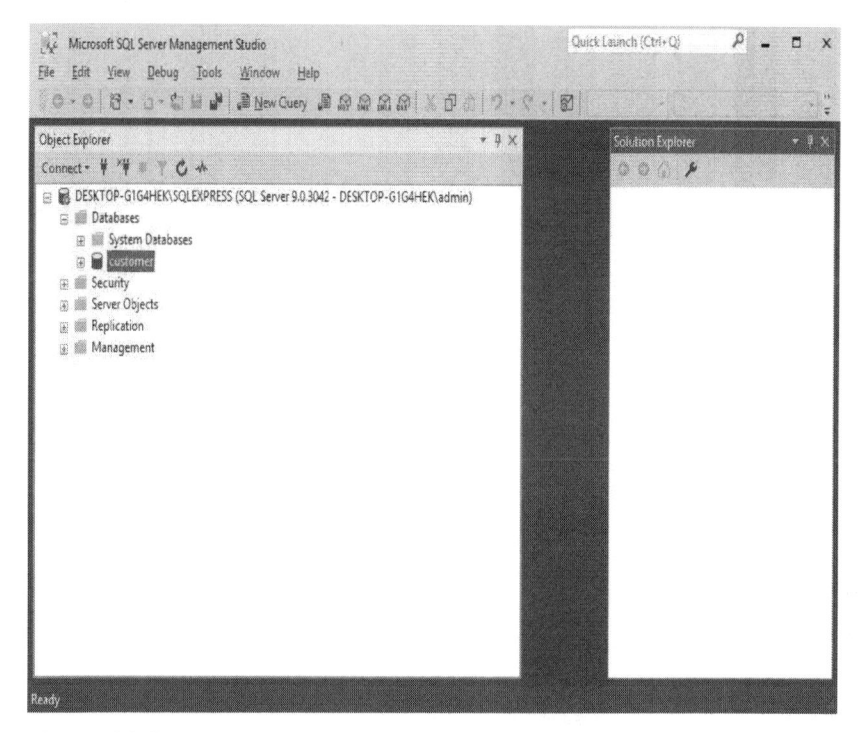

Figure 23.6

After creating the database, we need create table called cuslist. To create the table, expand the customer database and right click on table to bring up the table design window that allows you to key in the fields under column name and you can specify their data types such as string, numeric , money and so on. In our example, we create four fields, CusName, PhoneNum, State and Income. Save the table as cuslist.

To enter data in the table, right click on the table name to bring a list of options, select Edit Top 200 Rows from the options to bring up the table for you to enter the data, as shown in Figure 23.7.

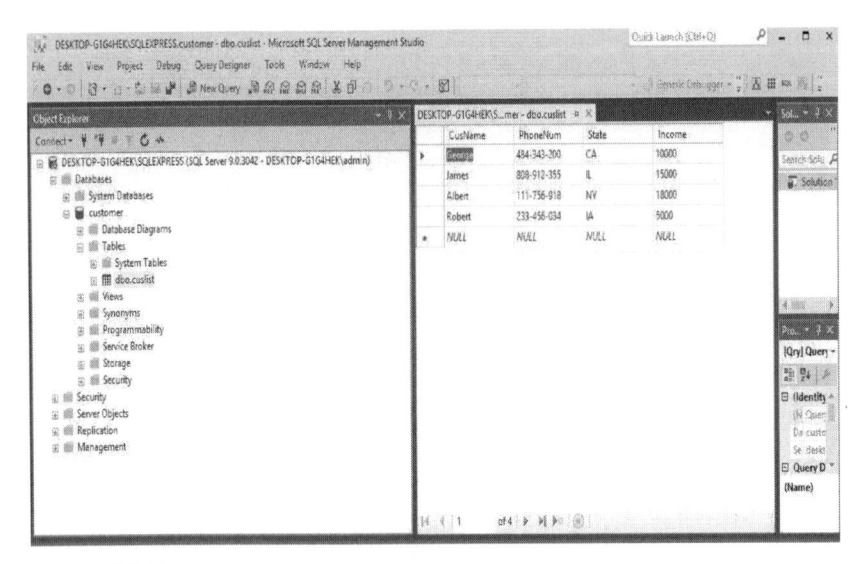

Figure 23.7

Now we are ready to write the code to access the database we have created. You may need to detach the file from SQL Server Management Studio and copy the file to another location before you can access it from Visual Basic 2019. To detach a database file, right click on the file and select Task, then click o Detach, as shown in Figure 23.8.

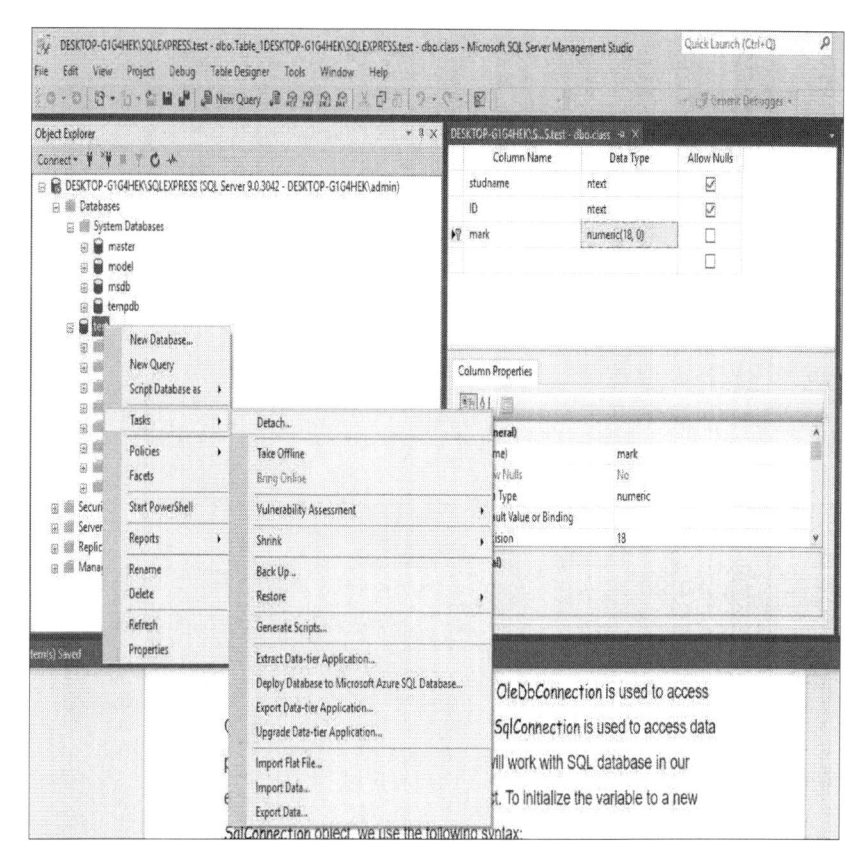

Figure 23.8

The ADO.NET object offers a number of connection objects such as `OleDbConnection`, `SqlConnection` and more. `OleDbConnection` is used to access OLEDB data such as Microsoft Access whilst `SqlConnection` is used to access data provided by Microsoft SQL server. Since we will work with SQL database in our example, we will use the `SqlConnection` object. To initialize the variable to a new `SqlConnection` object, we use the following syntax:

Private MyCn As New SqlConnection

Having created the instance of the **SqlConnecton** object, the next step is to establish a connection to the data source using the SQL **ConnectionString** property. The syntax is:

MyCn.ConnectionString ="Data Source=.\SQLEXPRESS;
AttachDbFilename=C:\Users\admin.DESKTOP-G1G4HEK\
Documents\My Websites\vbtutor\vb2019\customer.mdf;
Integrated Security=True;
Connection Timeout=30;" & "User Instance=True"

After establishing a connection to the database, you can open the database using the following syntax:

MyCn.Open()

23.4 Populating Data in ADO.NET

Establishing a connection to a database in Visual Basic 2019 using **SqlConnection** alone will not present anything tangible things to the user to manipulate the data until we add more relevant objects and write relevant codes to the project.

The next step is to create an instance of the **SqlDataAdpater** in our code so that we can populate the DataTable with data from the data source. Besides, you also need to create an instance of the **DataTable**. Other than that, you should also create an instance of the **SqlCommandBuilder** which is used to manipulate data such as updating and deleting data in the data table and send the changes back to the data source. The statements are:

```
Private MyDatAdp As New SqlDataAdapter
Private MyCmdBld As New SqlCommandBuilder
Private MyDataTbl As New DataTable
```

Besides that, we need to declare a variable to keep track of the user's current row within the data table. The statement is

```
Private MyRowPosition As Integer = 0
```

Having created the above of objects, you need to include the following statements in the Sub Form_Load event to start filling the DataTable with data from the data source. The statements are as follows:

```
MyDatAdp = New SqlDataAdapter("Select* from Contacts", MyCn)
MyCmdBld = New SqlCommandBuilder(MyDatAdp)
MyDatAdp.Fill(MyDataTbl)
```

After filling up the DataTable , we need to write code to access the data. To access data in the DataTable means that we need to access the rows in the table. We can achieve this by using the DataRow object. For example, we can write the following to access the first row of the table and present the data via two text boxes with the name txtName and txtState respectively:

```
Dim MyDataRow As DataRow = MyDataTbl.Rows(0)
Dim strName As String
Dim strState As String
strName = MyDataRow("ContactName")
strState = MyDataRow("State")
```

txtName.Text = strName.ToString

txtState.Text = strState.ToStringMe.showRecords()

* The two fields being referenced here are ContactName and State. Note Index 0 means first row.

showRecords() is a sub procedure created to show data in the text boxes. The code is as follows:

```
Private Sub showRecords()
If MyDataTbl.Rows.Count = 0 Then
txtName.Text = ""
txtState.Text = ""
Exit Sub
End If
txtName.Text = MyDataTbl.Rows(MyRowPosition)("ContactName").ToString
txtState.Text = MyDataTbl.Rows(MyRowPosition)("State").ToString
End Sub
```

The full Code is shown in Example 23.1

Example 23.1

```
Private MyDatAdp As New SqlDataAdapter
Private MyCmdBld As New SqlCommandBuilder
Private MyDataTbl As New DataTable
Private MyCn As New SqlConnection
Private MyRowPosition As Integer = 0
Private Sub Form1_Load(sender As Object, e As EventArgs)
```

```vb
Handles MyBase.Load
MyCn.ConnectionString ="Data Source=.\SQLEXPRESS;
AttachDbFilename=C:\Users\Documents\vb2019\customer.mdf;
Integrated Security=True; Connection Timeout=30;"
& "User Instance=True"
MyCn.Open()
MyDatAdp = New SqlDataAdapter("Select* from Contacts", MyCn)
MyCmdBld = New SqlCommandBuilder(MyDatAdp)
MyDatAdp.Fill(MyDataTbl)
Dim MyDataRow As DataRow = MyDataTbl.Rows(0)
Dim strName As String
Dim strState As String
Dim strPhone As String
Dim strIncome As Double
    strName = MyDataRow("CusName")
    strPhone = MyDataRow("PhoneNum")
    strState = MyDataRow("State")
    strIncome = MyDataRow("Income")
    TxtCusName.Text = strName.ToString()
    TxtContact.Text = strPhone.ToString()
    TxtState.Text = strState.ToString()
    TxtIncome.Text = strIncome.ToString()
Me.showRecords()

End Sub

  If MyDataTbl.Rows.Count = 0 Then
        TxtCusName.Text = ""
        TxtContact.Text = ""
        TxtState.Text = ""
```

```
            TxtIncome.Text = ""
            Exit Sub
        End If
TxtCusName.Text = MyDataTbl.Rows(MyRowPosition)
("CusName").ToString()
        TxtContact.Text = MyDataTbl.Rows(MyRowPosition)
("PhoneNum").ToString()
        TxtState.Text = MyDataTbl.Rows(MyRowPosition)
("State").ToString()
        TxtIncome.Text = MyDataTbl.Rows(MyRowPosition)
("Income").ToString()

End Sub
```

The output interface is shown in Figure 23.10

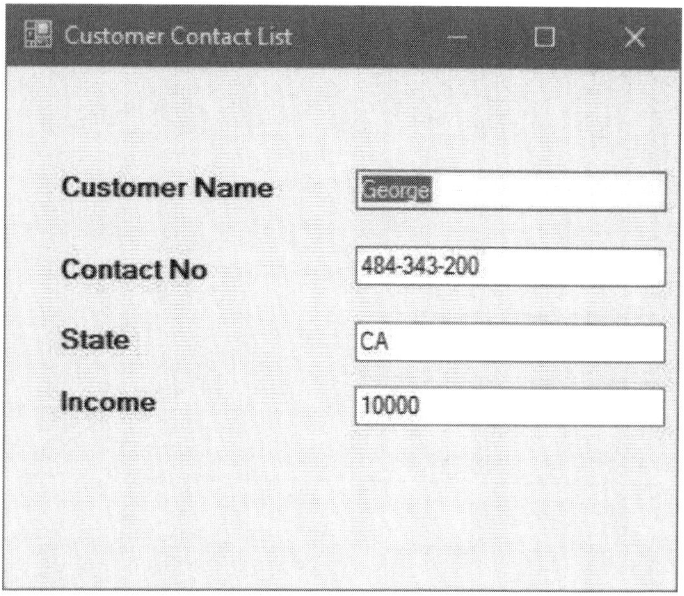

Figure 23.10

23.5 Browsing Records

In previous section, we have learned how to display the first record using the showRecords sub procedure. In this lesson, we will create command buttons and write relevant codes to allow the user to browse the records forward and backward as well as fast forward to the last record and back to the first record. The first button we need to create is for the user to browse the first record. We can use the button's text << to indicate to the user that it is the button to move to the first record and button's text >> to move to the last record. Besides we can use button's text < for moving to previous record and button's text > for moving to the next record.

The code for moving to the first record is

```
MyRowPosition = 0
Me.showRecords()
```

The code for moving to previous record is

If MyRowPosition > 0 Then
MyRowPosition = MyRowPosition - 1
Me.showRecords()
End If

The code for moving to next record is

If MyRowPosition < (MyDataTbl.Rows.Count - 1) Then
MyRowPosition = MyRowPosition + 1
Me.showRecords()
End If

The code for moving to last record is

If MyDataTbl.Rows.Count > 0 Then
MyRowPosition = MyDataTbl.Rows.Count - 1
Me.showRecords()
End If

23.6 Editing, Saving, Adding and Deleting Records

You can edit any record by navigating to the record and change the data values. However, you need to save the data after editing them. You need to use the update method of the SqlDataAdapter to save the data. The code is:

If MyDataTbl.Rows.Count <> 0 Then
MyDataTbl.Rows(MyRowPosition)("ContactName") = txtName.Text

```
MyDataTbl.Rows(MyRowPosition)("state") = txtState.Text
MyDatAdp.Update(MyDataTbl)
End If
```

You can also add new record or new row to the table using the following code:

```
Dim MyNewRow As DataRow = MyDataTbl.NewRow()
MyDataTbl.Rows.Add(MyNewRow)
MyRowPosition = MyDataTbl.Rows.Count - 1
Me.showRecords()
```

The code above will present a new record with blank fields for the user to enter the new data. After entering the data, he or she can then click the save button to save the data.

Lastly, the user might want to delete the data. Remember to add a primary key to one of the fields in the database, otherwise it will not work. The code to delete the data is:

```
If MyDataTbl.Rows.Count <> 0 Then
MyDataTbl.Rows(MyRowPosition) Delete()
MyDatAdp.Update(MyDataTbl)
MyRowPosition = 0
Me.showRecords()
End If
```

The complete code is shown in Example 23.2

Example 23.2

```
Private MyDatAdp As New SqlDataAdapter
Private MyCmdBld As New SqlCommandBuilder
```

```vb
Private MyDataTbl As New DataTable
Private MyCn As New SqlConnection
Private MyRowPosition As Integer = 0
Private Sub Form1_FormClosed(sender As Object, e As EventArgs) Handles
Me.FormClosed
MyCn.Close()
MyCn.Dispose()
End Sub
Private Sub Form1_Load(sender As Object, e As EventArgs)
 Handles MyBase.Load
MyCn.ConnectionString = "Data Source=.\SQLEXPRESS;
AttachDbFilename=C:\Users\Documents\vb2019\customer.mdf;
Integrated Security=True; Connection Timeout=30;"
& "User Instance=True"


MyCn.Open()
MyDatAdp = New SqlDataAdapter("Select* from cuslist", MyCn)
    MyCmdBld = New SqlCommandBuilder(MyDatAdp)
    MyDatAdp.Fill(MyDataTbl)
    Dim MyDataRow As DataRow = MyDataTbl.Rows(0)
    Dim strName As String
    Dim strState As String
    Dim strPhone As String
    Dim strIncome As Double
    strName = MyDataRow("CusName")
    strPhone = MyDataRow("PhoneNum")
    strState = MyDataRow("State")
    strIncome = MyDataRow("Income")
    TxtCusName.Text = strName.ToString()
```

```vb
        TxtContact.Text = strPhone.ToString()
        TxtState.Text = strState.ToString()
        TxtIncome.Text = strIncome.ToString()
        Me.showRecords()
    End Sub



Private Sub showRecords()
If MyDataTbl.Rows.Count = 0 Then
        TxtCusName.Text = ""
        TxtContact.Text = ""
        TxtState.Text = ""
        TxtIncome.Text = ""
        Exit Sub
    End If
TxtCusName.Text = MyDataTbl.Rows(MyRowPosition)
("CusName").ToString()
TxtContact.Text = MyDataTbl.Rows(MyRowPosition)
("PhoneNum").ToString()
TxtState.Text = MyDataTbl.Rows(MyRowPosition)
("State").ToString()
TxtIncome.Text = MyDataTbl.Rows(MyRowPosition)
("Income").ToString()
End Sub

Private Sub BtnMoveFirst_Click(sender As Object, e As EventArgs)
Handles BtnMoveFirst.Click
MyRowPosition = 0
```

```vb
        Me.showRecords()
    End Sub


    Private Sub BtnMovePrev_Click(sender As Object, e As EventArgs) Handles BtnMovePrev.Click
        If MyRowPosition > 0 Then
            MyRowPosition = MyRowPosition - 1
            Me.showRecords()
        End If
    End Sub
    Private Sub BtnMoveNext_Click(sender As Object, e As EventArgs) Handles BtnMoveNext.Click
        If MyRowPosition < (MyDataTbl.Rows.Count - 1) Then
            MyRowPosition = MyRowPosition + 1
            Me.showRecords()
        End If
    End Sub


    Private Sub BtnMoveLast_Click(sender As Object, e As EventArgs) Handles BtnMoveLast.Click
        If MyDataTbl.Rows.Count > 0 Then
            MyRowPosition = MyDataTbl.Rows.Count - 1
            Me.showRecords()
        End If
    End Sub


    Private Sub BtnAdd_Click(sender As Object, e As EventArgs) Handles BtnAdd.Click

        Dim MyNewRow As DataRow = MyDataTbl.NewRow()
        MyDataTbl.Rows.Add(MyNewRow)
```

```
MyRowPosition = MyDataTbl.Rows.Count - 1
Me.showRecords()
End Sub


Private Sub BtnDelete_Click(sender As Object, e As EventArgs)
Handles BtnDelete.Click
If MyDataTbl.Rows.Count <> 0 Then
MyDataTbl.Rows(MyRowPosition).Delete()
MyRowPosition = 0
MyDatAdp.Update(MyDataTbl)
Me.showRecords()
End If
End Sub


Private Sub BtnSave_Click(sender As Object, e As EventArgs)
 Handles BtnSave.Click
 If MyDataTbl.Rows.Count <> 0 Then
 MyDataTbl.Rows(MyRowPosition)("CusName") = TxtCusName.Text
 MyDataTbl.Rows(MyRowPosition)("PhoneNum") = TxtContact.Text
 MyDataTbl.Rows(MyRowPosition)("state") = TxtState.Text
 MyDataTbl.Rows(MyRowPosition)("Income") = TxtIncome.Text
 MyDatAdp.Update(MyDataTbl)
 End If
 End Sub
```

The output interface is as shown in Figure 23.11

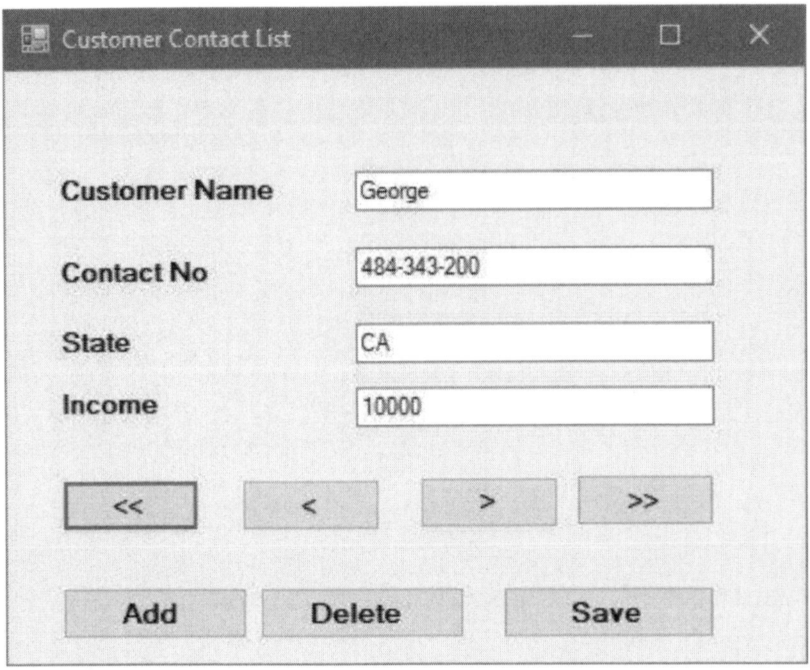

Figure 23.11

23.7 Accessing Database using DataGridView

Another method to access a database is to use the DataGridView control. DataGridView allows the user to browse the data in a database via a table that comprises rows and columns. To access the database, use the following statement:

Private Datastr As String = "Data Source=.\SQLEXPRESS;
AttachDbFilename=C:\Users\Documents\vb2019\customer.mdf;
Integrated Security=True; Connection Timeout=30;" &
 "User Instance=True"

To use the DataGridView control, drag it from the toolbox and insert it into the form. Next, insert a button and rename it as BtnShow. Click the button and enter the following code, as shown in Example 23.3

Example 23.3

```vb
Private Datastr As String = "Data Source=.\SQLEXPRESS;
AttachDbFilename=C:\Users\Documents\vb2019\customer.mdf;
Integrated Security=True; Connection Timeout=30;" &
 "User Instance=True"

Private Sub BtnShow_Click(sender As Object, e As EventArgs)
Handles BtnShow.Click
 Dim Mycon As New SqlConnection(Datastr)
 Dim MySelect As String = "Select CusName, PhoneNum,State,
 Income from cuslist"
Dim MyAdpt As New SqlDataAdapter(MySelect, Mycon)
Dim Myds As New DataSet()
MyAdpt.Fill(Myds, "cuslist")
DataGridView1.DataSource = Myds.Tables(0)
End Sub
```

The output is shown in Figure 23.12

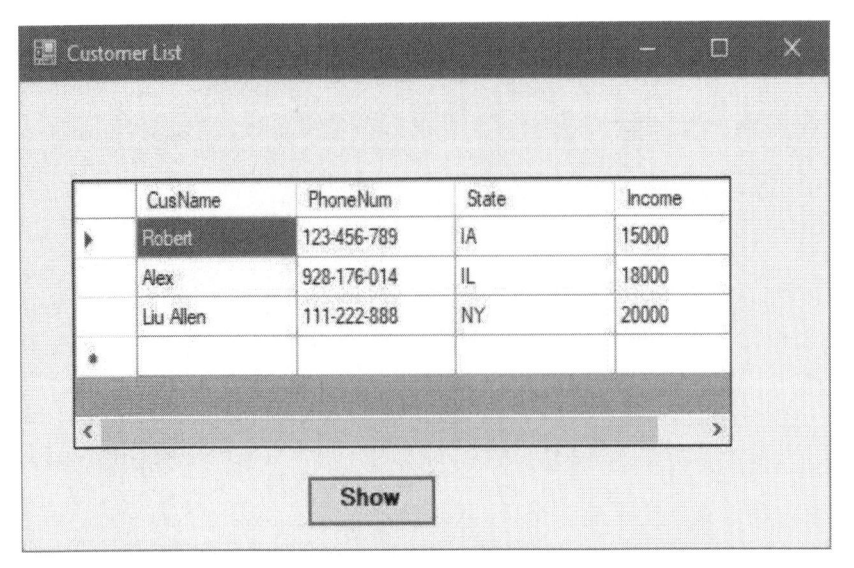

![Customer List form with data grid showing CusName, PhoneNum, State, Income columns]

Figure 23.12

23.8 Performing Arithmetic Calculations in a Database

In Visual Basic 2019, we can retrieve data from a database and perform arithmetic calculations. Let's create a simple database with two columns, name and income and save it as family.mdf in SQL server. For income, we need to specify it as money or numeric data type to enable calculation. We use money in our example.

In our example, we wish to calculate the sum of income for all the data. To perform this calculation, we use SQL keywords, as follows:

    Dim mySelectQuery As String = "Select SUM (Income) FROM mylist;"

We shall show modify the code in 23.7 but we add a button so that we can show the data in a data grid and calculate the total income, as shown in example 23.4.

Example 23.4

```
Private Datastr As String = "Data Source=.\SQLEXPRESS;
AttachDbFilename=C:\Users\Documents\vb2019\family.mdf;
Integrated Security=True; Connection Timeout=30;" &
"User Instance=True"
Private searchterm As String
Private Sub BtnShow_Click(sender As Object, e As EventArgs)
Handles BtnShow.Click
Dim Mycon As New SqlConnection(Datastr)
Dim MySelect As String = "Select Name, Income from mylist;"
Dim Adpt As New SqlDataAdapter(MySelect, Mycon)
Dim Myds As New DataSet()
   Adpt.Fill(Myds, "mylist")
   DataGridView1.DataSource = Myds.Tables(0)
End Sub

'Sub procedure to calculate the sum of income
Public Sub totalIncome(ByVal myConnString As String,
 ByVal searchValue As String)
Dim MyDatApt As New SqlDataAdapter
Dim Myds As New DataSet
Dim mySelectQuery As String = "Select SUM (Income) FROM mylist;"
Dim myConn As New SqlConnection(myConnString)
Dim myCommand As New SqlCommand(mySelectQuery, myConn)
myConn.Open()
MyDatApt.SelectCommand = myCommand
LblTotal.Text = Convert.ToString(Math.Round
(myCommand.ExecuteScalar, 2))
myConn.Dispose()    'To dispose the object to release more memory
End Sub
Private Sub BtnCalInc_Click(sender As Object, e As EventArgs)
```

Handles BtnCalInc.Click

totalIncome(Datastr, searchterm)

End Sub

The Output

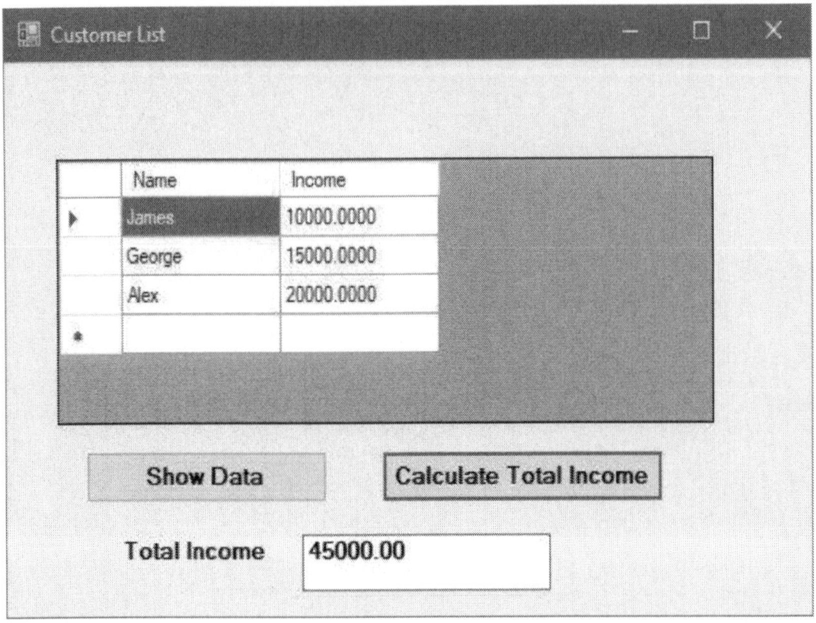

Figure 23.13

In the next example, we shall modify the code in Example 23.4 so that we can calculate the average income as well. In this example, we add a few more lines of code and a label to display the average income. The code is shown in Example 23.5

Example 23.5

```
Private Datastr As String = "Data Source=.\SQLEXPRESS;
AttachDbFilename=C:\Users\Documents\vb2019\family.mdf;
Integrated Security=True; Connection Timeout=30;" &
```

"User Instance=True"
Private searchterm As String
Private Sub BtnShow_Click(sender As Object, e As EventArgs)

Handles BtnShow.Click
Dim Mycon As New SqlConnection(Datastr)
Dim MySelect As String = "Select Name, Income from mylist"
Dim Adpt As New SqlDataAdapter(MySelect, Mycon)
Dim Myds As New DataSet()
Adpt.Fill(Myds, "mylist")
DataGridView1.DataSource = Myds.Tables(0)
End Sub
Public Sub Income(ByVal myConnString As String,

ByVal searchValue As String)
Dim MyDatApt As New SqlDataAdapter
Dim Myds As New DataSet
Dim mySelectQuery As String = "Select SUM (Income) FROM mylist;"
Dim mySelectQuery2 As String = "Select AVG (Income) FROM mylist;"
Dim myConn As New SqlConnection(myConnString)
Dim myCommand As New SqlCommand(mySelectQuery, myConn)
Dim myCommand2 As New SqlCommand(mySelectQuery2, myConn)
    myConn.Open()
    MyDatApt.SelectCommand = myCommand
    MyDatApt.SelectCommand = myCommand2
LblTotal.Text = Convert.ToString(Math.Round

(myCommand.ExecuteScalar, 2))
LblAvg.Text = Convert.ToString(Math.Round
(myCommand2.ExecuteScalar, 2))
    myConn.Dispose()
End Sub

Private Sub BtnCalInc_Click(sender As Object, e As EventArgs)

 Handles BtnCalInc.Click
    Income(Datastr, searchterm)
End Sub

The output is shown in Figure 23.14

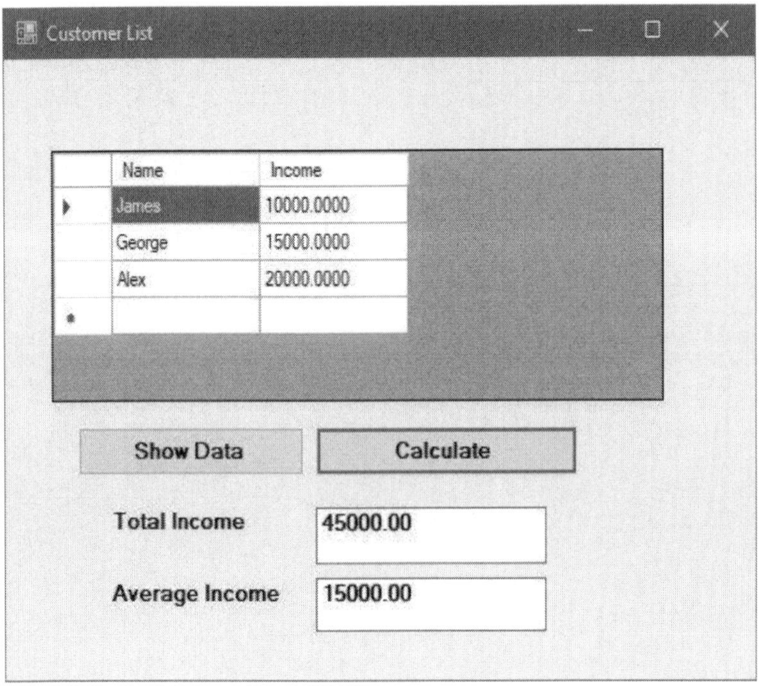

Figure 23.14

Besides the SUM and AVG sql Functions, there is also a COUNT function. The syntax is

SELECT COUNT(column_name) FROM table_name WHERE condition;

We shall show how it works in Example 23.6

Example 23.6

In this example, we add another label to show the count value. We impose a condition where count is executed for income <20000 with the following statement:

```
Dim mySelectQuery3 As String = "Select COUNT (Income)
FROM mylist WHERE Income<20000;"
```

Modify this part of the code in Example 23.5, as follows:

```
Public Sub Income(ByVal myConnString As String,
ByVal searchValue As String)
Dim MyDatApt As New SqlDataAdapter
Dim Myds As New DataSet
Dim mySelectQuery As String = "Select SUM (Income)
FROM mylist;"
Dim mySelectQuery2 As String = "Select AVG (Income)
 FROM mylist;"
Dim mySelectQuery3 As String = "Select COUNT (Income)
FROM mylist WHERE Income<20000;"
    Dim myConn As New SqlConnection(myConnString)
    Dim myCommand As New SqlCommand(mySelectQuery,
```

myConn)
   Dim myCommand2 As New SqlCommand(mySelectQuery2, myConn)
   Dim myCommand3 As New SqlCommand(mySelectQuery3, myConn)
   myConn.Open()
   MyDatApt.SelectCommand = myCommand
   MyDatApt.SelectCommand = myCommand2
LblTotal.Text=Convert.ToString(Math.Round(myCommand.ExecuteScalar, 2))
LblAvg.Text =Convert.ToString(Math.Round(myCommand2.ExecuteScalar, 2))
LblCount.Text =Convert.ToString(Math.Round(myCommand3.ExecuteScalar, 2))
   myConn.Dispose()
  End Sub

The output is shown in Figure 23.15

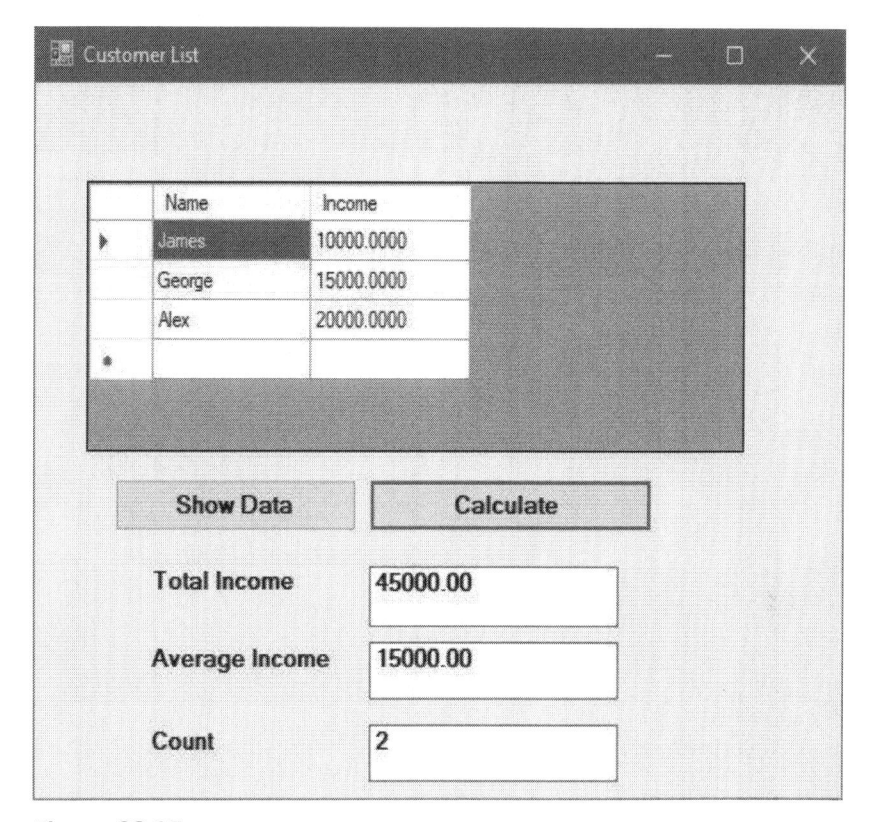

Figure 23.15

Summary

- In section 23.1, you have understood the concepts of database
- In section 23.2, you have learned how to create a database
- In section 23.3, you have learned how to create a connection to a database
- In section 23.4, you have learned how to populate a database
- In section 23.5, you have learned how to write code for browsing records
- In section 23.5, you have learned how to write code for editing, saving, adding and deleting records in a database

Chapter 24 Reading and Writing Text Files

24.1 Introduction

To be able to open a file and read the data from storage unit of a computer, such as a hard drive as well as able to save the data into the storage unit are important functions of a computer program. In fact, the ability to store, retrieve and modify data makes a computer a powerful tool in database management.

In this Chapter, we will learn how to create a text file that can store data. Using text file is an easy way to manage data, although it is not as sophisticated as full-fledged database management software such as SQL Server, Microsoft Access and Oracle. Visual Basic 2019 allows the user to create a text file, save the text file as well as to read the text file. It is relatively easy to write code for the above purposes in VB2019.

Reading and writing to a text file in VB2019 required the use of the StreamReader class and the StreamWriter class respectively. StreamReader is a tool that enables the streaming of data by moving it from one location to another so that the user can read it. For example, it allows the user to read a text file that is stored in a hard drive. On the other hand, the StreamWriter class is a tool that can write data input by the user to a storage device such as the hard drive.

24.2 Reading a Text File

To read a file from the hard disk or any storage device, we need to use the StreamReader class. To achieve that, first we need to include the following statement in the program code:

Imports System.IO

This line has to precede the whole program code as it is higher in hierarchy than the StreamReader Class. In Fact, this is the concept of object oriented programming where StreamReader is part of the namespace System.IO. You have to put it on top of the whole program (i.e. above the Public Class Form 1 statement). The word import means we import the namesapce System.IO into the program. Once we have done that, we can declare a variable of the streamReader data type with the following statement:

Dim FileReader As StreamReader

If we do not include the Imports System.IO, we have to use the statement

Dim FileReader As IO.StreamReader

each time we want to use the StreamReader class.

Now, start a new project and name it in whatever name you wish, we named it TxtEditor here. Now, insert the OpenFileDialog control into the form because we will use it to read the file from the storage device. We also need to declare a new OpenFileDialog object before we can use it, you can name it as **OpenFileDialog1**. The **OpenFileDialog** control will return a DialogResult value that can determine whether the user clicks the OK button or Cancel button. We will also insert a command button and change its displayed text to 'Open'. The user can use it to open and read a certain text file. The following statement will accomplish the task above.

```
Dim results As DialogResult
Dim OpenFileDialog1 As New OpenFileDialog()
results = OpenFileDialog1.ShowDialog
If results = DialogResult.OK Then
'Code to be executed if OK button was clicked
Else
'Code to be executed if Cancel button was clicked
End If
```

Next, we inserted a textbox ,name it TxtEditor and set its Multiline property to true. It is used for displaying the text from a text file. We also insert a button and name it BtnOpen. In order to read the text file, we need to create a new instant of the streamReader and connect it to a text file with the following statement:

```
FileReader = New StreamReader(OpenFileDialog1.FileName)
```

In addition, we need to use the ReadToEnd method to read the entire text of a text file and display it in the text box. The syntax is:

```
TxtEditor.Text = FileReader.ReadToEnd( )
```

Lastly, we need to close the file by using the Close() method. The entire code is shown in the box below:

The Code

```
Imports System.IO
Public Class Form1
Private Sub BtnOpen_Click(sender As Object, e As EventArgs)
 Handles BtnOpen.Click
Dim FileReader As StreamReader
```

```
Dim results As DialogResult
Dim OpenFileDialog1 As New OpenFileDialog()
results = OpenFileDialog1.ShowDialog
If results = DialogResult.OK Then
FileReader = New StreamReader(OpenFileDialog1.FileName)
TxtEditor.Text = FileReader.ReadToEnd()
FileReader.Close()
End If
End Sub
```

The Design Interface is shown in Figure 24.1

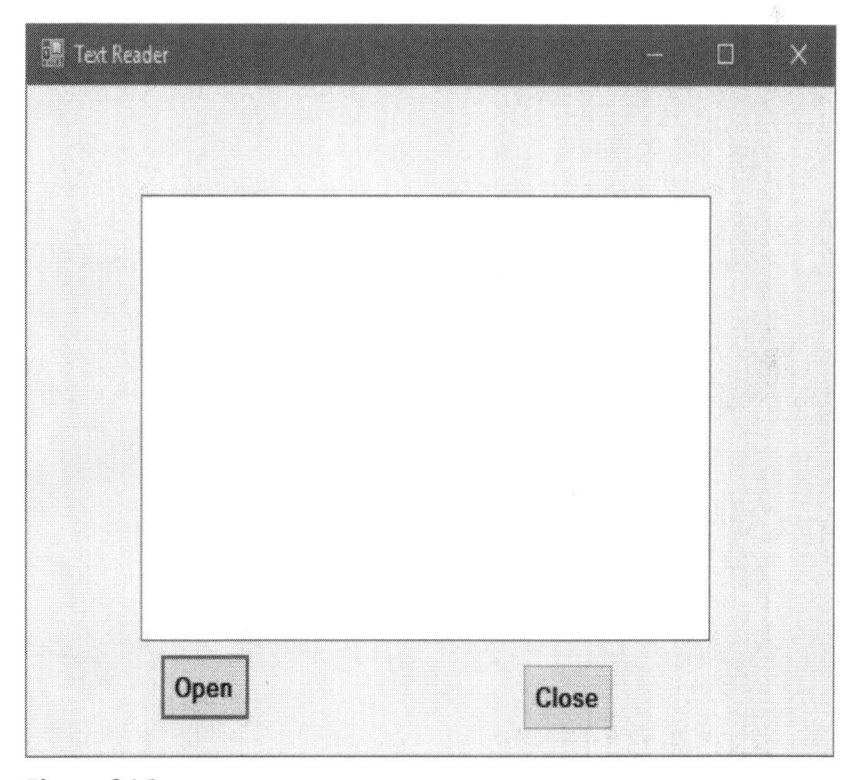

Figure 24.1

The Open Dialog box is shown in Figure 24.2

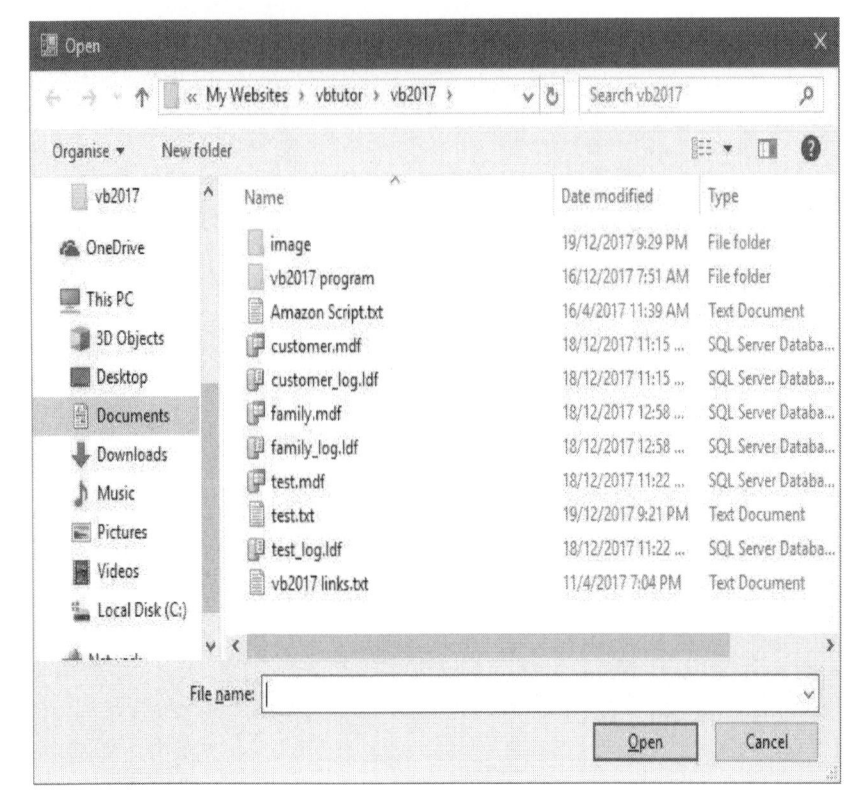

Figure 24.2

The Output Interface is shown in Figure 24.3

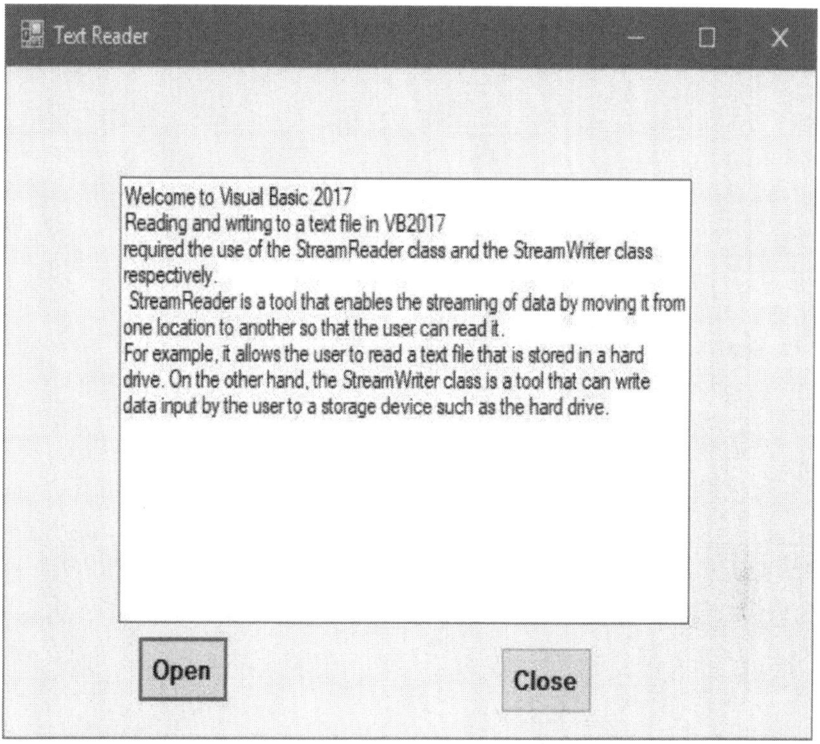

Figure 24.3

24.3 Writing to a Text File

Writing a text file means storing the text entered by the user via the textbox into a storage device such as a hard drive. It also means saving the file. To accomplish this task, we need to deploy the StreamWriter Class. You also need to insert the SaveFileDialog control into the form as it is used to save the data into the storage unit like a hard drive. You need to declare a new SaveFileDialog object before you can use it. You can name it as SaveFileDialog1. We also insert another button and name it as BtnSave. The Code is the same as the code for reading the file, you just change the StreamReader to StreamWriter, and the method from ReadToEnd to Write.

The code

```vb
Imports System.IO
Public Class Form1
Private Sub BtnSave_Click(sender As Object, e As EventArgs)
Handles BtnOpen.Click
Dim FileWriter As StreamWriter
Dim results As DialogResult
Dim saveFileDialog1 As New SaveFileDialog()
results = SaveFileDialog1.ShowDialog
If results = DialogResult.OK Then
FileWriter = New StreamWriter(SaveFileDialog1.FileName, False)
FileWriter.Write(TxtEditor.Text)
FileWriter.Close()
End If
End Sub
End Class
```

The Interface is shown in Figure 24.4

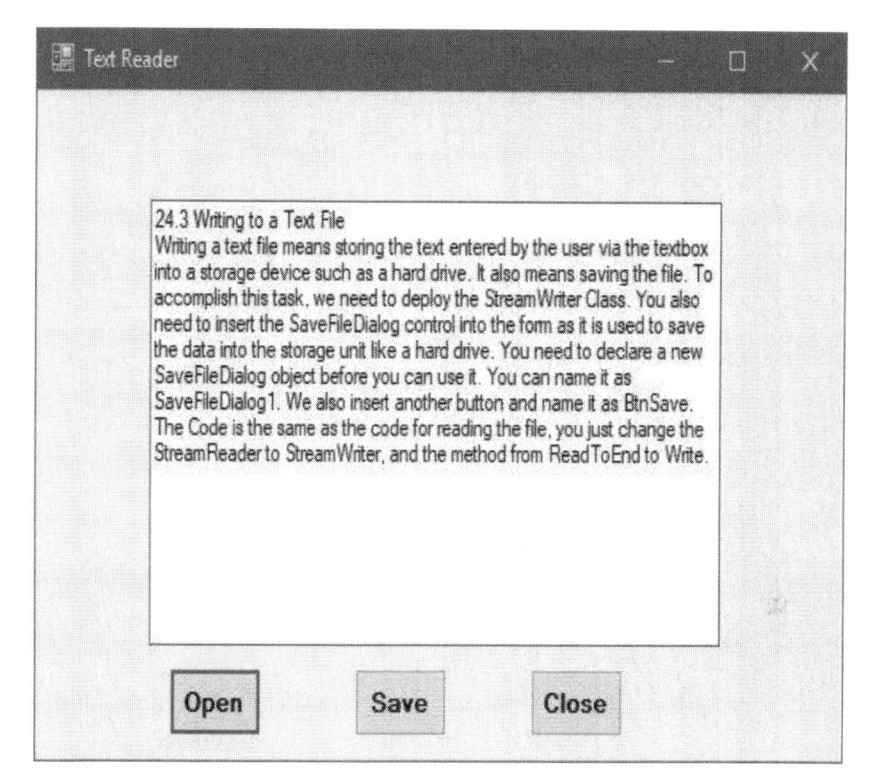

Figure 24.4

When you click the save button, the program will prompt you to key in a filename and the text will be saved as a text file. You can close the text editor and reopen the text file saved by you.

Summary

- In Section 24.1, you have understood the concepts of reading and writing a text file
- In section 24.2, you have learned how to write code to read a text file
- In Section 24.3, you have learned how to write code to write a text file.

Chapter 25 Building Console Applications

25.1 Introduction

In Visual Basic 2019, you can build console applications besides the Windows Form Applications. To start creating a console application, start Visual Basic 2019 and choose Console App(.NET Core) in the new project window, as shown in Figure 25.1 below:

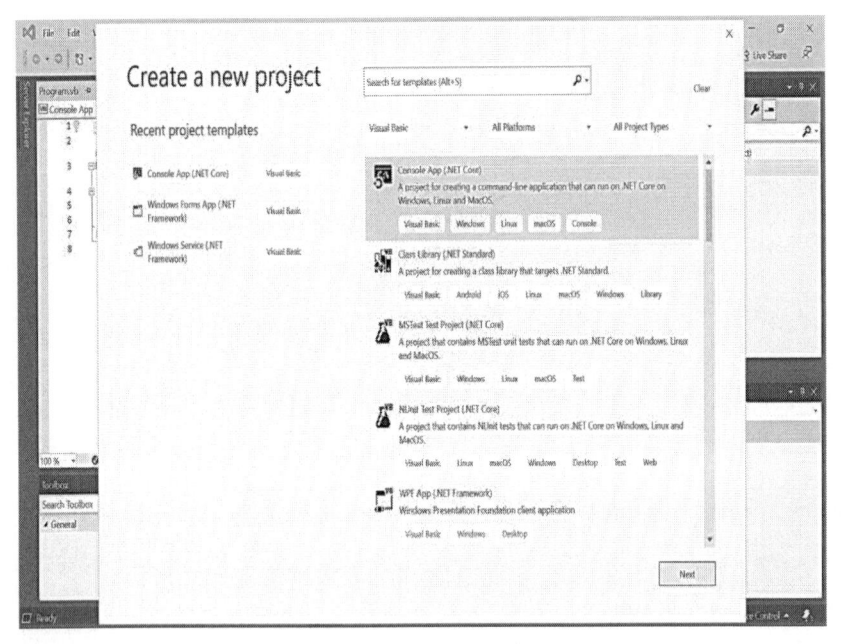

Figure 25.1

Retain the name as ConsoleApp or change it to the name of your choice.

Now, click on Console Application to bring up the code window. The default code is

```vb
Module Program

    Sub Main(args As String())

        Console.WriteLine("Hello World!")

    End Sub

End Module
```

as shown in Figure 25.2 below:

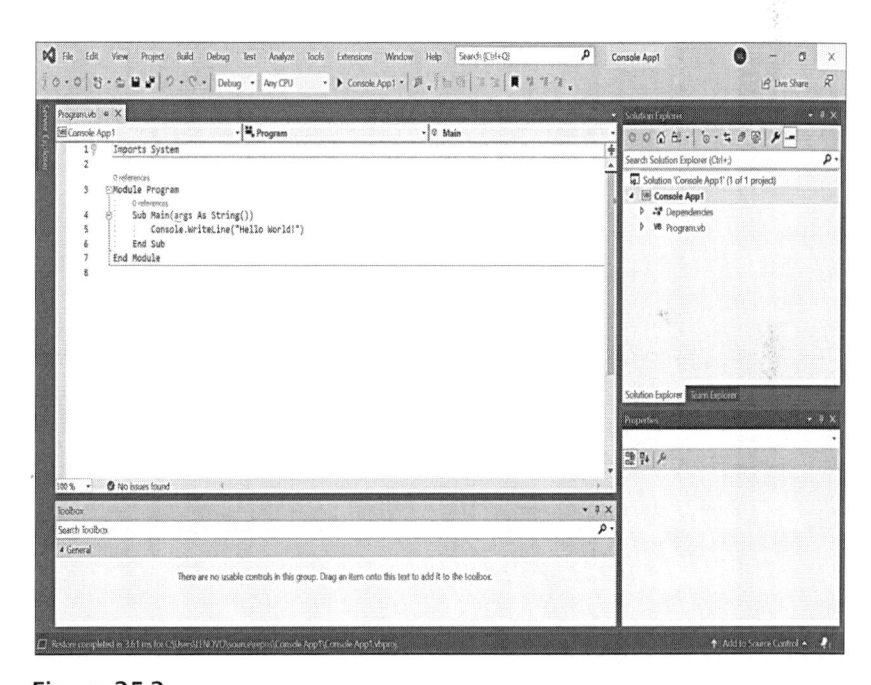

Figure 25.2

The console code window comprises modules, where the main module is module 1. You can add other modules by clicking on

Project on the menu bar and click Add Module, as shown in Figure 25.3 below:

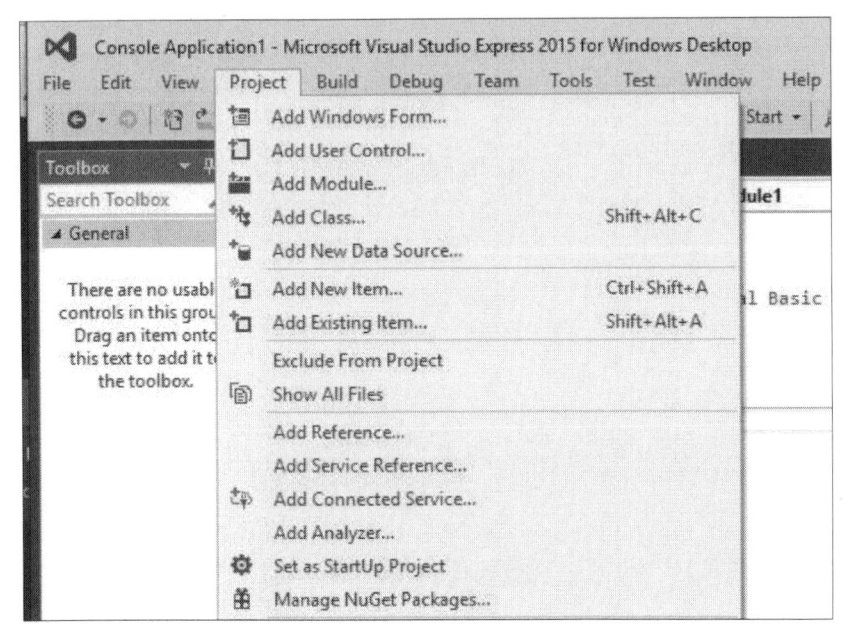

Figure 25.3

Now run the default code, the output is as shown in a command prompt window in Figure 25.4.

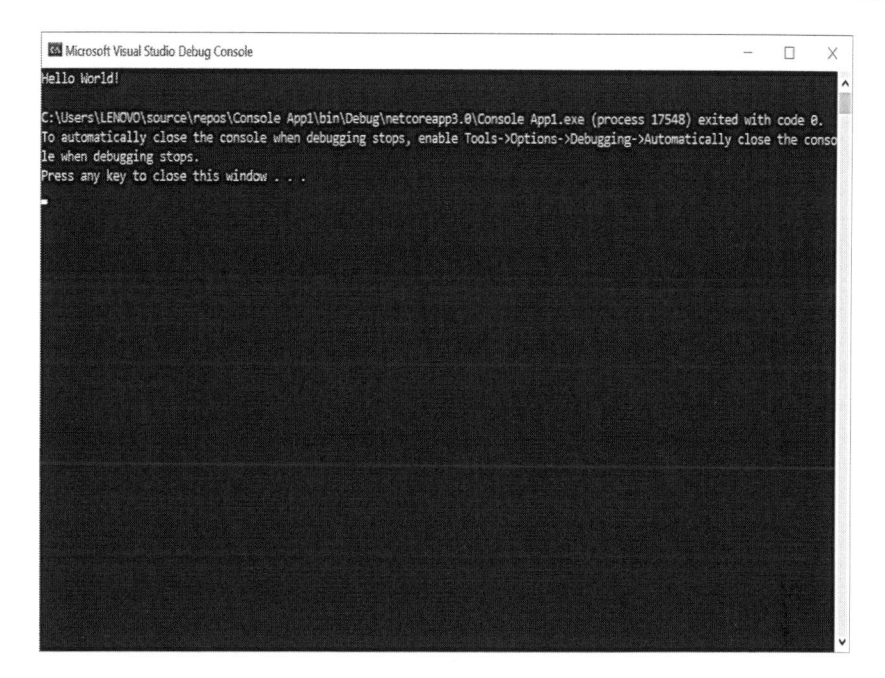

Figure 25.4

Example 25.1: Displaying a Message

The following program will perform a basic arithmetic operation.

```vb
Module Program

    Sub Main(args As String())

        Dim a, b, sum As Integer

        a = 2

        b = 3

        sum = a + b

        Console.WriteLine(sum)

    End Sub
```

End Module

The output is as shown in Figure 25.4

Figure 25.4 The output in command prompt console

25.2 Creating a Text File Writer in Console

We can write a Console app to create a text file in your hard drive or other storage devices. In order to write a text file to a hard drive or any storage devices, we need to use the StreamWriter class, as we have done the same thing in Lesson 24. The statement to write a text file with a file name mytext.txt to your hard drive is as follows:

Dim objWriter As New System.IO.StreamWriter("C:\Users\Documents\vb2019\mytext.txt")

It will create a text file in the specified location. In addition, we use the WriteLine() method to write text to the text file.

Example 25.2

```
Module Program

Sub Main(args As String())

Dim objWriter As New System.IO.StreamWriter
("C:\Users\Documents
\vb2019\mytext.txt")
objWriter.WriteLine("Welcome to Visual Basic 2019")
objWriter.WriteLine("Please follow our  Visual Basic 2019 Lessons")
objWriter.WriteLine("The Lessons are interesting")
objWriter.Close()
objWriter.Dispose()
End Sub
End Module
```

The text file as seen in the Notepad is what as shown in Figure 25.5

![Figure 25.5 - Notepad window showing mytext.txt with content: "Welcome to Visual Basic 2019 / Please follow our Visual Basic 2019 Lessons / The Lessons are interesting"]

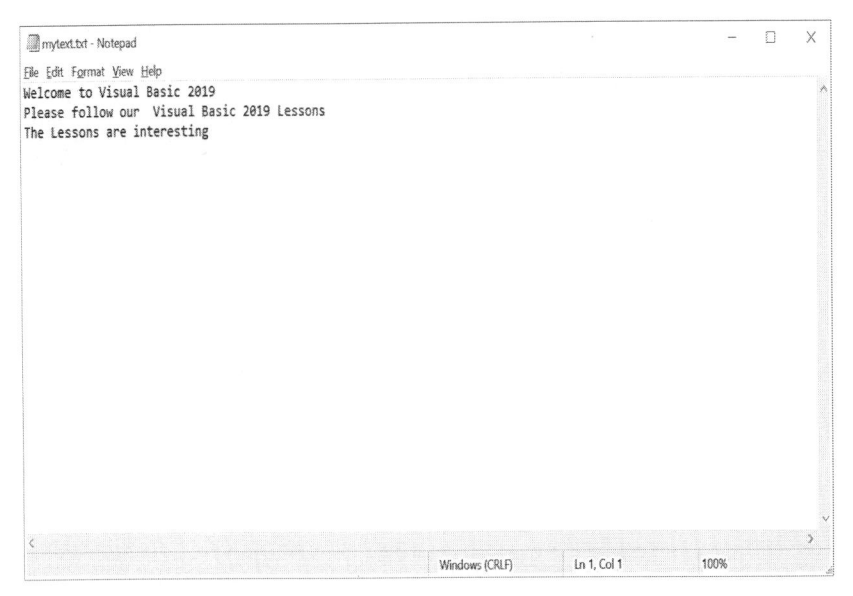

Figure 25.5

25.3 Creating a Text File Reader in Console

In order to read a text file from your hard drive or any storage devices, we need to use the `StreamReader` class, as we have done the same thing in Lesson 24.

Example 25.3
Module Program

Sub Main(args As String())

  Dim objReader As New System.IO.StreamReader("C:\Users\Documents\vb2019\mytext.txt")
    Dim strLine As String
    'Reading the first line
    strLine = objReader.ReadLine
    'Read until the end of the file.

```
        Do While Not strLine Is Nothing
            'Write the line to the Console window.
            Console.WriteLine(strLine)
            'Read the next line.
            strLine = objReader.ReadLine
        Loop


    End Sub
```

The output

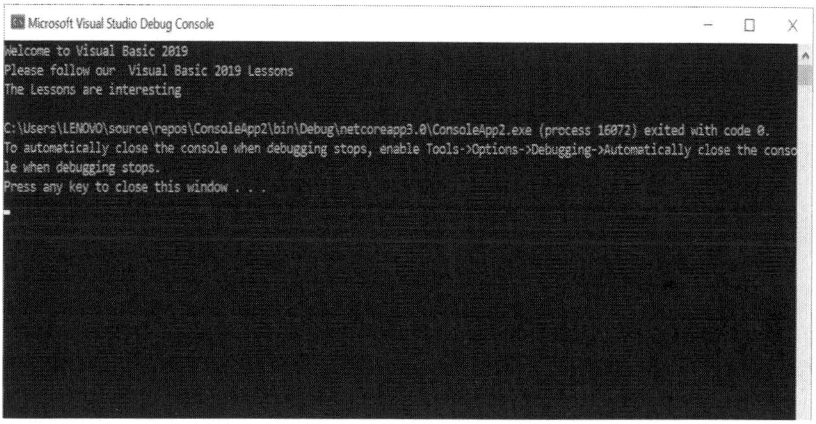

Figure 25.6

25.4 Creating a Console App using If...Then...Else

We can use If...Then...Else to create an Arithmetic program in the Console App.

Example 25.4

```
Module Program

    Sub Main(args As String())


        Dim answer As Boolean

        Dim x, y, sum As Single

        x = 5

        y = 100

        sum = x + y

        If sum = 105 Then

            answer = True

        Else

            answer = False

        End If

            Console.Write(answer)

    End Sub

End Module
```

When you run the application, you will be asked to enter a first number in an input box, as shown in Figure 25.7

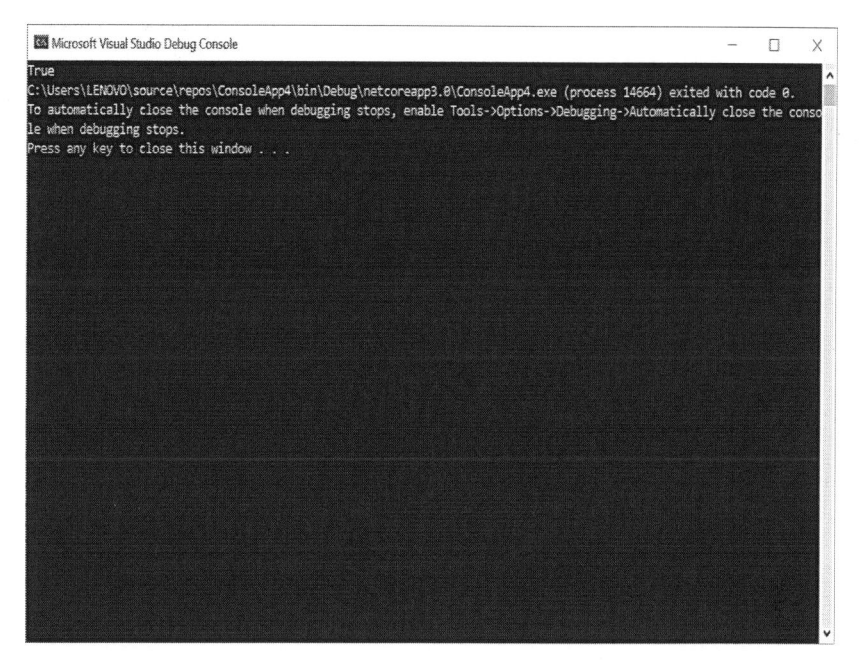

Figure 25.7

Summary

- In Section 25.1, you have created a Console App that display a Message
- In section 25.2, you have built a Console App that creates a text file
- In Section 25.3, you have built a Console App that read a text file.
- In Section 25.4 You have built a Console App that performs arithmetic calculations involving the usage of If...Then...Else

Chapter 26 Creating Menu Bar and Toolbar

In previous chapters, we have learned how to create buttons that will trigger an action or a series of actions when the user clicks on them. However, most standard Windows applications come with very few clickable buttons, instead, they provide menu bar and toolbar so that the user can click on the items on the menu bar or the icons on the toolbar. Besides, the user can also use the shortcut keys to access the items using the keyboard. In this chapter, we will show you how to create the menu items on the menu bar and the icons on the toolbar

26.1 Creating Menu Items on the Menu Bar

In this section, we will show you how to create Menu Items on the Menu Bar. We will use the text editor we have created in chapter 24 to demonstrates how to create the menu bar. Besides, we will delete the buttons as we will develop the menu bar and toolbar for navigation. Now, open the text editor in the design mode. Next, insert the MenuStrip control into the form. You will notice that the MenuStrip control will not appear on the form, instead, it lies below the form and remains invisible at runtime, as shown in Figure 26.1.

You will also notice that a text box will appear on the top of the form that displays the tip Type Here, this is where you can type in the top-level menu item. Here, we type &File in the text box, the ampersand sign is to display the menu item File with F underlined where the user can use hotkey Alt+F to access the item. After you type in the first top level item, the second text box will appear for you to enter the second item. You can enter as many top-level menu items as the form can accommodate. For our example, we create three top level menu items, File, Help and About. Next,

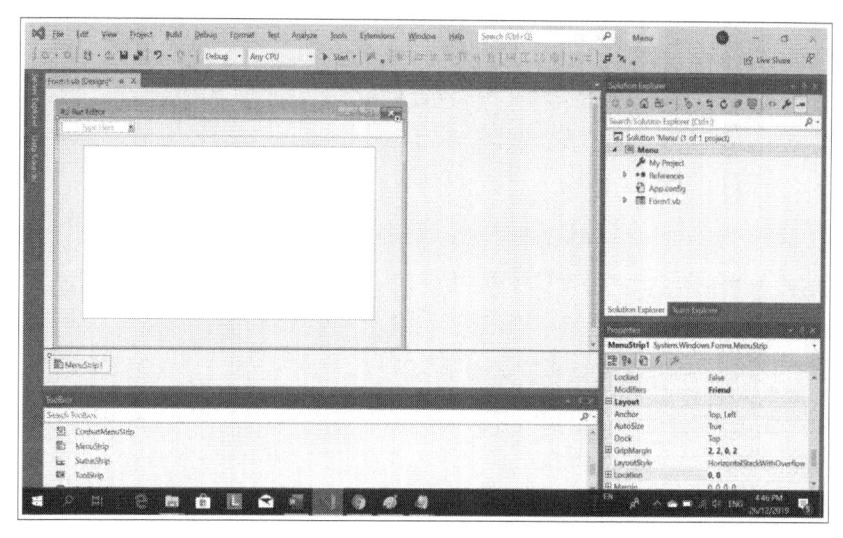

Figure 26.1

We shall now create a few items under the File menu item. To do this, click on the File item and you will get a drop-down text box will the Type Here tip, Enter &New as the first item. After you enter the first item, another drop-down text box below the New item will appear, enter Sa&ve in this text box. Enter &Open and E&xit for the next two text boxes. Now your design interface should look like the image shown in Figure 26.2. Notice the N is underlined for New; v is underlined for Save, O is underlined for Open and x is underlined for Exit.

Next, we need to write code for all the menu items so they can respond to events like clicking the mouse button or pressing a key on the keyboard. Before we write code for the items, let create two sub procedures first. One of them is to create a text file by writing the file to the hard drive or other storage devices and the other one is to open a text file from the hard drive or other storage devices. Let's name the first procedure as `WriteFile()` and enter the following code:

```
Sub WriteFile()
Dim FileWriter As StreamWriter
Dim results As DialogResult
Dim saveFileDialog1 As New SaveFileDialog()
   results = saveFileDialog1.ShowDialog
If results = DialogResult.OK Then
  FileWriter = New StreamWriter(saveFileDialog1.FileName, False)
  FileWriter.Write(TxtEditor.Text)
  FileWriter.Close()
End If
End Sub
```

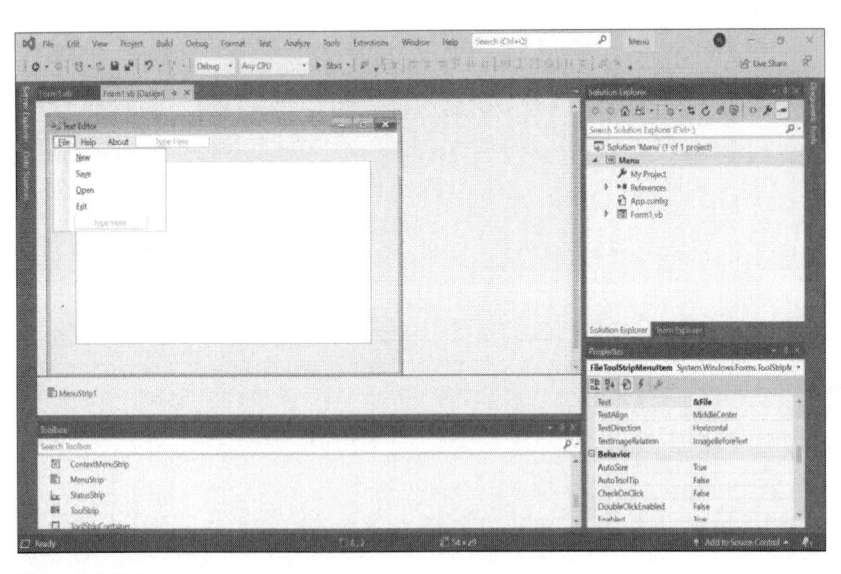

Figure 26.2

Next, create another sub procedure `ReadFile()` and enter the following code:

```
Sub ReadFile()
Dim FileReader As StreamReader
```

```vb
    Dim results As DialogResult
    Dim OpenFileDialog1 As New OpenFileDialog()
        results = OpenFileDialog1.ShowDialog
    If results = DialogResult.OK Then
        FileReader = New StreamReader(OpenFileDialog1.FileName)
        TxtEditor.Text = FileReader.ReadToEnd()
        FileReader.Close()
    End If
End Sub
```

For the New item, enter the following code:

```vb
Private Sub ToolStripNew_Click(sender As Object,
 e As EventArgs) Handles ToolStripNew.Click
      TxtEditor.Text = ""
End Sub
```

For the Save item, enter the following code:

```vb
Private Sub ToolStripSave_Click(sender As Object,
e As EventArgs) Handles ToolStripSave.Click
      Me.WriteFile()
End Sub
```

For the Open item, enter the following code:

```vb
Private Sub ToolStripOpen_Click(sender As Object,
 e As EventArgs)  Handles ToolStripRead.Click
      Me.ReadFile()
End Sub
```

For the Exit item, enter the following code:

```
Private Sub ExitToolStripMenuItem_Click(sender As Object,
e As EventArgs) Handles ExitToolStripMenuItem.Click
    TxtEditor.Dispose()
    Me.Close()
End Sub
```

For the Help button, enter the following code

```
Private Sub HelpToolStripMenuItem_Click(sender As Object,
e As EventArgs) Handles HelpToolStripMenuItem.Click
MsgBox(
"Type some text in the editor and click save to create a text file.
Click New to start a new text file. Click
Open to open a text file.")
End Sub
```

For the About button, just enter the text " Text Editor Ver 1.0" in the drop-down menu item, as shown in Figure 26.3

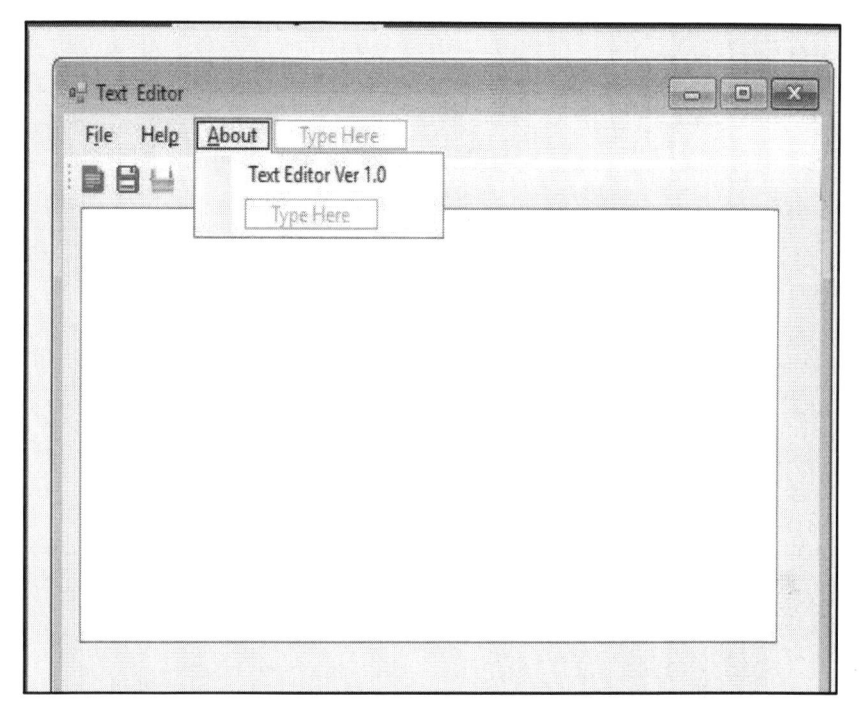

Figure 26.3

Now , run the program and enter some text, as shown in Figure 26.4

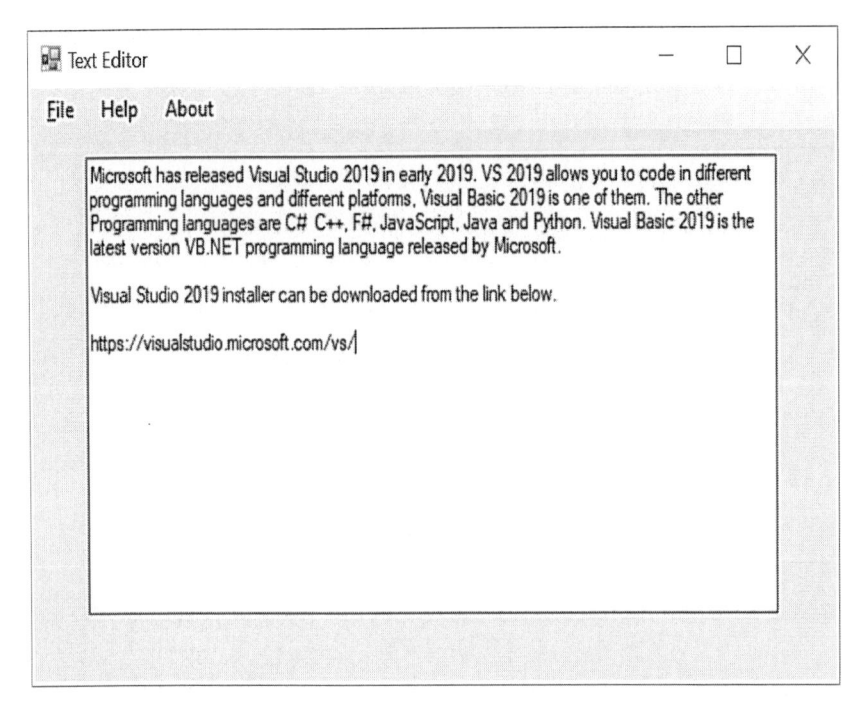

Figure 26.4

Next, click on File to bring up the drop-down menu, as shown in Figure 26.5.

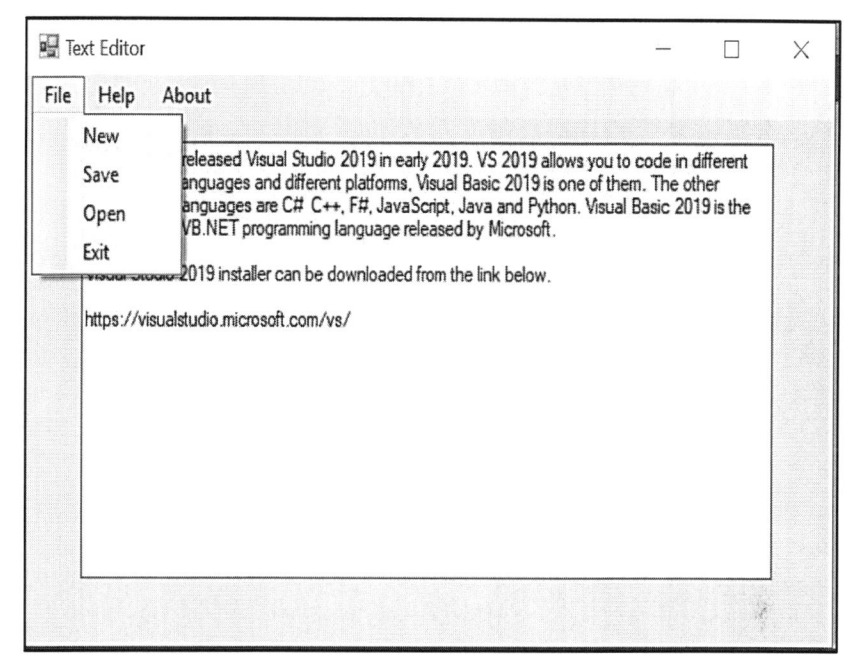

Figure 26.5

When you click on the Save button, the Save As dialog will appear, as shown in Figure 26.6. Save the file as vb2019me.txt.

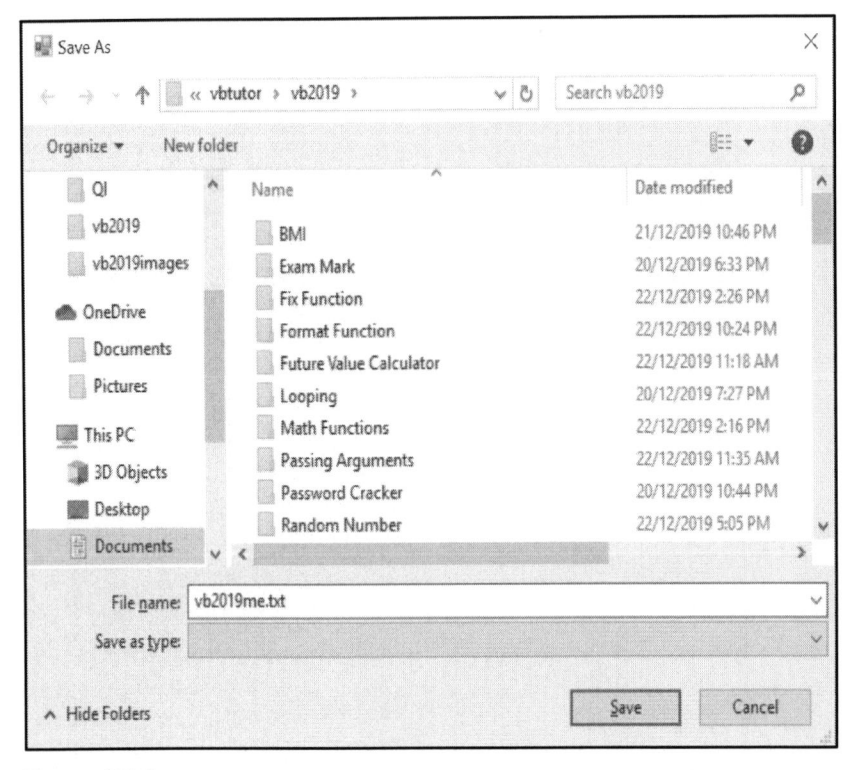

Figure 26.6

You can now click New to clear the text and type some other text and save another file. You can also open a text file by clicking the open button, and the Open dialog will appear, as shown in Figure 26.7

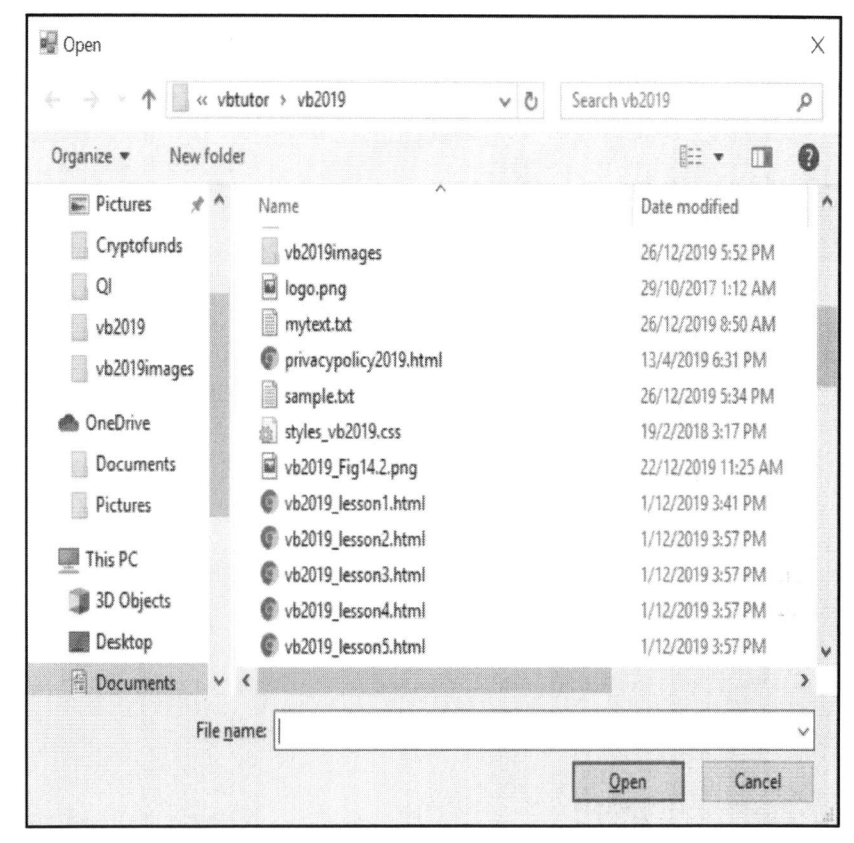

Figure 26.7

Let select mytext.txt and click the Open button, you will open this text file in the text editor, as shown in Figure 26.8

Figure 26.8

If you want to show the opened file name appear as the caption of the form, you enter the following line under the ReadFile() sub procedure,

   Me.Text = OpenFileDialog1.FileName

Now, when you open a text file, its name will appear as the caption of the text editor, as shown in Figure 26.9

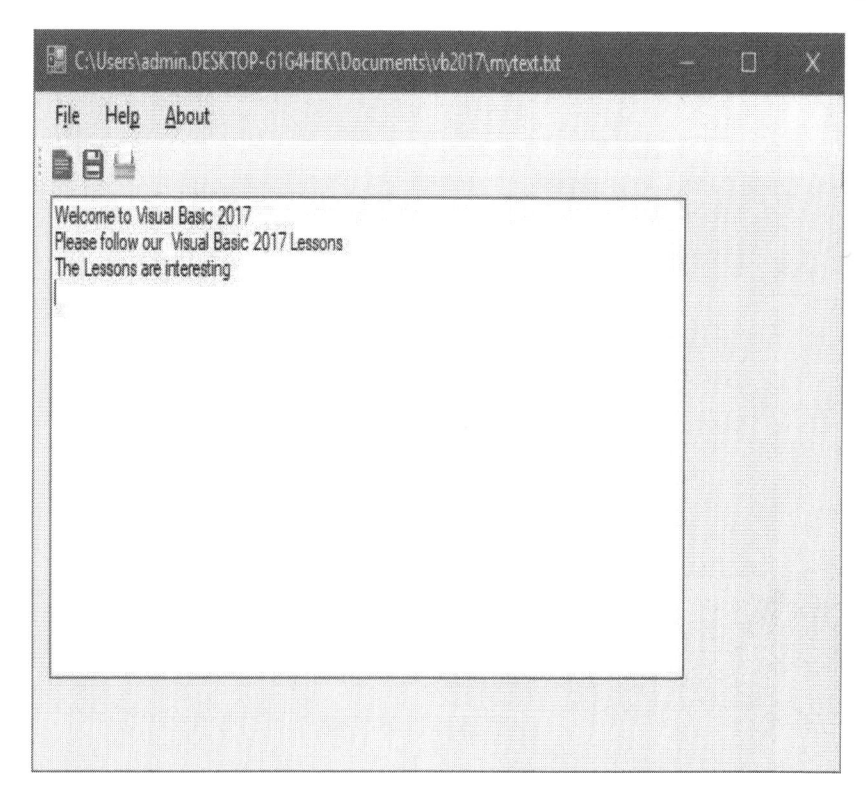

Figure 26.9

26.2 Creating the Toolbar

To create the toolbar, you need to insert the ToolStrip Control into the form. It will stay below the form and remains invisible at runtime, as shown in Figure 26.10

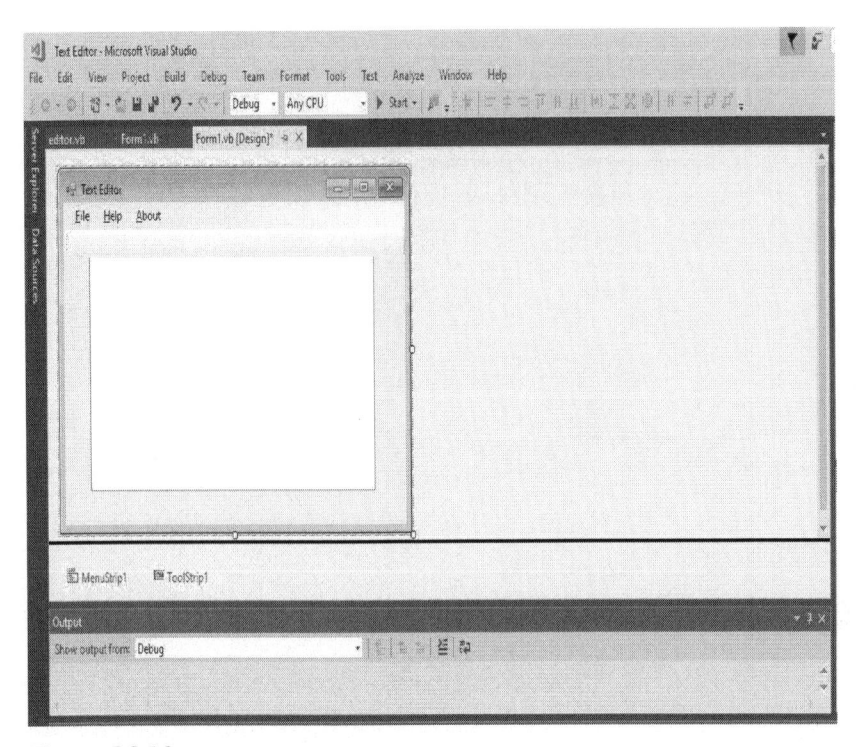

Figure 26.10

Now, click on the far left corner of the form just below the menu bar, click to bring up the first ToolStrip button with the default name ToolStripButton1. You can rename it to ToolStripNew. Now click on the image property to bring up the Select Source dialog and import an image as icon, as shown in Figure 26.11

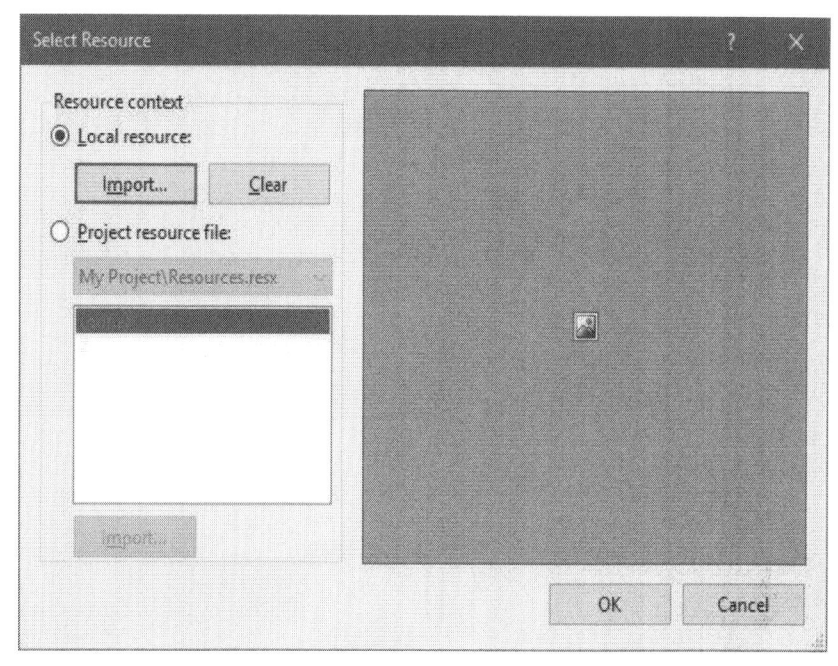

Figure 26.11

After opening an image folder and selected an image file, the image will appear in the Select Source window, as shown in Figure 26.12

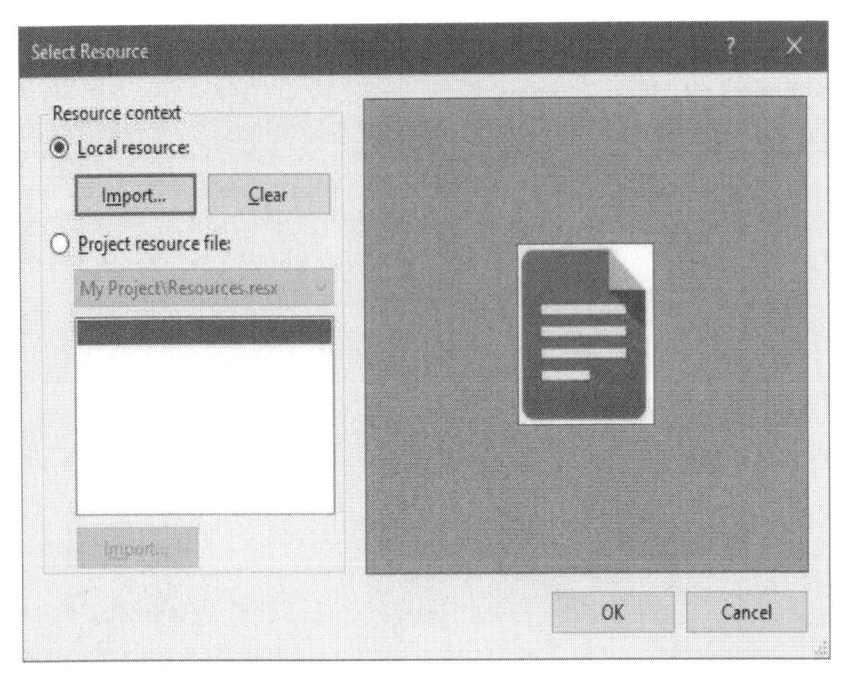

Figure 26.12

After clicking the OK button, the image will appear as an icon to replace the default toolstrip button on the toolbar, as shown in Figure 26.13

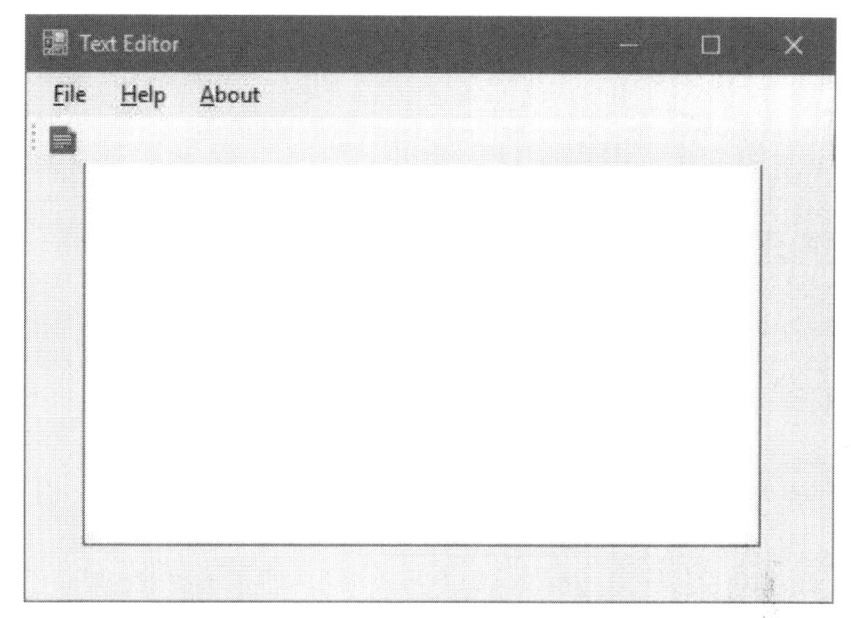

Figure 26.13

In addition, you might want to add the Tooltip Text in the properties window to the toolstrip button, so that the tip will appear when the mouse hover about this toolstrip button on the toolbar. You add the Tooltip text as shown in Figure 26.14

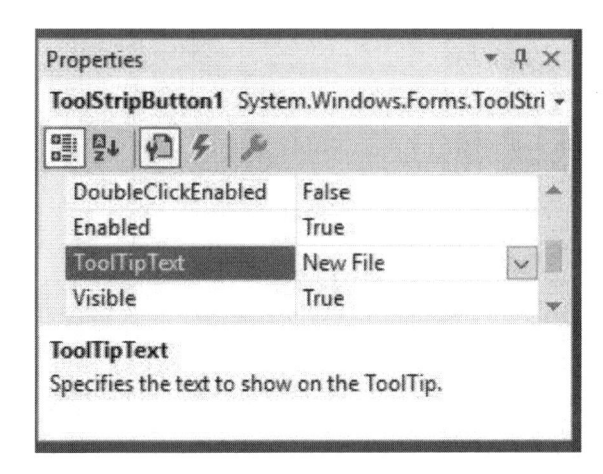

Figure 26.14

When you run the application and place the mouse over the 'New' toolstrip button, the tip "New File" will appear, as shown in Figure 26.15

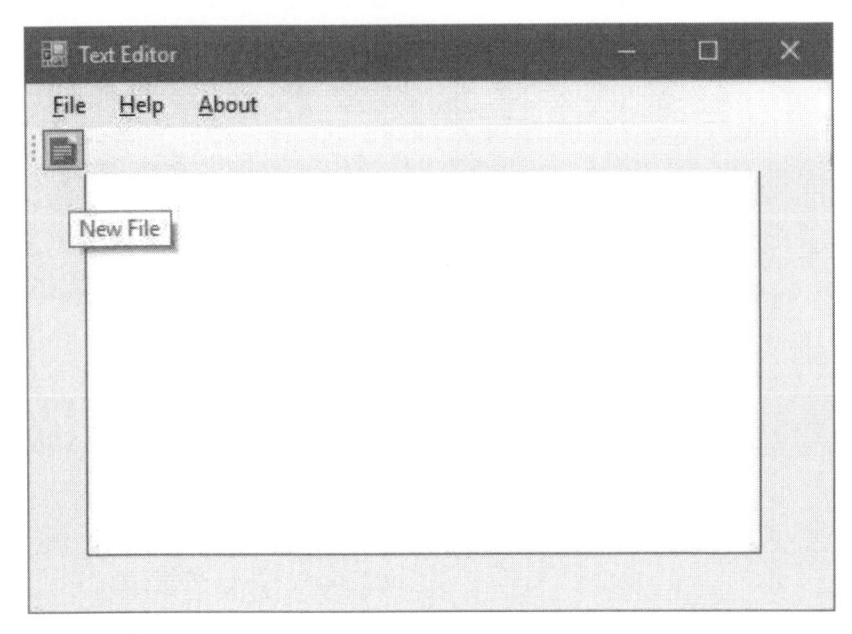

Figure 26.15

Next, continue to add two more toolbar buttons (one for saving file and the other one for opening file) on the toolbar until you obtain the design interface, as shown in Figure 26.16.

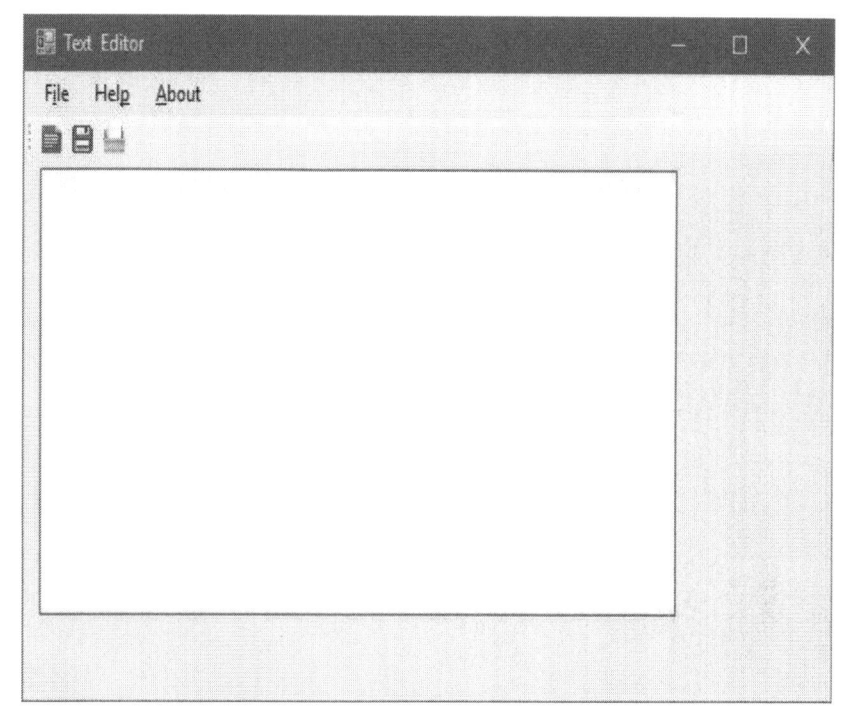

Figure 26.16

Now, it is time to write code for the three toolstrip buttons on the toolbar.

For the 'New' toolbar button, enter the following code:

Private Sub ToolStripNew_Click(sender As Object,
e As EventArgs) Handles ToolStripNew.Click
    TxtEditor.Text = ""
End Sub

For the "Save" toolbar button, enter the following Code:

Private Sub ToolStripSave_Click(sender As Object,

```
   e As EventArgs) Handles ToolStripSave.Click
       Me.WriteFile()
   End Sub
```

For the "Open" toolbar button, enter the following Code:

```
   Private Sub OpenToolStripMenuItem_Click(sender As Object,
     e As EventArgs) Handles OpenToolStripMenuItem.Click
       Me.ReadFile()
   End Sub
```

Finally, you have added both the functional menu bar and toolbar. You can add more menu items and toolstrip buttons and experiment with them.

Summary

- In Section 26.1, you have learned how to create a menu bar by adding top-level menus as well as menu items. You have also learned how to write code for the menu items.
- In section 262, you have built the toolbar by adding toolstrip buttons to it. You have also learned how to write code for the toolstrip buttons.

Chapter 27 Deploying your VB 2019 Applications

Having developed a Visual Basic 2019 application, you might want to publish and distribute it to the users.

Before deploying your application, you need to test and debug your application to ensure it is error-free.

Publishing your application is a quite easy procedure, it just requires a few clicks. First, load your application in Visual Basic 2019. In this example, we wish to publish the Draw Text application. In the Visual Basic 2019 IDE, choose Build and then select Publish Draw text, as shown in Figure 27.1

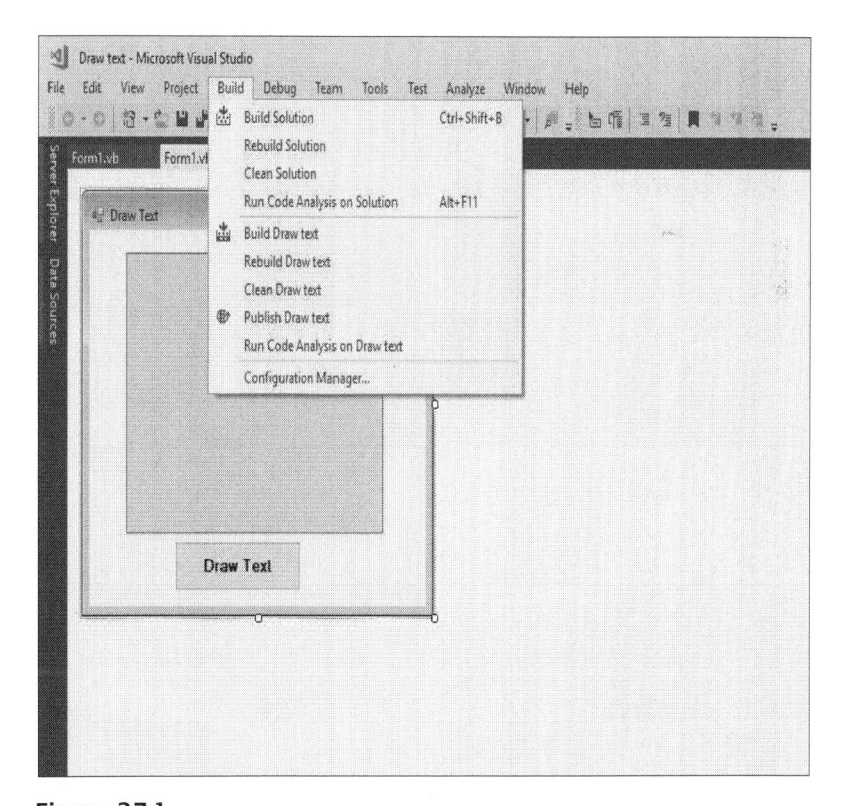

Figure 27.1

After clicking Publish Draw Text, the Publish Wizard will ask you to choose a location that you want to publish this application. You may publish the application on your local drive or to a remote location via FTP, as shown in Figure 27.2.

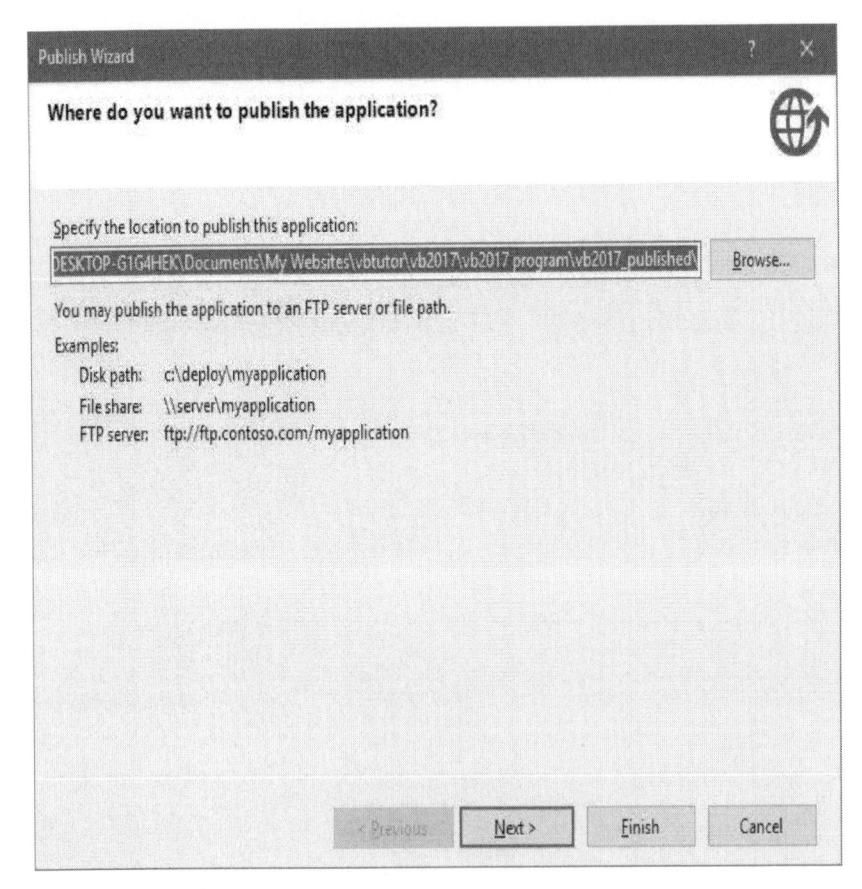

Figure 27.2

Click the Next button to continue. Now, the Publish Wizard will ask you how users will install the application. There are three options, from a website, from a UNC path or file share and from a CD-ROM or DVD-ROM. In this example, we choose CD-ROM or DVD-ROM, as shown in Figure 27.3

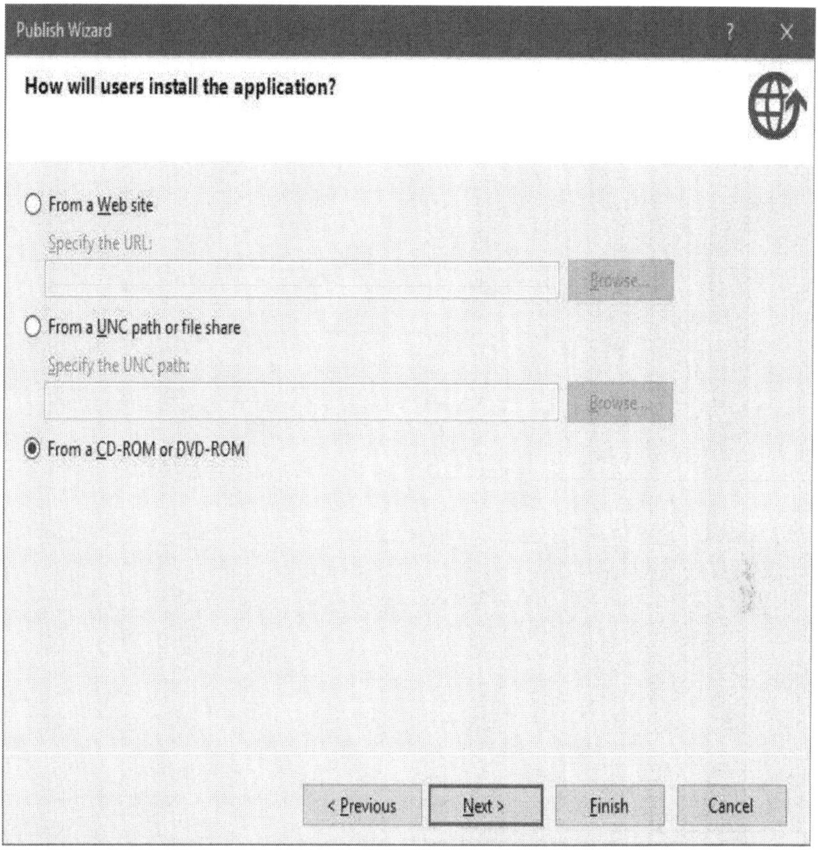
Publish Wizard
How will users install the application?
From a Web site
Specify the URL:
Browse...
From a UNC path or file share
Specify the UNC path:
Browse...
From a CD-ROM or DVD-ROM
< Previous
Next >
Finish
Cancel

Figure 27.3

You may click the Next button to continue with the Publish Wizard or the Finish button to complete the publishing process. If you click the Next button, the Publish Wizard will ask where will the application check for updates. In our example, we choose that the application will not check for updates, as shown in Figure 27.4

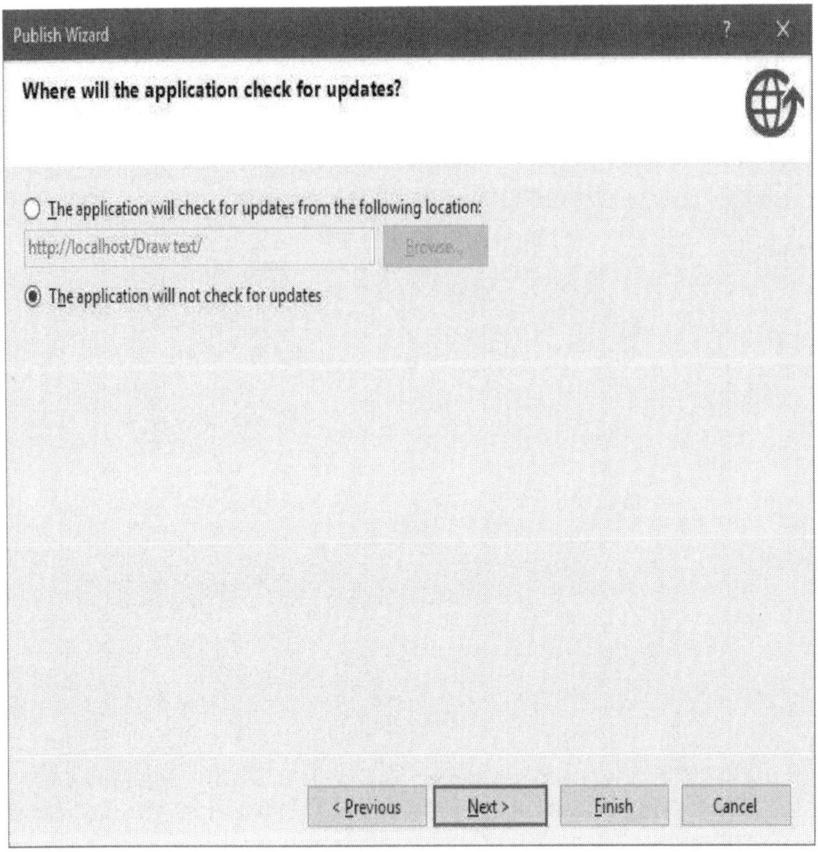

Figure 27.4

After clicking the Next button, the final screen of the Publish Wizard will show you where the application will be published to, as shown in Figure 27.5

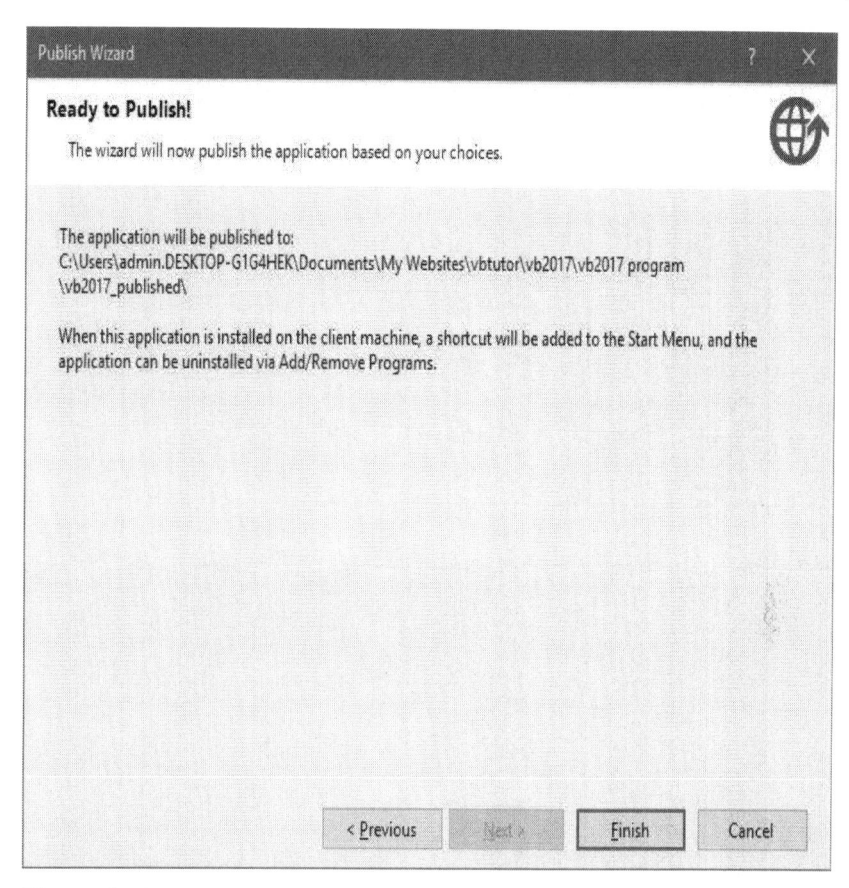

Figure 27.5

Upon clicking the Finish button, the installation files and folder will be saved to the specified location. In our examples, the folder is Application files and the files are Draw text.application and setup.exe. You may now burn the folder and files into a CD-ROM, DVD-ROM or upload them to a website for distribution to the users.

Summary

- In this chapter, you have learned how to create installation files to deploy your Visual Basic 2019 Applications.

Index

,

, keypress · 36

A

Add() method · 46, 47, 50, 59
ADO.NET · 234, 235, 242, 243
animation · 64, 218, 224
array · 82, 83, 84, 85, 87, 186, 187, 188, 191
Arrays · 82, 83
ASCII code · 102

B

`BackColor` · 25, 29, 30, 34, 170
background color · 25, 27, 34, 43, 64, 169
BMI Calculator · 90, 134
Boolean · 73, 77, 279
Boolean data types · 73
button · 22, 23, 32, 36, 37, 41, 42, 45, 49, 51, 52, 55, 56, 62, 64, 65, 68, 81, 89, 99, 107, 109, 114, 116, 117, 128, 130, 148, 161, 167, 169, 171, 181, 185, 225, 226, 229, 235, 236, 248, 249, 254, 256, 265, 266, 269, 271, 283, 286, 288, 289, 290, 293, 295, 296, 297, 298, 300, 301, 302, 303
ByRef · 138, 139, 140, 141
ByVal · 76, 89, 90, 91, 93, 94, 96, 97, 100, 106, 113, 116, 117, 119, 125, 126, 138, 139, 140, 141, 180, 257, 259, 261

C

`Case IS` · 117
Check box · 161
checkbox · 32, 161, 166, 167
Chr function · 102

Class · 38, 39, 111, 178, 179, 180, 265, 266, 269, 270

click · 16, 21, 23, 32, 34, 36, 38, 44, 45, 56, 57, 61, 64, 65, 67, 68, 107, 109, 130, 148, 161, 166, 179, 181, 185, 224, 235, 237, 240, 241, 249, 271, 272, 273, 282, 283, 286, 287, 288, 289, 290, 293, 301

Close() method · 266

code window · 23, 29, 33, 36, 38, 52, 134, 180, 272, 273

combobox · 32, 57, 61, 62, 63

ComboBox · 41, 57, 59

command button · 265

conditional operators · 104, 106, 110, 115, 121

ConnectionString · 243, 245, 250

Console · 272, 273, 275, 276, 278, 279, 280, 281

Const · 80, 161, 164

constant · 71, 74, 80, 81

controls · 21, 25, 32, 34, 35, 36, 40, 41, 67, 161, 183

Create a new project · 18, 19, 20

Creating Motion · 224

D

Dash · 196

DashDot · 196

DashDotDot · 196, 197

DashStyle value · 196, 197

data · 41, 71, 73, 74, 75, 78, 79, 82, 93, 94, 104, 105, 121, 138, 177, 178, 233, 234, 235, 240, 242, 243, 244, 245, 249, 254, 256, 264, 265, 269

database · 233, 234, 235, 237, 238, 240, 241, 242, 243, 249, 254, 256, 262, 263, 264

DataGridView · 254

DataTable · 234, 243, 244, 245, 250

Date data types · 73

Declaring Variables · 75

dialog box · 21, 23, 64, 67, 68, 78, 161

DialogResult · 68, 265, 266, 270, 284

Dim statement · 75, 83

Do Loop · 123, 126, 127

Do While · 123, 278

`Do...Loop` · 49

`Do...Loop Until` · 49

double-click · 36

drag-drop · 36

DrawCurve method · 191

DrawCurve() method · 188

`DrawEllipse` method · 199, 201

DrawLine method · 185

DrawPie method · 210

`DrawRectangle` method · 195

DrawString method · 203

drop-down list · 25, 36, 57

E

ellipse · 183, 198, 199, 201, 211, 213, 214, 217

encapsulation · 177

`End Sub` · 23, 29, 31, 38, 39, 42, 43, 47, 48, 50, 52, 53, 54, 56, 59, 60, 62, 63, 67, 68, 76, 78, 80, 84, 85, 86, 89, 90, 91, 93, 94, 96, 97, 99, 101, 106, 108, 111, 114, 117, 118, 119, 120, 125, 127, 128, 129, 131, 132, 135, 137, 139, 143, 144, 145, 147, 148, 149, 152, 155, 156, 157, 159, 162, 164, 165, 168, 170, 174, 175, 179, 181, 185, 187, 189, 192, 194, 197, 200, 201, 204, 206, 208, 210, 211, 212, 214, 215, 217, 219, 220, 222, 225, 227, 230, 245, 246, 250, 251, 252, 253, 255, 257, 259, 262, 267, 270, 273, 275, 277, 278, 280, 284, 285, 286, 297, 298

Error handling · 172

event procedure · 36, 38, 128

event-driven programming · 14, 36

event-driven programming language · 14, 36

F

`FillEllipse` · 212, 214

`FillPie` · 212, 216, 217

FillPolygon · 212, 215

FillRectangle · 212

fixed-length string · 76

FixedSingle · 64

floating point numbers · 71

For...Next · 55, 121

For...Next loop · 55, 121

Formatting Date and time · 156, 158

function · 23, 38, 41, 43, 44, 47, 57, 60, 88, 96, 97, 98, 100, 101, 102, 103, 107, 130, 134, 138, 139, 141, 142, 143, 145, 146, 147, 148, 149, 150, 151, 153, 160, 190, 192, 193, 218, 221, 260

G

geometric progression · 49

graphics · 64, 183, 185, 208, 210, 217, 226

Groupbox · 169

I

If ...Then...ElseIf · 106

If...End If · 55

If...Then...Else · 104, 106, 107, 112, 131, 167, 279, 281

If...Then...ElseIf · 112, 113

inheritance · 177

inherits · 39

InputBox · 47, 48, 53, 60, 86, 99, 101, 107, 181, 205, 206

instant of a class · 39

intellisense · 212

L

label · 32, 43, 51, 55, 56, 62, 63, 99, 116, 142, 144, 164, 167, 172, 173, 218, 229, 230, 258, 260

Lcase function · 102
listbox · 32, 47, 48, 49, 53, 55, 56, 63
ListBox · 41, 44, 45, 46
Literals · 73
load · 36, 38, 64, 67, 69, 70, 229, 299
logical operators · 104, 105, 106, 115
Loop Until · 50, 124, 228
Loop While · 123

M

Math · 142, 143, 144, 145, 147, 149, 193, 257, 259, 261
Math class · 142, 145
mathematical functions · 142
mathematical operators · 88
`MaximizeBox` property · 218
menu bar · 32, 33, 179, 273, 282, 293, 298
MenuStrip control · 282
Microsoft SQL server · 233, 234, 242
Mid Function · 98
MsgBox · 23, 38, 39, 42, 76, 78, 80, 84, 85, 93, 94, 95, 96, 97, 107, 108, 114, 131, 139, 286
Multiline property · 266
multimedia · 64
MultipleSimple · 55

N

non-numeric data type · 71
numeric data · 41, 43, 71, 73, 81, 94, 104, 105, 173, 256

O

object · 14, 29, 39, 46, 73, 177, 178, 180, 182, 183, 184, 185, 190, 195, 196, 199, 201, 203, 205, 208, 210, 212, 213, 215, 216, 217, 224, 225, 226, 234, 242, 243, 244, 257, 265, 269

object-oriented programming · 14, 39, 177

OleDbConnection · 242

On Error GoTo · 172, 173

OpenFileDialog · 67, 70, 265, 266, 284

P

Pen Object · 184, 196

picture box · 32, 34, 64, 65, 67, 69, 184, 193, 205, 224, 226

Polygon · 207, 215

polymorphism · 177, 178

Private · 23, 29, 30, 38, 39, 41, 43, 46, 47, 50, 51, 52, 53, 55, 56, 59, 60, 62, 67, 68, 76, 78, 79, 80, 84, 85, 86, 89, 90, 91, 93, 94, 96, 97, 99, 100, 106, 111, 113, 116, 117, 119, 125, 126, 129, 131, 132, 134, 135, 137, 138, 139, 142, 144, 145, 146, 148, 149, 152, 154, 156, 157, 159, 161, 162, 163, 164, 165, 167, 169, 173, 175, 178, 179, 181, 185, 187, 189, 191, 193, 196, 200, 201, 204, 206, 208, 209, 211, 212, 214, 215, 216, 219, 220, 222, 224, 227, 230, 242, 244, 245, 250, 251, 252, 253, 254, 255, 256, 257, 258, 259, 266, 270, 285, 286, 297, 298

project configuration page · 20

properties windows · 35, 55

Public · 38, 39, 79, 80, 83, 107, 111, 134, 178, 179, 180, 257, 259, 261, 265, 266, 270

Pythagorean Theorem · 90

Q

quadratic curve · 190

Quadratic Curve · 190

R

radio button · 32, 167
Radio Button · 167
ReadToEnd method · 266
RGB color code · 26
Rnd · 78, 107, 111, 130, 131, 132, 147, 148, 150, 221, 222, 226, 227, 229, 230

S

SaveFileDialog · 269, 270, 284
Select Case · 115, 116, 118, 119, 121, 226, 227, 230
Sin function · 193
Sine Curve · 192
SizeMode · 64
Solid · 196
Solution Explorer · 21, 25, 33
SQL Server Management Studio · 235, 236, 241
SqlCommandBuilder · 243, 244, 245, 250
SqlConnection · 234, 242, 243, 245, 250, 255, 256, 257, 258, 261
SqlDataAdpater · 243
Static · 79
StreamReader · 264, 265, 266, 269, 278, 284
StreamWriter · 264, 269, 270, 276, 277, 283
StretchImage · 64
string · 39, 41, 43, 73, 74, 76, 77, 78, 93, 94, 95, 96, 98, 102, 103, 105, 172, 240
String · 41, 45, 51, 57, 62, 73, 76, 77, 83, 84, 85, 86, 93, 96, 97, 99, 100, 111, 113, 116, 167, 169, 178, 179, 206, 244, 246, 250, 254, 255, 256, 257, 258, 260, 261, 273, 275, 276, 278, 279
String Collection Editor · 45, 51, 57, 62
sub procedure · 128, 133, 134, 226, 245, 247, 284, 291
suffixes · 73, 81
SweepAngle · 210, 216

syntax · 41, 43, 46, 50, 53, 75, 76, 77, 80, 83, 96, 97, 98, 100, 101, 102, 103, 106, 107, 124, 142, 143, 151, 153, 158, 172, 185, 186, 188, 190, 191, 193, 195, 196, 201, 207, 208, 210, 212, 213, 215, 216, 226, 229, 242, 243, 260, 266

System.Windows.Forms.Form · 39

T

textbox · 32, 116, 142, 144, 266, 269

TextBox · 41, 43

TimeOfDay() · 218

timer · 32, 130, 157, 218, 219, 221, 224, 226, 229, 230

Toolbox · 21, 32, 33

ToString method · 161

TranslateTransform method · 190, 193

Try...Catch...End Try · 174, 176

U

user interface · 25, 36

V

Val · 41, 42, 43, 78, 113, 129, 135, 142, 143, 144, 145, 147, 149, 220

variable · 47, 48, 50, 73, 74, 75, 76, 77, 78, 79, 81, 82, 83, 128, 169, 175, 184, 195, 221, 226, 242, 244, 265

variable-length string · 76

VB.net · 183

VBMath · 148

Visual Basic 2019 IDE · 21, 24, 32, 169, 179, 183, 235, 299

Visual Basic Studio 2019 · 24

W

While...End While · 121, 126, 127

Windows Forms App · 19

WriteFile() · 283, 285, 298

WriteLine() method · 276

Printed in Great Britain
by Amazon